SCIENCE VISUAL RESOURCES

SPACE AND ASTRONOMY

An Illustrated Guide to Science

The Diagram Group

CHELSEA HOUSE
PUBLISHERS
An imprint of Infobase Publishing

Space and Astronomy: An Illustrated Guide to Science

Copyright © 2006 The Diagram Group

Editorial:	Tim Furniss, Gordon Lee, Jamie Stokes
Design:	Anthony Atherton, Richard Hummerstone, Lee Lawrence, Trevor Mason, Roger Pring, Phil Richardson
Illustration:	Trevor Mason, Peter Wilkinson
Picture research:	Neil McKenna
Indexer:	Martin Hargreaves

Chelsea House
An imprint of Infobase Publishing
132 West 31st Street
New York NY 10001

For Library of Congress Cataloging-in-Publication data,
please contact the publisher.

ISBN 0-8160-6168-8

Chelsea House books are available at special discounts when purchased in bulk quantities for businesses, associations, institutions, or sales promotions. Please call our Special Sales Department in New York at 212/967-8800 or 800/322-8755.

You can find Chelsea House on the World Wide Web at
http://www.chelseahouse.com

Printed in China

CP Diagram 10 9 8 7 6 5 4 3 2 1

This book is printed on acid-free paper.

Introduction

Space and Astronomy is one of eight volumes of the **Science Visual Resources** set. It contains eight sections, a comprehensive glossary, a Web site guide, and an index.

Space and Astronomy is a learning tool for students and teachers. Full-color diagrams, graphs, charts, and maps on every page illustrate the essential elements of the subject, while parallel text provides key definitions and step-by-step explanations.

The Universe provides an overview of the physical dimensions of space and current theories concerning its origin and eventual fate. This section also defines and illustrates the main classes of objects, from black holes to binary stars, that populate the known universe.

The Sun's Family examines our solar system and defines the various classes of celestial bodies that it includes. There are detailed comparisons of all nine planets as well as information about asteroids, meteoroids, planetary moons, and the Sun itself.

Astronomy is concerned with the human effort to observe and understand objects beyond Earth from the earliest civilizations to the present day. It describes the different methods of astronomy that are used to examine the universe across the entire electromagnetic spectrum.

Space Travel is an overview of the practical and theoretical challenges of getting into space and traveling through it. All aspects of space travel are covered, from the basics of celestial mechanics to the relative pros and cons of different types of propulsion.

Uncrewed Exploration is a history of the exploration of space by uncrewed spacecraft.

Crewed Exploration is a history of manned expeditions in space, from Yuri Gagarin to the contemporary crews of the *International Space Station*.

The Space Shuttle and **Using Space** are concerned with the economic and scientific importance of space today. The many classes of satellite that provide the world with telecommunications and vital data are examined here.

Contents

1 THE UNIVERSE

2 THE SUN'S FAMILY

3 ASTRONOMY

4 SPACE TRAVEL

5 UNCREWED EXPLORATION

6 CREWED EXPLORATION

7 THE SPACE SHUTTLE

8 USING SPACE

APPENDIXES

Key words

galaxy	Milky Way
galaxy group	Oort cloud
galaxy	solar system
supercluster	star
Local Group	
Local	
Supercluster	

The universe

- The universe is the entirety of all matter, energy, and phenomena.
- The origins and ultimate fate of the universe are uncertain.

Cubes of space

- Each cube has sides 100 times longer than the preceding cube.
- Each cube has a volume one million times greater than the preceding cube.

1 **0.015 light years**
The solar system.

2 **1.5 light years**
The Oort cloud.

3 **150 light years**
The nearest stars to the Sun.

4 **15,000 light years**
Part of a spiral arm of the Milky Way.

5 **1,500,000 light years**
The Local Group of galaxies.

6 **150 million light years**
The Local Supercluster of galaxies.

7 **15 billion light years**
All known galaxies.

8 **1,500 billion light years**
Unknown.

Size and scale

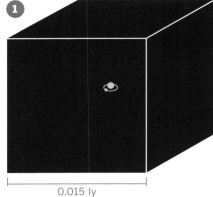

0.015 ly

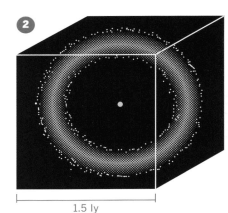

1.5 ly

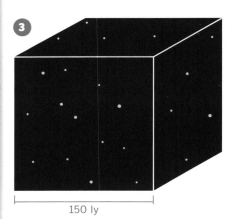

150 ly

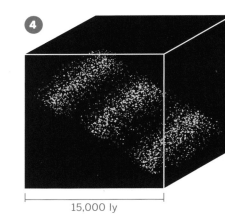

15,000 ly

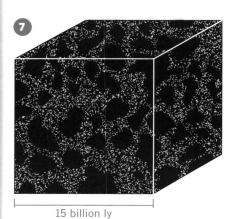

1,500,000 ly

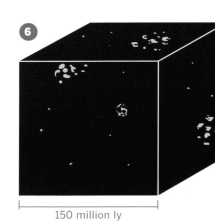

150 million ly

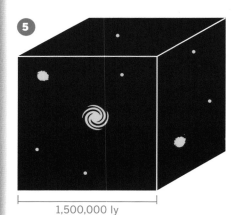

15 billion ly

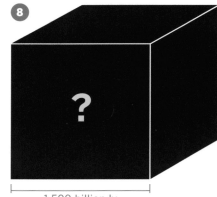

1,500 billion ly

Distances

Traveling distance

Journey Apollo to the Moon	Furthest flight (*Pioneer 10*)	Apollo to Proxima Centauri	Voyager across our galaxy
Distance 238,328 miles 383,551.7 km	7 billion miles 384,400 km	4.2 ly 11 billion km	100,000 ly
Time 3 days	30 years	900,000 years	1,904,760,000 yrs

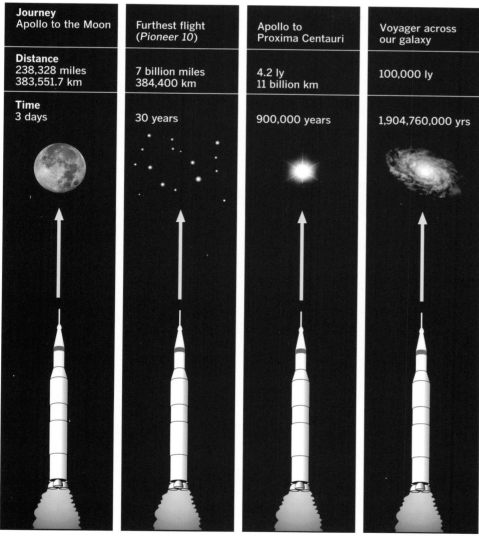

Key words

astronomical unit	light year (ly)
(au)	megaparsec
kiloparsec (kpc)	(Mpc)
light day	parallax
light month	parsec (pc)
light second	solar system

Measuring distances
- Astronomical distances are too large to be usefully measured in miles or kilometers.
- Astronomers use much larger units of measurement.

Astronomical unit (au)
- An *astronomical unit* (*au*) is the mean distance between Earth and the Sun.
- It is used to describe distances within solar systems.

Light year (ly)
- A *light year* (*ly*) is the distance traveled by light in a vacuum in one year.
- It is used to describe the distances between stars or the dimensions of galaxies.
- Terms such as *light second*, *light day*, or *light month* are also used to denote distances traveled by light in other time spans.

Parsec (pc)
- *Parsec* (*pc*) is an abbreviation of "parallax second."
- This denotes the distance at which a baseline of 1 au subtends an angle of 1 arc second.
- It is used to describe distances between galaxies.
- The terms *kiloparsec* (*kpc*) and *megaparsec* (*Mpc*) are also used to denote distances of 1,000 parsecs and one million parsecs respectively.

Defining a parsec

- Earth (**a**) orbits the Sun (**b**) at a distance of 1 au.
- Over a period of about three months, Earth moves from position **1** to position **2**.
- A nearby star (**c**) will change position against the background of more distant stars when observed from Earth at position **1** and then position **2**.

- This change in angular position (**p**) is known as *parallax*.
- When a star's parallax is exactly 1 arc second (1/3600 of a degree) that star is exactly one parsec distant from Earth.
- The distance in parsecs of any star that is close enough to have an observable parallax can be calculated from this relationship.

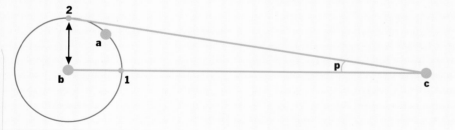

Astronomical distances

1 au	93 million miles (149.6 million km)
1 ly	5.878 trillion miles (9.460 trillion km)
1 parsec	19.174 trillion miles (30.857 trillion km)

Key words

big bang	gravity
cosmic	Hubble's
microwave	constant
background	Hubble's law
radiation (CMB)	quantum gravity
element	quasar
galaxy	

Big bang theory

- The view that the universe began at a single point in space and time at which all matter and energy came into existence is called the *big bang* theory.
- It arose in response to the discovery that the universe appears to be constantly expanding.
- A constantly expanding universe suggests that the expansion must have started at some point in the past.
- This point is referred to as the big bang.
- *Hubble's law* allows astronomers to extrapolate backwards from the current size and rate of expansion of the universe to determine when the big bang must have occurred.
- The calculation can only be performed by determining a value for *Hubble's constant*: the actual rate of expansion.
- Current estimates set the time of the big bang at about 13.7 billion years ago.

Big bang concepts

- Matter did not expand out from the big bang into space over a period of time: space and time came into existence with the big bang and have been expanding ever since.
- The universe was very different in the past to what it is now, and will be very different in the future.
- The origins of the big bang itself are unknown. A theory of gravity on very small scales—*quantum gravity*—is needed to explain processes within the big bang.

Beginnings of the universe

Expansion of space and time since the big bang

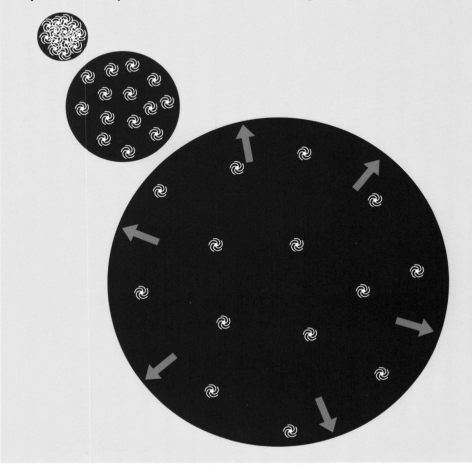

Big bang evidence

Cosmic microwave background radiation

- In the early universe temperatures would have been so high that subatomic particles would have been too energetic to form atoms. This would have resulted in a universe opaque to light.
- Evidence for this period appears as *cosmic microwave background radiation* (*CMB*): a uniform background haze of radiation at about 2.725 kelvins.

Abundance of elements

- The relative abundance of helium-4, helium-3, deuterium, and lithium-7 in the universe are very close to the levels predicted by the theory.
- No other theory attempts to explain why there should be, for example, more helium than deuterium.

Quasars and galaxies

- The observable universe is more or less isotropic in space, but not in time.
- Objects at a great distance are seen as they were long ago in the past. Closer objects are seen as they were more recently.
- Different kinds of objects are more often seen at great distances than at close distances, suggesting that they evolved at various stages in the universe's history when conditions were different.
- For example, no *quasars* have been observed close to Earth. Beyond a certain distance, many are seen. Beyond a greater distance, there are none. This suggests that quasars only evolved during a certain period. This in turn suggests that the universe is itself evolving.

Endings of the universe

Closed universe

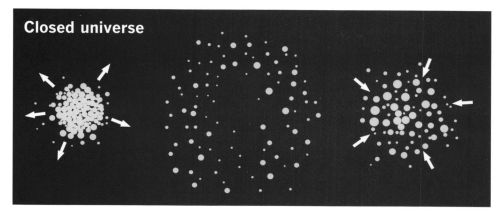

Open universe

Static universe

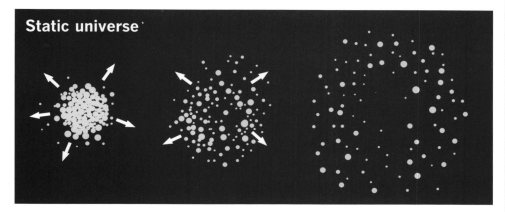

Key words

big bang	gravitational
big crunch	attraction
black hole	heat death
closed universe	MACHO
dark matter	missing mass
entropy	open universe
galaxy	WIMP
galaxy cluster	
galaxy	
supercluster	

Fate of an expanding universe

- If the universe began with the big bang and is currently expanding, there are three possible future scenarios:

Closed universe

- The gravitational attraction of all the matter in the universe may be high enough to slow the expansion and eventually reverse it.
- The universe will reach a maximum extent and then contract back to a singularity (the *big crunch*).

Open universe

- If there is insufficient matter in the universe for gravity to slow its expansion, the universe will go on expanding forever.
- Entropy will ensure that, eventually, all star formation will stop, all matter will decay into dispersed subatomic particles, and black holes will evaporate.
- This ultimate conclusion of entropy is known as the *heat death* of the universe.

Static universe

- If there is just enough matter in the universe to slow and eventually stop its expansion, but not enough to cause it to collapse again, the universe will reach a maximum extent and become static.
- In this scenario the universe will also eventually undergo a heat death.

Dark matter

- In order to predict the fate of the universe accurately, astronomers must know how much matter it contains.
- The structure of galaxies, galaxy clusters, and galaxy superclusters cannot be explained without assuming that a large proportion of the matter they contain cannot be observed (the *missing mass* problem).
- This matter is known as *dark matter* and is thought to make up 90–95 percent of the mass of the universe.

- There are two explanations for what dark matter consists of:
- *Massive Compact Halo Objects* (*MACHO*s) are large dense pieces of baryonic matter such as brown dwarfs.
- *Weakly Interacting Massive Particles* (*WIMP*s) are elementary particles other than electrons, protons, and neutrons that have mass but interact only very rarely with other matter.
- Current theories suggest that dark matter consists of both MACHOs and WIMPs.

Key words

absolute magnitude
apparent magnitude
constellation
luminosity
magnitude
Northern Hemisphere
spectral type
star

Star magnitude

- Astronomers describe the brightness of a star as its *magnitude*.
- *Apparent magnitude* is a measure of how bright a star appears to be in the night sky. This does not distinguish between stars that appear bright because they are close and those that are intrinsically bright.
- *Absolute magnitude* is a measure of how bright a star would appear to be if it were ten parsecs (32.6 ly) away. This is a measure of a star's intrinsic brightness.
- For example, Sirius is the brightest star in the sky and Canopus is the second-brightest. In fact Canopus is about 600 times more luminous than Sirius, but it is much farther away so it appears dimmer.
- Absolute magnitude is measured in two ways: if the distance to a star is known, its apparent magnitude can be scaled up or down to match a distance of ten parsecs. Alternatively a star's luminosity can be estimated according to its spectral type.

Magnitude scales

- Stars with lower magnitude measurements (apparent or absolute) are brighter than stars with higher magnitude measurements.
- A magnitude 1 star is brighter than a magnitude 2 star and a magnitude –1 star is brighter still.
- Both magnitude scales are logarithmic: each step in the scale represents a 2.512 multiple increase in brightness. This means that a star of magnitude 1 is 100 times brighter than a star of magnitude 5.

Bright stars

The 12 brightest stars in the sky

Name	Constellation	Apparent magnitude	Absolute magnitude	Distance (light years)
Sirius	Canis major	−1.44	+1.5	8.6
Canopus	Carina	−0.62	−5.5	313.0
Alpha Centauri	Centaurus	−0.01	+4.1	4.39
Arcturus	Boötes	−0.05	−0.3	37.0
Vega	Lyra	+0.03	+0.6	25.0
Capella	Auriga	+0.08	−0.5	42.0
Rigel	Orion	+0.18	−6.7	773.0
Procyon	Canis minor	+0.40	+2.7	11.4
Betelgeuse	Orion	+0.45	−5.1	427
Achernar	Eridanus	+0.45	−2.8	144.0
Hadar	Centaurus	+0.61	−5.4	525.0
Altair	Aquila	+0.76	+2.2	16.8

Northern Hemisphere sky

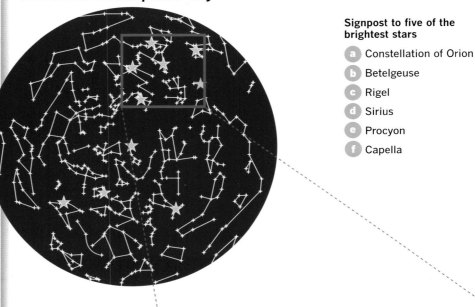

Signpost to five of the brightest stars

- a Constellation of Orion
- b Betelgeuse
- c Rigel
- d Sirius
- e Procyon
- f Capella

Close stars

The ten nearest stars

Name	Constellation	Apparent magnitude	Distance (light years)
1 Proxima Centauri	Centaurus	+11.1	4.24
2 Alpha Centauri	Centaurus	−0.01	4.39
3 Barnard's Star	Ophiuchus	+9.5	6.0
4 Wolf 358	Leo	+13.6	7.8
5 Lalande 21185	Ursa Major	+7.7	8.2
6 Luyten 726.8	Cetus	+12.3	8.5
7 Sirius	Canis Major	−1.44	8.6
8 Ross 154	Sagittarius	+10.5	9.6
9 Ross 248	Andromeda	+12.2	10.3
10 Epsilon Eridani	Eridanus	+3.7	10.6

Visibility of the nearest stars

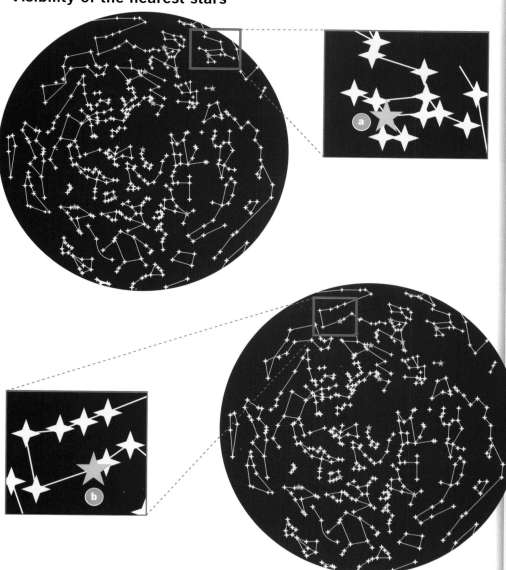

Of the ten stars closest to Earth only two can be seen with the naked eye from the Northern Hemisphere:

a Sirius in the constellation Canis Major;

b Epsilon Eridani in the constellation Eridanus.

Key words

apparent magnitude	Milky Way
binary star system	multiple star system
constellation	Northern Hemisphere
galaxy	star
magnitude	

Closest stars

- The Milky Way galaxy contains about 200 billion stars.
- About 100 stars lie within 20 light years of the Sun.
- About 30 stars lie within 12 light years of the Sun.
- The closest star, Proxima Centauri, is 4.24 light years from the Sun.

Alpha Centauri system

- Proxima Centauri is a member of a triple star system with Alpha Centauri A and Alpha Centauri B, both 4.34 light years from the Sun.
- Proxima Centauri is the dimmest star of the system and is not visible to the naked eye.
- Alpha Centauri A and B are separated by a distance of about 23 au and are not discernible as individual bodies to the naked eye.
- Alpha Centauri A, also known as Rigil Kentaurus, is very similar to the Sun and is the fourth brightest star in the sky.

Local space

- The nature and distribution of the stars within 12 light years of Earth allows some conclusions to be made about local space.
  - Stars are on average about eight light years apart.
  - More than 50 percent of them belong to multiple star systems.
- Most are dimmer than the Sun.

© Diagram Visual Information Ltd.

Key words

accretion disc	Lagrange point
astrometric	multiple star
binary	system
binary star	neutron star
system	orbit
black hole	Roche lobe
contact binary	star
detached binary	visual binary
eclipsing binary	X-ray binary

Binary stars

- A binary star system consists of two stars orbiting each other around a common center of mass.
- Three, four, or more stars may orbit each other in the same way.
- Astronomers estimate that about 50 percent of all stars are part of binary or multiple star systems.
- The closest star to the Sun, Proxima Centauri, is part of a triple star system.

Binary star types

- *Eclipsing binaries* are binary systems in which, from the point of view of an observer, one star periodically passes in front of the other.
- *Astrometric binaries* are binary systems in which only one member of the system is bright enough to be observed. The existence of the other member is inferred by its gravitational effects.
- *Contact binaries* are binary systems in which both member stars fill their Roche lobes. Their upper atmospheres form a common envelope.
- *Detached binaries* are binary systems in which both member stars are within their Roche lobes and have no significant effect on each other's evolution.
- *Visual binaries* are stars that appear to be members of a binary system from the point of view of an observer, but which are not actually gravitationally linked.
- *X-ray binaries* are binary systems that periodically emit powerful X-rays. This is thought to occur when one system member is a neutron star or a black hole with an accretion disc formed from material drawn from the other member.

Star pairs

Binary system

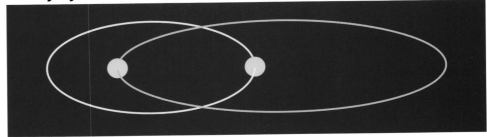

Visual binary

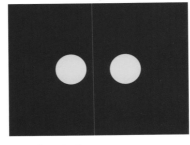

Roche lobe

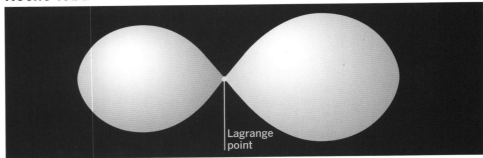

Lagrange point

Roche lobe

- A *Roche lobe* is the region around a star in a binary system within which material is gravitationally bound to that star.
- The Roche lobes of two stars in a binary system are tear-shaped volumes of space with their apexes touching at the *Lagrange point* of the system.

- If a star expands so that some of its surface lies outside of its Roche lobe, that material may be drawn into the Roche lobe of its companion.
- The overflow of material from one Roche lobe into another is thought to be responsible for the formation of *accretion discs*.

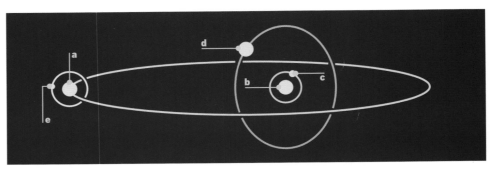

The Mizar-Alcor multiple system
Alcor (**a**) takes 10 million years to orbit Mizar (**b**). Mizar also has two, closer companions (**c**, **d**). Alcor also has a close companion (**e**).

Variable stars

Mira variable

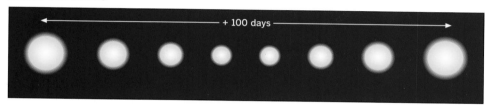

+ 100 days

Cepheid variable

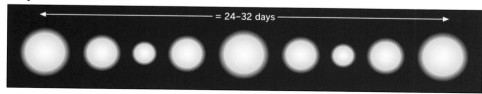

= 24–32 days

Eclipsing binary

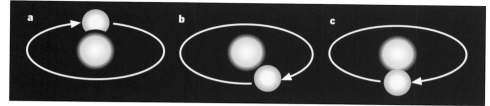

a The star is bright as seen from Earth because its companion is on the "far side."
b The companion begins to move in front of the main star.

c The companion is in front of the main star, causing its light to dim.

1 A white dwarf sucks material from a red giant.

2 Captured material is shed in an explosion.

Cepheid variables

- Cepheid variables are a form of intrinsic variable star.
- They are very useful to astronomers because their period of luminosity variability closely correlates to their absolute luminosity.
- For example, a Cepheid variable with a luminosity period of three days has an absolute luminosity of about 800 Suns. A Cepheid variable with a luminosity period of 30 days has an absolute luminosity of 10,000 Suns.
- These correlations were initially calculated by observing relatively close Cepheid variables whose distances had already been calculated by other methods such as parallax observations.

- Understanding this correlation allows astronomers to determine the distance of a Cepheid variable based solely on its observed period of luminosity. This is done by calculating the distance that a star with a known absolute magnitude (determined by its period of luminosity) must be in order to have its apparent magnitude observed.
- Because Cepheid variables tend to be very bright stars, they are visible across great distances. By determining the distance to a Cepheid variable in another galaxy, astronomers are able to determine the approximate distance to that galaxy as a whole.

Key words

absolute magnitude	irregular variable
accretion disc	luminosity
apparent magnitude	magnitude
	Mira variable
Cepheid variable	parallax
eclipsing binary	semiregular variable
extrinsic variable	star
galaxy	variable star
intrinsic variable	

Variable star

- A star that undergoes a great change in luminosity over a relatively short time period is a *variable star*.
- For comparison, the Sun varies in luminosity by about 0.1 percent over an 11 year cycle but is not considered to be a variable star.
- Some variable stars have regular cycles of variation, others are irregular.

Intrinsic variables

- Stars that vary in luminosity because of features intrinsic to those stars are *intrinsic variables*.
- *Mira variables* are old, giant red stars. Their luminosity varies because they expand and contract over periods of 100 days or more.
- *Cepheid variables* are giant yellow stars. Their luminosity varies because they periodically expand and contract.
- *Semiregular variables* are giant or supergiant stars that have variations in luminosity that are usually regular but can be irregular.
- *Irregular variables* are stars that vary in luminosity irregularly.

Extrinsic variables

- *Extrinsic variables* are stars that appear to vary in luminosity because of extrinsic factors.
- The most common are eclipsing binary stars in which luminosity is affected by one star passing in front of another.
- Less common are binary systems in which the luminosity of the members is affected by accretion discs and other interactions.

Key words

astrometry	neutron star
Doppler method	orbit
exoplanet	planet
gas giant	pulsar
gravitational	pulsar timing
lensing	spectral line
main sequence	star
millisecond	transit method
pulsar	

Exoplanet

- *Exoplanet* means "extra-solar planet."
- An extra-solar planet is a planet in orbit around a star other than the Sun.

Finding exoplanets

- More than 130 exoplanets have been confirmed to date.
- None can be observed directly with current technology: they are too dim and distant.
- The first exoplanets were discovered in 1992. Three planets were detected in orbit around the millisecond pulsar PSR B 1257+12 at a distance of about 2,630 light years from Earth.
- *Pulsar timing* is the detection of irregularities in the pulse periods of pulsars caused by the gravitation effects of planets orbiting them. The first exoplanets were found using this method.
- *Astrometery* is the measurement of irregularities in the proper motion of stars caused by orbiting planets. Current technologies are not sensitive enough to make this method reliable.
- *Doppler method* is the measurement of irregularities in a star's spectral lines caused by orbiting planets. It is best at locating close-orbit planets.
- *Gravitational lensing* is the detection of the lensing effect of a star and its planets on light from a distant star in the background. It relies on the correct alignment of Earth with the target star and the distant star.
- *Transit method* is the detection of a planet's shadow when it passes in front of a star. It also relies on the correct alignment of Earth, star, and planet.

Exoplanets

Comparison of solar systems

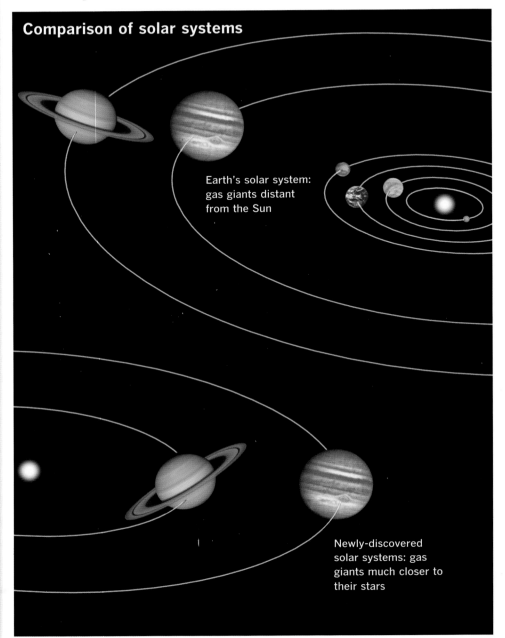

Earth's solar system: gas giants distant from the Sun

Newly-discovered solar systems: gas giants much closer to their stars

Exoplanet observations

- The oldest exoplanet so far discovered is thought to be about 13 billion years old. That is more than twice the age of Earth and only about one billion years younger than the universe.
- Its existence challenges accepted theories of planet formation.
- Most of the exoplanets discovered so far are gas giants like Jupiter, but have orbits much closer to their stars than Jupiter's is to the Sun.
- This also undermines assumptions about solar system formation.
- The observed dissimilarity between other solar systems and our own may be due to the limitations of current methods of detection since planets smaller than gas giants cannot yet be reliably detected.

Stellar evolution

Color of star	Temperature °C	Spectral type	Example
Blue	30,000–10,000	O, B	Spica (**a**)
White	10,000–7,000	A, F	Polaris (**b**)
Yellow	7,000–5,000	G	Capella (**c**)
Orange	5,000–3,000	K	Aldebaran (**d**)
Red	3,000	M	Betelgeuse (**e**)

Hertzsprung-Russell diagram

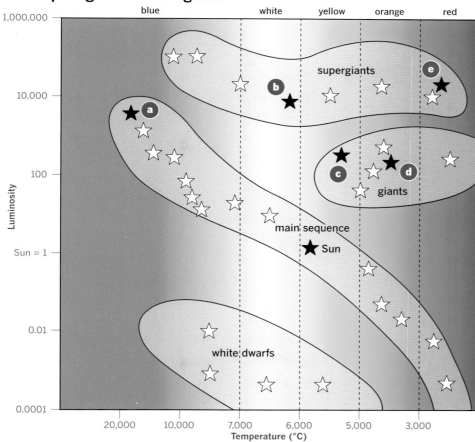

Key words

absolute	protostar
magnitude	red giant
Hertzsprung-	spectral type
Russell diagram	star
luminosity	stellar evolution
magnitude	T-Tauri star
main sequence	white dwarf
Morgan-Keenan	
classification	

Star color

- The variation in the observed color of stars is apparent even to the naked eye.
- Instruments are able to discern very small variations in color between stars.
- The color of a star is closely related to its temperature.

Spectral types

- Stars are commonly classified according to their surface temperatures using the Morgan-Keenan spectral classification scheme.
- A mnemonic for the order of the spectral classes (O, B, A, F, G, K, M) is "Oh Be A Fine Girl, Kiss Me."
- Within each class, stars are further classified with numbers from 0 to 9. For example, A0 denotes the hottest stars in the A class and A9 the coolest.

Hertzsprung-Russell diagram

- Different versions of the H-R diagram can show the relationships between absolute magnitude, luminosity, star classification, and surface temperature.
- The majority of stars fall into a few regions of the graph.
- The *main sequence* is a diagonal spread of stars from the top left to the bottom right of the diagram.
- Stars appear at different points on the diagram at different stages of their life spans.

Stellar evolution

- As a star evolves over time its position on a Hertzsprung-Russell diagram changes.
- A protostar is cool but very large, so it has a high luminosity. It appears in the top right corner of an H-R diagram.
- Once the star has evolved to become a T-Tauri star, it has contracted and become hotter. It appears very close to the main sequence.
- Once stability has been achieved by hydrogen burning, the star appears within the main sequence.
- Exactly where a star joins the main sequence will depend on its mass.
- More massive stars will be hotter and larger (and therefore more luminous) and will join the main sequence farther to the top left of an H-R diagram than less massive stars. The Sun is at this point in its life and appears near the middle of the main sequence.
- When hydrogen burning stops and helium burning begins, a star rapidly departs from the main sequence as it becomes larger (and therefore more luminous) but cooler.
- A star that reaches a new equilibrium as a red giant or red supergiant appears near the center top of an H-R diagram.
- When helium burning stops in a red giant, the star quickly shrinks in size (and therefore becomes less luminous) until it stabilizes as a white dwarf, which appears near the center bottom of the diagram.

Key words

brown dwarf	nuclear fusion
galaxy	plasma
gravitational	protostar
attraction	star
infrared	supernova
nebula	

Gas cloud

- Most of the empty space in a galaxy actually contains very low concentrations of gas and dust.
- In some regions this concentration is higher: these "clouds" or *nebulae* are the birthplaces of stars.
- Most clouds are in a state of equilibrium.
- The equilibrium of some clouds may be disrupted by supernova shock waves or the close approach of another cloud or massive object.
- These disruptions may cause changes in the density of parts of the cloud so that gravity overcomes kinetic energy.
- As particles clump together, larger and larger concentrations are formed, which in turn attract more matter.

Protostar

- As a cloud contracts, it increases in temperature. Gravitational energy is converted into thermal kinetic energy.
- At first, most of the thermal energy escapes as infrared radiation.
- As the contracting cloud becomes denser, it becomes increasingly opaque to infrared radiation and the rate of heating rises.
- If enough mass is present to raise temperatures to 15,000,000 kelvins, a plasma forms.
- As contraction continues and temperatures rise further, the nuclear fusion of hydrogen may occur.

Brown dwarf

- If not enough mass is present to generate the temperatures needed for nuclear fusion, a *brown dwarf* results.
- Brown dwarfs typically have masses between 13 and 75 times the mass of Jupiter.
- Some astronomers believe that brown dwarfs may be the most common objects in our galaxy.

Stellar beginnings

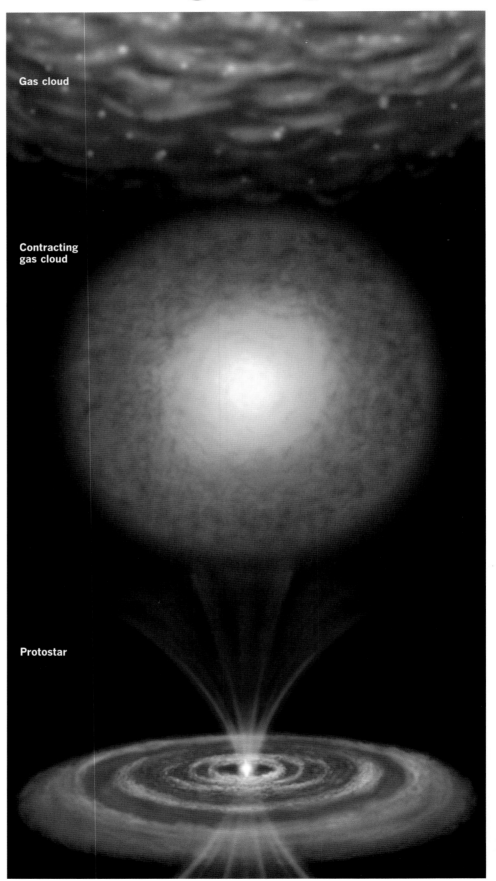

Gas cloud

Contracting gas cloud

Protostar

Stellar birth

© Diagram Visual Information Ltd.

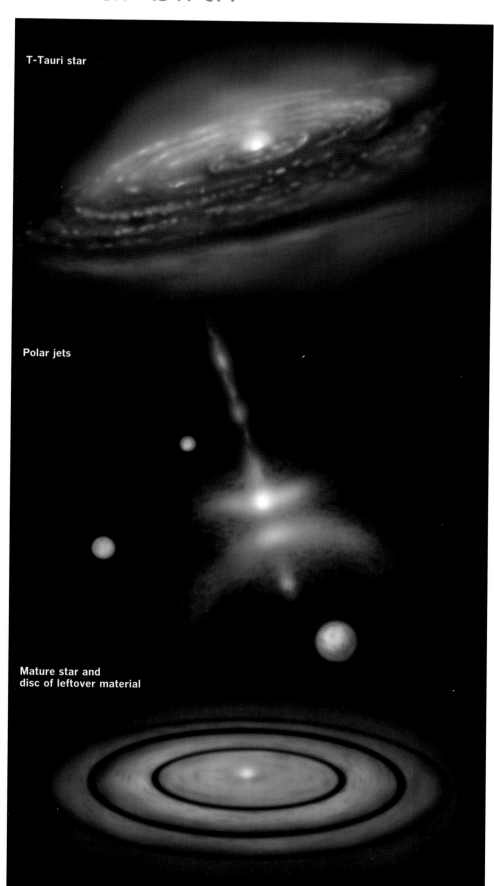

T-Tauri star

Polar jets

Mature star and disc of leftover material

Key words

accretion disc	nuclear fusion
core	polar jet
Hertzsprung-	protostar
Russell diagram	star
main sequence	T-Tauri star
mature star	

T-Tauri star

- If temperatures become high enough for the nuclear fusion of hydrogen nuclei to occur, a protostar becomes a T-Tauri star.
- T-Tauri stars are situated just above the main sequence on a Hertzsprung-Russell diagram.
- Their fusion processes are restricted to a small central core.
- The star is still contracting gravitationally and some material is still falling onto its surface from an accretion disc.
- Strong winds push some material away and the star may emit polar jets of energetic radiation.
- Equilibrium has not been achieved.

Mature star

- Eventually, the outward pressure generated by nuclear fusion balances the inward pressure of gravitation and the star achieves a stable diameter.
- Equilibrium is achieved and the star is situated on the main sequence of an H-R diagram.

Life span

- The stable phase of a star's life is usually its longest.
- This is because the nuclear fusion of hydrogen into helium is the most efficient of the nuclear burning stages.
- The length of time that a star remains in the main sequence is closely related to its mass.
- More massive stars have shorter spans of stable maturity than less massive stars.

© Diagram Visual Information Ltd.

Key words

black dwarf	white dwarf
core	
nuclear fusion	
planetary nebula	
red giant	

Red giant

- Once all the hydrogen in a star has undergone nuclear fusion into helium, fusion processes stop.
- Without the outward pressure generated by fusion, the star undergoes rapid gravitational contraction.
- This contraction raises the temperature and density of the core until the nuclear fusion of helium nuclei becomes possible.
- The pressure generated by helium fusion forces the star to expand again.
- A new equilibrium is reached, leaving the star with a diameter 100–200 times greater than it was during the hydrogen burning phase.
- The surface temperature and overall density are lower, but the density of the core is higher.

White dwarf

- Once all the helium in a red giant has been fused into carbon, fusion processes stop again.
- The star undergoes rapid gravitational contraction again.
- If the star has a mass of less than about 3.4 times the mass of the Sun, this contraction will not produce enough heat to initiate the fusion of carbon nuclei.
- The star's outer layers (about 80 percent of its mass) are ejected to form a *planetary nebula*.
- The remaining mass (about 20 percent of its original mass) contracts to form a *white dwarf*.
- It is thought that white dwarfs eventually cease shining, and become black dwarfs.

Regular star death

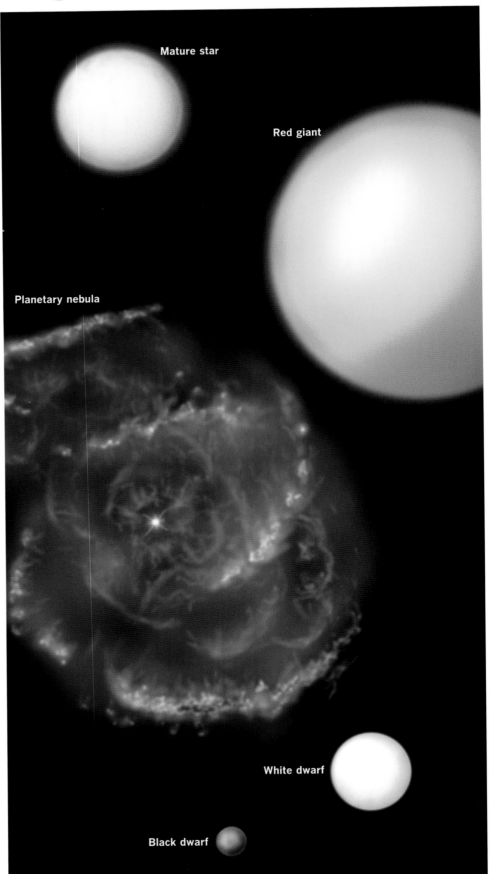

Mature star

Red giant

Planetary nebula

White dwarf

Black dwarf

Large star death

Mature star

Red supergiant

Type II supernova

Neutron star

Key words

binary star system	nuclear fusion
black hole	red supergiant
core	supernova
neutron star	white dwarf

Red supergiant

- Massive stars evolve into stars burning helium in the same way as stars with masses similar to the mass of the Sun.
- They swell to sizes much greater than those achieved by Sun-like stars and are known as red supergiants.
- Their greater masses allow them to achieve temperatures at which carbon and other, heavier, elements undergo nuclear fusion.
- Helium is fused into carbon, carbon into oxygen, oxygen into silicon, and silicon into iron.
- Massive stars are likely to suffer a supernova explosion once sustained fusion can no longer take place.

Chandrasekhar limit

- The Chandrasekhar limit describes the maximum sustainable mass of a white dwarf: about 1.44 times solar mass.
- This is the mass at which a body's tendency to contract due to gravitation can no longer be balanced by degeneracy pressure.
- This limit defines whether the core of a star will collapse to become a white dwarf, a neutron star, or a black hole.
- It refers only to that portion of a star's mass that undergoes gravitational collapse when fusion reactions stop.
- For example, a massive star may lose a large proportion of its mass in the form of a planetary nebula and the remaining mass may be below the Chandrasekhar limit.

Type I and II supernovas

- Type II *supernovas* result from the gravitational collapse of massive stars.
- Type I supernovas result when a white dwarf in a binary star system acquires additional mass from another star in that system, which causes it to exceed its Chandrasekhar limit.
- Type I supernovas are many times more powerful than Type II supernovas.

© Diagram Visual Information Ltd.

Key words

black hole	star
core	supernova
neutron star	
nuclear fusion	
red supergiant	

Giant stars

- The most massive stars undergo the same stages of evolution as large stars.
- No star is thought to be large enough to enable the sustained nuclear fusion of iron to occur in its core.
- Giant stars are eventually torn apart in supernova explosions.

Supernova

- At the point where no more fusion reactions are possible the core of a red supergiant undergoes a very rapid gravitational collapse.
- The core collapses to a diameter of about six miles (10 km) in a fraction of a second.
- Material from the outer envelope collapses more slowly and is thought to rebound from the collapsed core.
- This rebound is incredibly energetic and causes the envelope to be ripped apart and ejected in a supernova.
- A supernova may release more energy in a second than the Sun will produce in its entire 10 billion-year life span.
- The surviving core may be a neutron star or, if it is more massive, may collapse further to become a black hole.

Supernova seeding

- Only massive stars form relatively heavy elements such as oxygen, silicon, and iron through the fusion of lighter, more abundant elements.
- When a supernova occurs, these heavy elements are ejected into interstellar space at high speeds.
- Planets such as Earth, and the living things that exist on it, are partly made up of these heavy elements.
- Without red supergiant fusion and the subsequent seeding of its fusion products, rocky planets and life may not be possible.

Giant star death

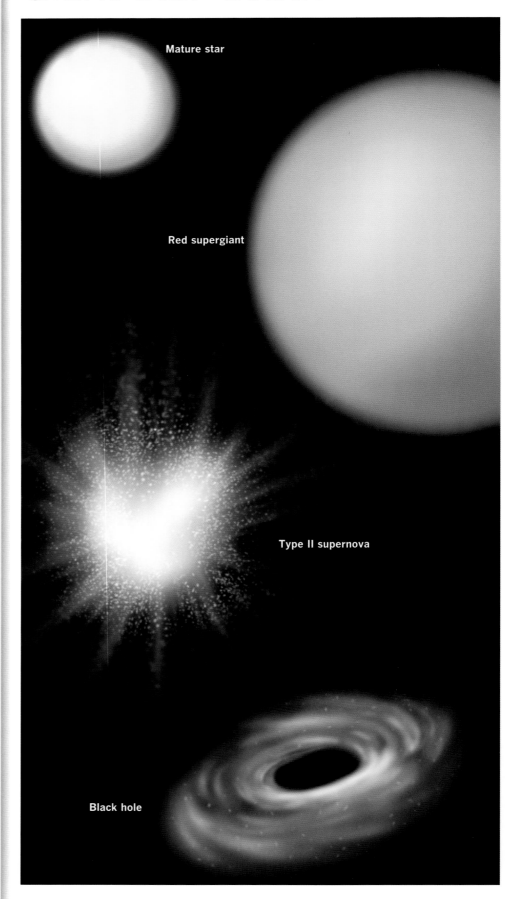

Mature star

Red supergiant

Type II supernova

Black hole

Neutron stars

Size

By comparing a neutron star with Manhattan Island on the same scale, the neutron star's very small size can be visualized.

neutron star

Manhattan Island

Miles

0   6   12

Neutron star

- A *neutron star* is a small but extremely dense object composed almost entirely of neutrons.
- A neutron star may be only six miles (10 km) in diameter but have between 1.4 and three times the mass of the Sun.
- Neutron stars are thought to be the collapsed remnants of massive stars that have exploded in supernovas.

Neutron star features

- Neutron stars rotate very rapidly. The most rapid have rotation periods of hundredths of a second and the slowest of 30 seconds.
- This rapid rotation is due to the conservation of angular momentum: the slow rotation of the original massive star speeds up as the object shrinks.
- Rotation periods very slowly become longer over time: younger neutron stars rotate more rapidly than older ones.

Mass

A neutron star is the result of the collapse of a giant star many millions of times larger in size. As a result of this compression, neutron stars are very dense.

A cubic centimeter of matter from a neutron star would weigh about as much as 3,500 fully-laden Saturn V rockets on Earth.

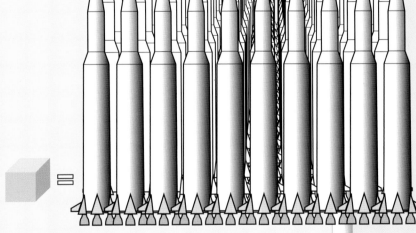

Neutron star types

- *Magnestars* are neutron stars with magnetic fields that are at least 1,000 times more intense than Earth's. Their magnetic fields become weaker over time.
- *X-ray bursters* are neutron stars that have accretion discs formed from material drawn from orbiting companion stars. Friction in the accretion disc results in the periodic emission of powerful X-ray bursts.

Pulsars

- Pulsars are neutron stars that emit a stream of X-rays and gamma rays from their poles. These are recorded as regular pulses whenever an observer is in line of sight of one of the poles.
- As with all neutron stars, a pulsar's rate of rotation slows as time passes. As its rotation slows, the frequency of the pulses is also reduced.
- However, millisecond pulsars are very old pulsars (one billion years or more) with very high rotation rates (pulse periods of less than 25 milliseconds).
- Millisecond pulsars are thought to form when material from a companion star falls onto a pulsar, causing it to spin more and more rapidly.
- The first exoplanets to be discovered are in orbit around millisecond pulsars.

Key words

accretion disc	pole
active galaxy	red shift
axis	singularity
black hole	star
blue shift	stellar mass
escape velocity	black hole
event horizon	supermassive
galaxy	black hole
gravitational	X-ray
lensing	

Black holes

- A *black hole* is a region of space with a gravity field so strong that nothing, including light, can escape from it: it has an escape velocity greater than the speed of light.
- A black hole is thought to result from the gravitational collapse of a massive star at the end of its life.
- Black holes may also be created in the centers of young galaxies.

Black hole features

- No matter or information can flow from the inside of a black hole to the outside universe.
- The *event horizon* is the "surface" of a black hole. It is the perimeter at which the escape velocity is exactly the speed of light.
- At the center of a black hole there is a singularity where gravity and escape velocity become infinite.
- Astronomers suspect there are two classes of black hole: *stellar mass* and *supermassive*.
- Stellar mass black holes have masses between four and 15 times the mass of the Sun.
- Supermassive black holes have masses many billions of times greater than the Sun.
- Supermassive black holes are thought to form at the centers of active galaxies.

Black holes

Cygnus X-1

An X-ray source known as Cygnus X-1 may be related to the presence of a black hole in orbit around the star Eta Cygni.

a blue giant star Eta Cygni
b proposed orbiting black hole
c material drawn from Eta Cygni by the black hole's gravitation
d heated material gives off X-rays as it accelerates toward the black hole

Detecting black holes

The evidence

- Only indirect evidence for black holes has been observed.
- Evidence for the existence of black holes comes from the observation of phenomena close to where a black hole might be.

Accretion disc

- Matter falling toward a black hole, but still outside the event horizon, is thought to form a rapidly spinning accretion disc.
- Friction between different zones of the accretion disc is thought to cause the emission of large amounts of X-rays.
- Narrow jets of particles moving at close to the speed of light are thought to be emitted along the polar axis of an accretion disc.

Red and blue shifts

- Material orbiting a black hole would be moving away from an observer for one half of its orbit and toward the same observer for the other half.
- Velocity and direction of motion can be ascertained by measuring the blue shift or red shift of its emissions.
- Material orbiting a supermassive black hole at very high speeds would exhibit a large red shift on one half of its orbit and a large blue shift on the other.

Other evidence

- Stars that appear to be orbiting a region of space where no matter is visible may be orbiting black holes.
- Gravitational lensing may distort light from objects behind and far beyond a black hole.

Quasars

Key words

blue shift	radio loud
galaxy	radio quiet
luminosity	red shift
Milky Way	solar system
quasar	star
quasi-stellar object (QSO)	supermassive black hole

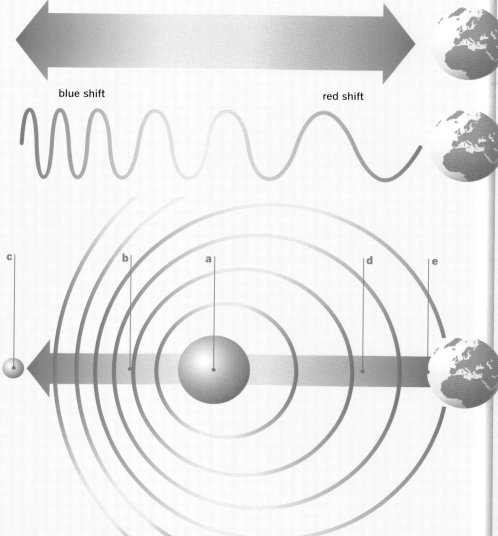

blue shift

red shift

a A distant star receding from Earth at high velocity.
b Light waves emitted in front of the star are squashed closer together.
c An observer aboard a craft in the path of the star sees a blue-shifted image of the star.
d Light waves emitted behind the star are stretched further apart.
e An observer on Earth sees a red-shifted image of the star.

Quasars

- The word *quasar* is derived from "quasi-stellar radio source."
- Quasars are also known as *QSOs* or *quasi-stellar objects*.
- They appear as bright blue point sources through an optical telescope.
- Some have strong radio emissions (they are "radio loud") but most do not (they are "radio quiet").

Quasar features

- The emissions from all quasars exhibit very high red shifts, indicating that they are very distant and therefore receding at very high velocities.
- Despite their great distance, they are very bright.
- A typical quasar has the same luminosity as about 1,000 Milky Way galaxies.
- Quasar luminosities vary over time periods of months, weeks, days, or hours.
- These relatively short periods of variation in luminosity indicate that they are relatively small (no effect can propagate across an object faster than the speed of light).
- Taken together, these features indicate that quasars are about the size of the solar system, but emit as much energy as a thousand large galaxies.

Quasar origins

- Quasars are thought to be the active cores of very ancient galaxies.
- Their energy is thought to be produced by the effects of supermassive black holes on matter surrounding them.

Red shift and blue shift

- Red shift is a phenomenon used by astronomers to determine the distance of objects.
- Light travels in waves and its color depends upon its wavelength. When an object, such as a star, moving at high velocity gives out light, the light waves ahead of it are squashed closer together and the light waves behind it are stretched further apart.
- Light with longer (stretched) wavelengths is redder. Light with shorter (squashed) wavelengths is bluer.
- Objects receding from an observer at high velocity appear to be redder than they actually are (called red shift).
- The faster an object is receding from Earth the larger its red shift. The faster an object is traveling the farther away it must be, if it is true that the universe is constantly expanding.

Key words

black hole
galactic center
galactic plane
galaxy
globular cluster

Local Arm
Milky Way
spiral galaxy
supermassive
black hole

The Milky Way

The Milky Way

- The *Milky Way* is visible as an irregular band of faint light across the night sky.
- This band is the arm of our galaxy in which the Sun is located.
- Astronomers refer to our galaxy as a whole as the Milky Way.

Our galaxy

- Our galaxy is a spiral galaxy with four major arms.
- It is thought to be unusually large.
- It contains about 100 billion stars.
- The central bulge is densely populated with old red stars.
- The arms are mostly populated by young blue stars.
- A spherical halo of old dull stars surrounds the main disc.
- Clusters of old stars (between 10,000 and a million) known as globular clusters also surround the main disc.
- Some astronomers believe there may be a supermassive black hole at the galactic center.

The Sun's place

- The Sun is situated in one of the Milky Way's spiral arms known as the Orion or Local Arm.
- It is about 28,000 light years from the galactic center and about 20 light years above the center of the galactic plane.

Components of the Milky Way

1 A dense bulging center with a high concentration of stars.
2 A surrounding halo of stars.
3 Trailing arms with less concentration of stars.
4 Our Sun, about 30,000 ly from the center.

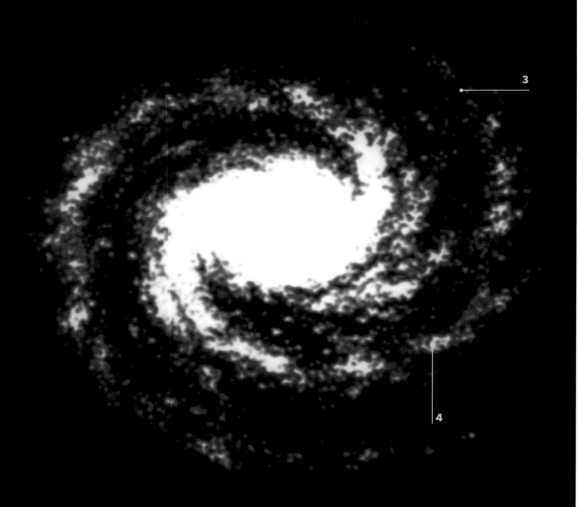

2,000 light years

100,000 light years

Galaxy types

Elliptical galaxy

NGC 4472 in Virgo

Spiral galaxy

M 51: the Whirlpool galaxy

Barred spiral galaxy

NGC 1300 in Eridanus

Irregular galaxy

Large Magellanic Cloud

Galaxy

- A *galaxy* is a collection of stars, gas, and dust bound together by gravity.
- The universe contains many billions of galaxies.
  - They typically contain millions to hundreds of billions of stars.
  - There are four main types: elliptical, spiral, barred spiral, and irregular.

Elliptical galaxies

- *Elliptical galaxies* are the most common kind of galaxy.
- They have a smooth rounded appearance, without complex regular structural features.
- They contain little gas or dust.
- They contain few hot bright stars and many dull old stars.

Spiral galaxies

- *Spiral galaxies* resemble a flattened disc with outlying spiral arms in the same plane.
- The central disc is dense and contains mainly older stars.
- The spiral arms contain gas, dust, and younger stars.
- They are surrounded by a halo of older stars and dense clusters of older stars.
- Our galaxy is a spiral galaxy.

Barred spiral galaxies

- A *barred spiral galaxy* is a spiral galaxy in which the arms originate from the ends of a bar through the galactic core.

Irregular galaxies

- *Irregular galaxies* have no regular shape or symmetrical features.
- Many contain a lot of gas, dust, and young stars.

Key words

galaxy	*Local*
galaxy cluster	*Supercluster*
galaxy group	*Milky Way*
galaxy	
supercluster	
local group	

Clusters

- *Galaxies* are not randomly distributed in space.
- They are clumped together in *groups*, *clusters*, and *superclusters*.
- A group contains fewer than 50 galaxies and has a diameter of about two Megaparsecs (Mpc).
- A cluster contains 50–1,000 galaxies and has a diameter of about eight Mpc.
- A supercluster contains thousands of clusters and groups and may be millions of megaparsecs in extent.

Voids, sheets, and filaments

- About 90 percent of space seems to consist of bubble-like voids in which very few galaxies are observed.
- Most voids are about 25 Mpc in diameter. The largest known, the Boötes void, has a diameter of about 124 Mpc.
- Galaxies are concentrated in sheets and filaments separated by these voids.
- Superclusters occur at the intersections of sheets and filaments.
- No structures larger than superclusters have been confirmed.

Local group

- The Milky Way is a member of the Local Group of galaxies, which consists of about thirty other galaxies including the Andromeda galaxy and the Large and Small Magellanic Clouds.
- The Local Group is a member of the Virgo or Local Supercluster, which consists of about 100 other groups and clusters of galaxies, including the Virgo cluster.

Galaxy groups

Distribution of galaxies

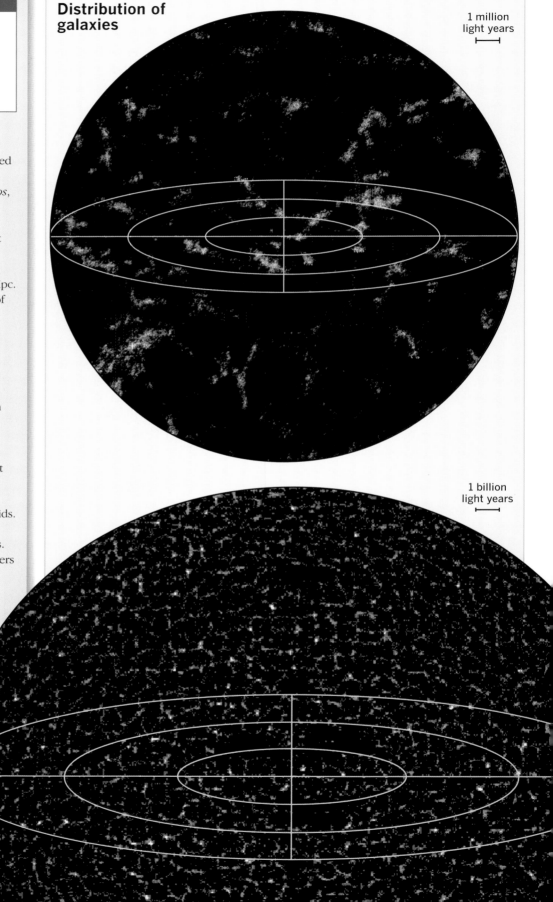

1 million light years

1 billion light years

Hubble's law

Key words

galaxy
Hubble's
  constant
Hubble's law
red shift

Hubble's constant

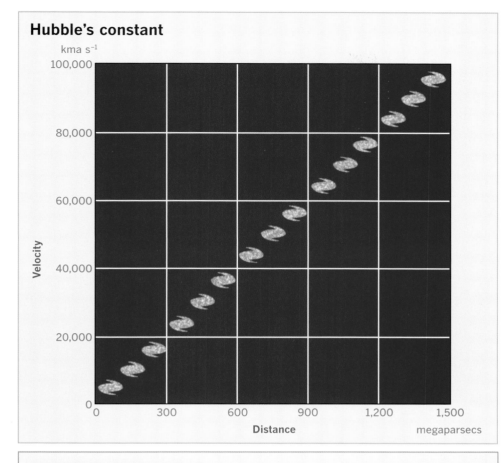

kma s⁻¹

Velocity

Distance   megaparsecs

Hubble's law

- U.S. astronomer Edwin Hubble (1889–1953) proved the existence of galaxies other than our own.
- He discovered that the universe is many times larger than previously thought.
- *Red shift* analysis showed that all objects outside our galaxy were receding.
- More distant objects were receding at greater velocities.
- He concluded that the universe is constantly expanding in all directions.
- Hubble's law states: the further away an object is, the faster its rate of recession, and that this relationship is constant.

Hubble's constant

- *Hubble's constant* is the actual ratio of the speed of recession of an object to its distance from the observer.

The raisin cake analogy

- In an uncooked raisin cake (**1**) one raisin is chosen to represent Earth **a** and the distances from it to other raisins in the cake are measured.
- After an hour, yeast in the cake has caused it to expand uniformly in all directions so that it is now twice the size (**2**).
- The distances between the "Earth" raisin and the other raisins are measured again and all distances are now twice what they were before. This means that more distant raisins **b** have covered much larger distances relative to the "Earth" raisin than nearby raisins **c**. They have covered this distance in the same time, so they are moving at a greater velocity than nearby raisins.

1

2

© Diagram Visual Information Ltd.

Key words

ecliptic	rocky planet
gas giant	solar system
inner planet	solar wind
orbit	
planet	

Observations

- A good theory of solar-system formation has to explain certain facts observed in our own solar system:
- In our own solar system the planets orbit very close to the plane of the *ecliptic* (the plane of Earth's orbit around the Sun).
- All of the planets orbit around the Sun in the same direction.
- The inner planets are much smaller and have very different compositions to the outer gas giants.

Modern theory

- The Sun was formed from a condensing cloud of gas and dust.
- As this cloud shrank, any rotation it had would have been accelerated by the conservation of angular momentum.
- This caused the cloud to flatten into a broad rotating disc. The planets are thought to have formed from material in the outer part of this disc. The Sun is thought to have formed from material in the inner part of the same disc.
- Temperatures were higher in the regions of the disc closer to the proto-Sun than they were in more distant regions.
- Higher temperatures and a strong solar wind would have driven lighter elements out of the inner solar system allowing only small dense planets to form.
- Lower temperatures farther away from the proto-Sun would allow lighter elements to clump together, resulting in large gaseous planets.

Beginnings of the solar system

Temperature and formation of the solar system

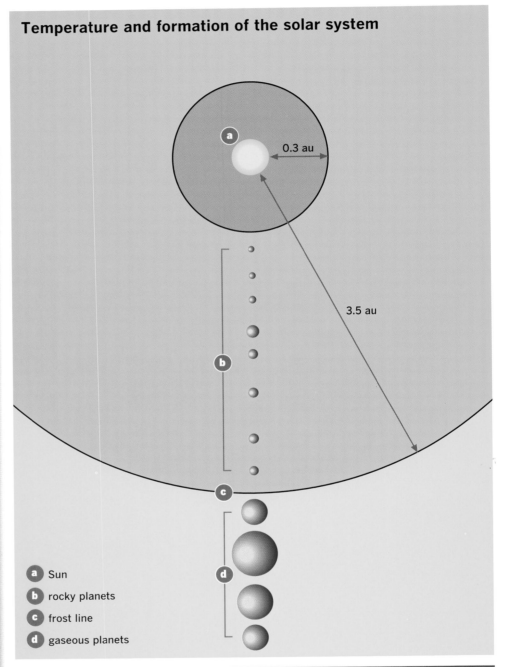

0.3 au

3.5 au

- **a** Sun
- **b** rocky planets
- **c** frost line
- **d** gaseous planets

Two types of planet

- Within about 0.3 au of the Sun temperatures are too high for rocks, metals, or hydrogen compounds to exist as solids. No planets have been formed within this limit.
- Between about 0.3 au and 3.5 au of the Sun temperatures are low enough for rocks and metals to condense as solids, but too high for hydrogen compounds to do so. Rocky planets have formed within this band.
- Beyond about 3.5 au of the Sun (known as the "frost line") temperatures are low enough for hydrogen compounds such as CO_2 and H_2O to condense as solids. Gaseous planets have formed beyond this limit.

Sizes

© Diagram Visual Information Ltd.

Key words

gas giant
Jovian planet
orbit
rocky planet
terrestrial planet

trans-Neptunian
object (TNO)

Terrestrial planets

- The *terrestrial planets*, or *rocky planets*, are those similar in size and composition to Earth.
- They are smaller and denser than the Jovian planets.
- The terrestrial planets are Mercury, Venus, Earth, and Mars.
- They orbit closest to the Sun.

Jovian planets

- The *Jovian planets*, or *gas giants*, are those similar in size and composition to Jupiter: Saturn, Uranus, and Neptune.
- They are larger and less dense than the terrestrial planets.
- They orbit farthest from the Sun.

Trans-Neptunian objects

- A *trans-Neptunian object* is any object within the solar system with an orbit that is entirely or mostly beyond the orbit of Neptune.
- Pluto is classified as a trans-Neptunian object. Some astronomers believe that Pluto is too dissimilar to the other planets to be classified as a planet in its own right.
- Pluto is believed to consist mostly of ice and has a highly irregular orbit.
- Several other recently discovered bodies, including Sedna, Quaoar, and Varuna are similar in composition, size, and orbit to Pluto but are not regarded as planets.
- It is likely that, if Pluto were discovered today, it would not be classified as a planet.

Planet	Diameter miles (km)	Planet	Diameter miles (km)
a Pluto	1,420 (2,280)	f Neptune	30,780 (49,530)
b Mercury	3,030 (4,879)	g Uranus	31,760 (51,120)
c Mars	4,220 (6,790)	h Saturn	74,900 (120,540)
d Venus	7,520 (12,100)	i Jupiter	89,350 (142,980)
e Earth	7,930 (12,760)		

Distances

Key words

eccentricity
inner planet
outer planet
orbit
planet

Sun distances

- Each planet's distance from the Sun varies because each has an elliptical orbit.
- Planetary distances are commonly given as their mean distances from the Sun during the course of an orbit.
- Pluto has the most eccentric orbit: for about 20 years of its 248-year orbits it is closer to the Sun than Neptune.

Earth distances

- The distances between Earth and the other planets constantly change because the orbits of the planets are not synchronized.
- For example, when Venus is on the same side of the Sun as Earth it approaches Earth to within 26 million miles (42 million km), but when it is on the opposite side of the Sun it reaches a distance of about 160 million miles (258 million km).

Distance visualization

- The inner planets are much more closely grouped together than the outer planets.
- The mean distance between Mars, the last of the inner planets, and Jupiter, the first of the outer planets, is three times greater than the space that spans the mean orbits of the inner planets combined.
- On average the mean distances between the orbits of the outer planets is about 22 times greater than the mean distances between the orbits of the inner planets.

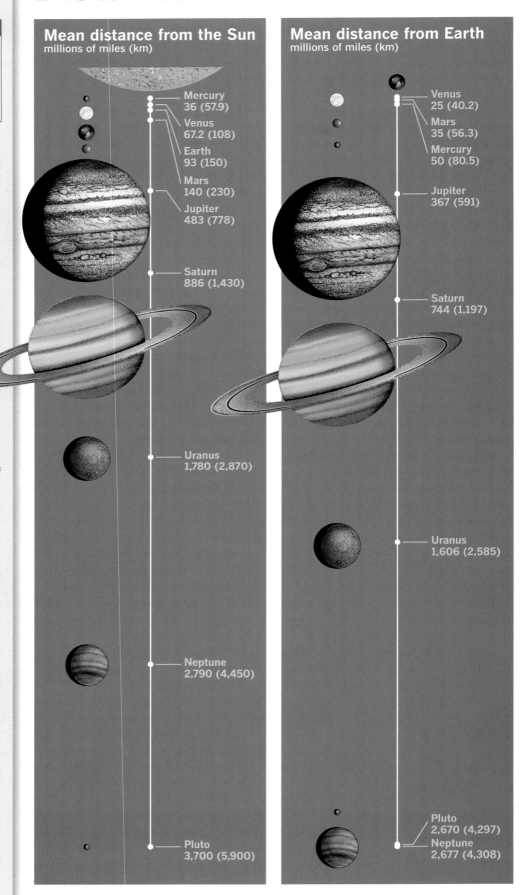

Mean distance from the Sun
millions of miles (km)

Mercury
36 (57.9)

Venus
67.2 (108)

Earth
93 (150)

Mars
140 (230)

Jupiter
483 (778)

Saturn
886 (1,430)

Uranus
1,780 (2,870)

Neptune
2,790 (4,450)

Pluto
3,700 (5,900)

Mean distance from Earth
millions of miles (km)

Venus
25 (40.2)

Mars
35 (56.3)

Mercury
50 (80.5)

Jupiter
367 (591)

Saturn
744 (1,197)

Uranus
1,606 (2,585)

Pluto
2,670 (4,297)

Neptune
2,677 (4,308)

Temperatures

Masses of the planets

Approximate Earth mass
= 6,000,000,000,000,000,000,000 tons

Key words

albedo
atmosphere
orbit
planet

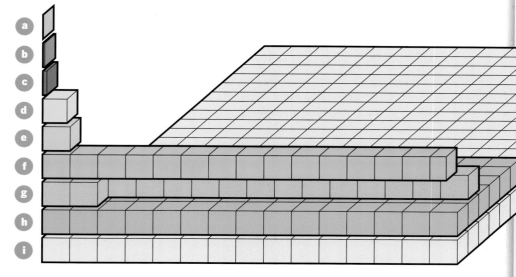

Planet	Mass
a Pluto	0.002
b Mercury	0.06
c Mars	0.11
d Venus	0.82
e Earth	1.0
f Uranus	14.6
g Neptune	17.2
h Saturn	95.2
i Jupiter	317.9

Planet	Average surface temperature °F (°C)
a Venus	864°F (462°C)
b Mercury	−279° to +801°F (−173° to +427°C)
c Earth	57°F (14°C)
d Mars	−225° to 63°F (−143° to 17°C)
e Jupiter	−250°F (−157°C)
f Saturn	−288°F (−178°C)
g Uranus	−357°F (−216°C)
h Neptune	−353°F (−214°C)
i Pluto	−387° to −369°F (−233° to −223°C)

Temperature

- The average temperature on the surface of a planet is determined by two main factors:
- The first factor is the distance from the Sun. The closer a planet's orbit lies to the Sun, the more heat it receives.
- Atmospheric composition is the second factor. This determines how much of the Sun's heat is retained.
- Earth and the Moon receive about the same amount of heat from the Sun. Since the Moon has no appreciable atmosphere however, very little of that heat is retained.
- Mercury is closer to the Sun than Venus, but average surface temperatures on Venus are higher than they are on Mercury because the composition of Venus' atmosphere traps heat.

Albedo

- *Albedo* is a measure of the reflectiveness of a planet or other celestial body.
- It is expressed as a percentage of the amount of sunlight that a body reflects back into space.
- Earth has an average albedo of about 38 percent. The Moon has an albedo of about 12 percent.
- Different regions have different albedos. A snow-covered landscape may have an albedo of 90 percent, but a deciduous forest only has about 13 percent.
- Albedo has a significant influence on surface temperatures.

Surface temperatures of the planets

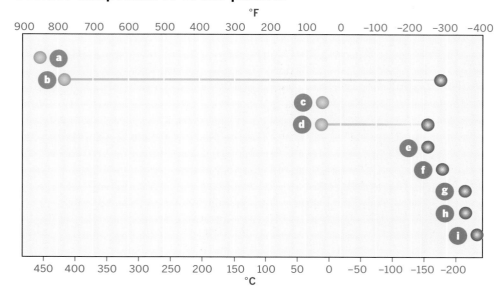

© Diagram Visual Information Ltd.

Key words

axis	orbital speed
eccentricity	planet
ecliptic	rotational period
inclination	sidereal period
orbit	

Describing orbits

- *Rotational period* is the time taken for a planet to complete one revolution on its axis (a local day).
- *Sidereal period* is the time taken for a planet to make one orbit of the Sun (a local year).
- *Orbital speed* is the average velocity at which a planet orbits the Sun.
- *Eccentricity* is a measure of how far an orbit departs from being a perfect circle (all planetary orbits are ellipses).
- *Inclination* is the angle between the plane of a planet's orbit and a fixed reference plane (usually the plane of Earth's orbit around the Sun, known as the *ecliptic*).

Observations

- All the planets except Pluto orbit in planes very close to the ecliptic.
- All the planets orbit in the same direction around the Sun.
- Pluto has the largest eccentricity to its orbit.
- All the planets except Venus have rotational periods shorter than their sidereal periods (a local day is longer than a local year on Venus).

Orbits

Planetary orbits
The yellow line indicates the distance traveled around the Sun in one Earth year.

Rotation periods

	Planet	Days (Earth)	Hours	Minutes
a	Mercury	59	0	0
b	Venus	243	0	0
c	Earth		23	56
d	Mars		24	37
e	Jupiter		9	55
f	Saturn		10	39
g	Uranus		17	8
h	Neptune		16	7
i	Pluto	6	0	0

Orbital speeds

Planet	Miles per sec (km per sec)
Mercury	28.74 (46.24)
Venus	21.0 (33.78)
Earth	17.88 (28.77)
Mars	14.46 (23.27)
Jupiter	7.86 (12.65)
Saturn	5.76 (9.27)
Uranus	4.08 (6.56)
Neptune	3.24 (5.21)
Pluto	2.82 (4.54)

Sidereal periods

Planet	Earath years	Earth days
Mercury		88.0
Venus		224.7
Earth		365.256
Mars		687.0
Jupiter	11.86	
Saturn	29.46	
Uranus	84.01	
Neptune	164.80	
Pluto	248.54	

Moons

Number of known moons

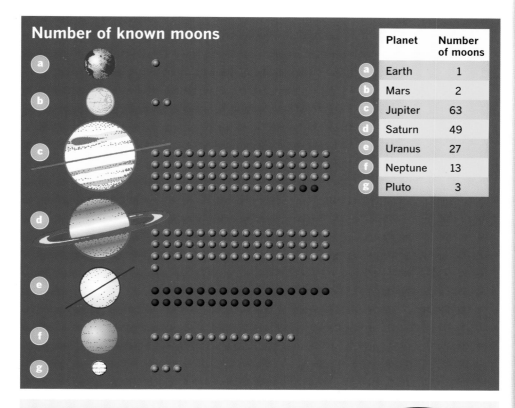

Planet	Number of moons
a Earth	1
b Mars	2
c Jupiter	63
d Saturn	49
e Uranus	27
f Neptune	13
g Pluto	3

Sizes of moons

Moons can be larger than planets:

a Mercury is 3,030 miles (4,879 km) in diameter

b Pluto is 1,420 miles (2,280 km) in diameter

Moon	Of planet	Diameter miles (km)
c Ganymede	Jupiter	3,293 (5,270)
d Titan	Saturn	3,200 (5,120)
e Callisto	Jupiter	3,012 (4,820)
f Io	Jupiter	2,286 (3,659)
g Europa	Jupiter	1,906 (3,050)

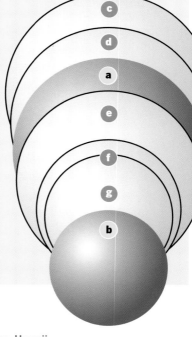

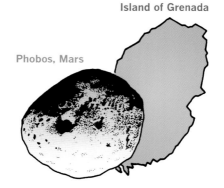

Island of Grenada

Phobos, Mars

Kahoolawe, Hawaii

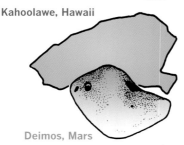

Deimos, Mars

Key words

asteroid	orbit
binary planet	planet
system	satellite
exoplanet	solar system
Jovian planet	tidally locked
moon	

Moon

- A *moon* is a natural satellite of a planet, although the natural companions of some non-planets (such as asteroids) may also be referred to as moons.
- There are more than 140 recognized moons in the solar system and more are continually being discovered.
- Mercury and Venus do not have moons.
- Earth has one large satellite (the Moon). Some astronomers refer to Earth and the Moon as a *binary planet system* because of the relatively large size of the Moon.
- Mars has two small irregularly shaped moons.
- The Jovian planets each have large numbers of moons.
- Pluto has one large and two much smaller moons. It is also considered to be part of a binary planet system by some astronomers because of the relative size of its largest moon, Charon.
- Theories of planet formation suggest that planets outside of the solar system, known as *exoplanets*, should also have moons, but none have yet been detected.

Moon orbits

- All moons are *tidally locked* to the planets they orbit.
- No moons have moons of their own because the orbit that the moon of a moon would have to occupy would be inherently unstable.

Key words

gravitational
  attraction
gravity
orbit
planet

Gravity

- Gravity is the tendency of masses to move toward each other.
- *Gravitational attraction* is the way in which this tendency is usually described. According to Albert Einstein's generally accepted theory of gravity there is no such force as gravitational attraction, but the phrase is used when discussing the motion of celestial bodies and spacecraft.
- The gravitational attraction exerted by a body depends on its mass. More massive bodies exert greater gravitational attraction than less massive bodies.

Planet gravities

- Because the planets have different masses, their gravitational attractions are also different.
- For example, it takes less energy to launch a spacecraft from the surface of Mars into orbit than it does to launch the same spacecraft from the surface of Earth. This is because Earth has a greater mass and therefore a greater gravitational attraction than Mars.

Gravities

Planetary high jumps

An athelete capable of making a vertical jump of 3 feet (0.91 m) on Earth would achieve these heights on the other planets.

	Planet	Height
a	Jupiter	1 foot 3.5 inches (0.39 m)
b	Neptune	2 feet 6.5 inches (0.77 m)
c	Uranus	2 feet 6.75 inches (0.78 m)
d	Saturn	2 feet 7.25 inches (0.79 m)
e	Venus	3 feet 4.75 inches (1.04 m)
f	Mars	7 feet 10.75 inches (2.41 m)
g	Mercury	8 feet 1.25 inches (2.47 m)
h	Pluto	Not known

	Planet	Comparative gravity (Earth gravity = 1.0)		Planet	Comparative gravity (Earth gravity = 1.0)
a	Jupiter	2.64	e	Venus	0.88
b	Neptune	1.2	f	Mars	0.38
c	Uranus	1.17	g	Mercury	0.38
d	Saturn	1.15	h	Pluto	Not known

Planet summaries

	Mercury	Venus	Earth
Diameter	3,030 miles (4,879 km)	7,520 miles (12,100 km)	7,930 miles (12,760 km)
Mean distance from Sun	36 million miles (57.9 million km)	67.2 million miles (108 million km)	93 million miles (150 million km)
Surface temperature	−279° to +801°F (−173° to +427°C)	864°F (462°C)	57°F (14°C)
Rotation period	59 days	243 days	23 hours 56 mins
Sidereal period	88 days	224.7 days	365.26 days

	Mars	Jupiter	Saturn
Diameter	4,220 miles (6,790 km)	89,350 miles (142,980 km)	74,900 miles (120,540 km)
Mean distance from Sun	140 million miles (230 million km)	483 million miles (778 million km)	886 million miles (1,430 million km)
Surface temperature	−225° to +63°F (−143° to +17°C)	−250°F (−157°C)	−288°F (−178°C)
Rotation period	24 hours 37 minutes	9 hours 55 minutes	10 hours 39 minutes
Sidereal period	687 days	11.86 years	29.46 years

	Uranus	Neptune	Pluto
Diameter	31,760 miles (51,120 km)	30,780 miles (49,530 km)	1,420 miles (2,280 km)
Mean distance from Sun	1,780 million miles (2,870 million km)	2,790 million miles (4,450 million km)	3,700 million miles (5,900 million km)
Surface temperature	−357°F (−216°C)	−353°F (−214°C)	−387° to −369°F (−233° to 223°C)
Rotation period	17 hours 8 minutes	16 hours 7 minutes	6 days
Sidereal period	84.01 years	164.80 years	248.54 years

Key words

aphelion	orbit
atmosphere	perihelion
axis	pole
equator	rotational period
greenhouse gas	sidereal period

Diameter

- None of the planets in the solar system are perfect spheres.
- The equatorial diameters of all of the planets are slightly greater than their polar diameters.

Mean distance from the Sun

- The orbits of all of the planets are elliptical.
- This means that there is a point on a planet's orbit where it makes its closest approach to the Sun and a point where it is at its most distant.
- The closest point to the Sun is known as *aphelion* and the most distant point as *perihelion*.

Surface temperature

- Planets closer to the Sun are generally warmer than planets farther away from the Sun, but the nature of a planet's atmosphere has a great impact on surface temperature.
- For example, Venus has a very thick atmosphere laden with greenhouse gases, which gives it a very high and almost constant surface temperature. Mercury is much closer to the Sun but has a very thin atmosphere that does not trap heat. Consequently there is a great temperature difference between the side of Mercury facing the Sun and the side facing away from it.

Rotational period

- A planet's *rotational period* is the length of time it takes that planet to rotate once on its axis. This can be thought of as a local "day."

Sidereal period

- A planet's *sidereal period* is the length of time it takes to complete one orbit around the Sun. This can be thought of as a local "year." Not all planets have sidereal periods (years) that are longer than their rotational periods (days).

Sunspots and flares

Key words

atmosphere
solar flare
sunspot

Sunspots

- A *sunspot* is a region of the Sun's surface that is cooler than its surroundings at about 8,500°F (4,700°C) rather than 10,300°F (5,700°C).
- They are darker because they are cooler.
- Sunspots are also slight depressions in the Sun's surface.
- They are associated with magnetic fields surrounding the Sun.
- Different parts of the Sun's surface rotate at different speeds, which results in lines of magnetic flux becoming twisted, with their ends puncturing the Sun's surface. These puncture points are sunspots.
- Sunspots appear in pairs, each with opposite magnetic polarity, and fade after about two weeks.

Solar flares

- A *solar flare* is a rapid and energetic eruption of material from the Sun's surface.
- They are explosive events that typically last for no more than a few minutes.
- Solar flare strength is categorized as A, B, C, D, M, or X (with X being the most powerful). Each class is ten times more powerful than the preceding class.
- Increased solar flare activity corresponds with increased sunspot activity.
- The streams of energized particles emitted in a solar flare may interact with Earth's atmosphere and cause interference with electronic and radio equipment.

Typical sunspot distribution

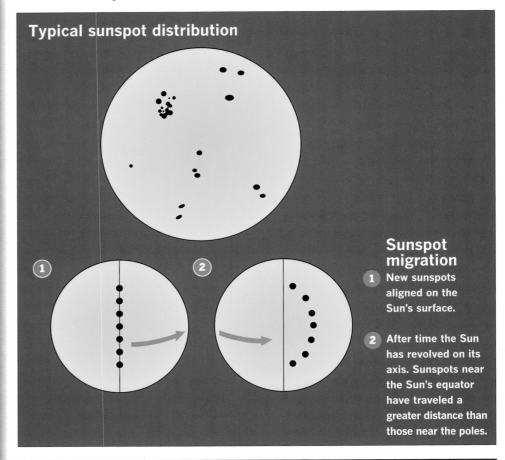

Sunspot migration

1 New sunspots aligned on the Sun's surface.

2 After time the Sun has revolved on its axis. Sunspots near the Sun's equator have traveled a greater distance than those near the poles.

Elements of a solar flare

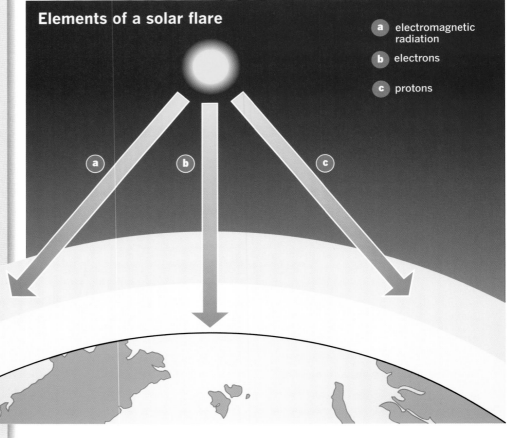

a electromagnetic radiation

b electrons

c protons

Solar wind

Solar prominence

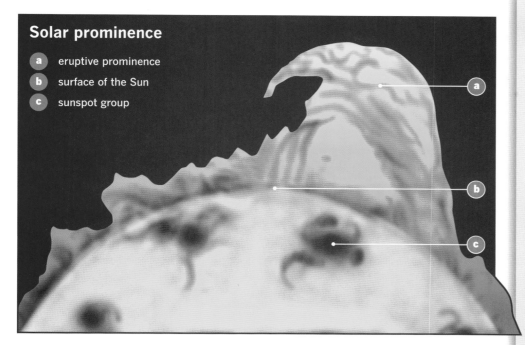

- **a** eruptive prominence
- **b** surface of the Sun
- **c** sunspot group

Solar wind

- *Solar wind* is the high-energy plasma constantly emitted into space from the surface of the Sun.
- It consists of a stream of ionized particles (mostly protons) with the same composition as the Sun's corona. The volume of space influenced by the solar wind is known as the *heliosphere*.
- The *heliopause* is the boundary of the solar wind's influence.
  - The actual distance of the heliopause from the Sun is unknown. It certainly lies far beyond the orbit of Pluto.
  - The position of the heliopause probably varies depending on the density of the local interstellar medium and the velocity of the wind.

Solar prominences

- A *solar prominence* is a prominent structure of energetic material formed in the Sun's chromosphere.
- An *eruptive prominence* is an arched structure following lines of magnetism that may persist for several hours.
- A *quiescent prominence* is a patch of energized gas that hangs in the Sun's chromosphere for days.
- Prominences are associated with sunspots.

Solar wind

- **a** Sun
- **b** solar winds moving along lines of magnetism
- **c** "bow shock" region where solar wind is deflected by the magnetosphere
- **d** magnetosphere (Earth's magnetic field)
- **e** Earth
- **f** distortion of the magnetosphere by solar wind creates a magnetotail
- **g** interstellar gases and radiation deflected by heliosphere

© Diagram Visual Information Ltd.

Mercury

Comparative sizes of Mercury and Earth

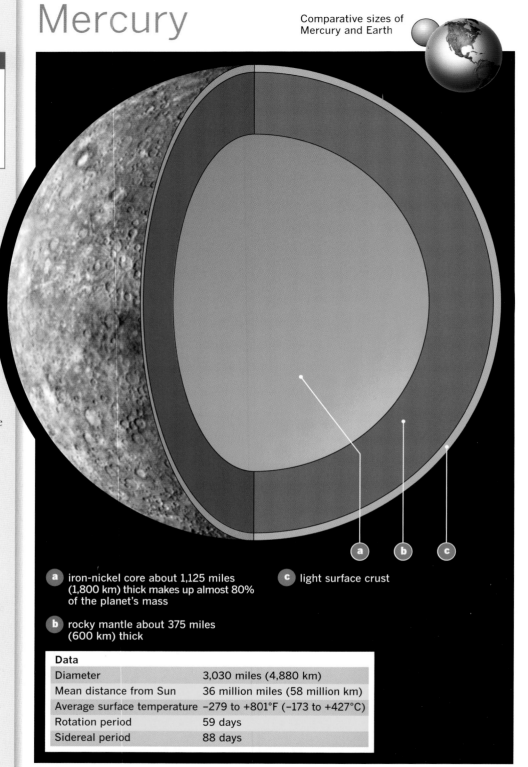

Key words

atmosphere	orbit
axis	retrograde
core	rotational period
crust	sidereal period
impact crater	tidally locked
mantle	

Atmosphere

● Mercury has a trace atmosphere consisting of oxygen, potassium, and sodium.

Surface

● The surface is heavily cratered.
● There are many scarps caused as cooling and shrinking of the core wrinkled the surface.
● The Caloris basin is a prominent impact crater 840 miles (1,350 km) wide.

Composition

● Mercury has a relatively large iron core that composes 42 percent of the planet's volume (Earth's core composes just 17 percent of its volume).

Orbit and rotation

● It spins on its axis three times for every two orbits of the Sun.
● It is not tidally locked to the Sun as originally thought.
● An observer on the surface would see the Sun in retrograde motion (moving backwards across the sky) for the period during which Mercury's orbital velocity exceeds it rotational velocity.

a iron-nickel core about 1,125 miles (1,800 km) thick makes up almost 80% of the planet's mass

b rocky mantle about 375 miles (600 km) thick

c light surface crust

Data	
Diameter	3,030 miles (4,880 km)
Mean distance from Sun	36 million miles (58 million km)
Average surface temperature	−279 to +801°F (−173 to +427°C)
Rotation period	59 days
Sidereal period	88 days

Mercury

Venus

Comparative sizes of
Venus and Earth

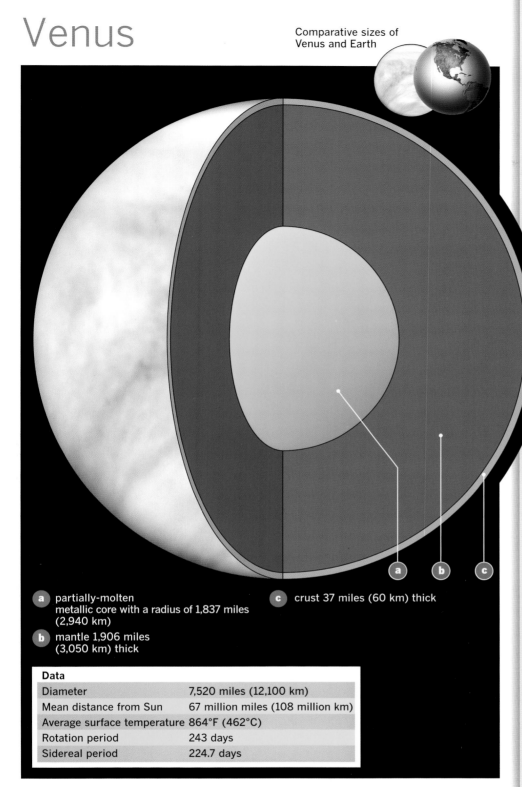

a partially-molten
metallic core with a radius of 1,837 miles
(2,940 km)

b mantle 1,906 miles
(3,050 km) thick

c crust 37 miles (60 km) thick

Data	
Diameter	7,520 miles (12,100 km)
Mean distance from Sun	67 million miles (108 million km)
Average surface temperature	864°F (462°C)
Rotation period	243 days
Sidereal period	224.7 days

Key words

atmosphere	mantle
axis	meteorite
core	orbit
crater	retrograde
crust	rotational period
greenhouse effect	sidereal period

Atmosphere

- Venus has a very dense atmosphere consisting of carbon dioxide and nitrogen.
  - Atmospheric pressure at the surface is about 90 times that on Earth.
  - The carbon dioxide-rich atmosphere produces a strong greenhouse effect.
  - Dense clouds composed of sulfur dioxide and sulfuric acid droplets completely obscure the surface.

Surface

- Most of the surface (90 percent) is composed of solidified lava and there are few craters.
- The dense atmosphere is thought to burn up all but the largest meteorites before they can impact the surface.
- The surface rock is young. Venus may undergo periodic resurfacing events caused by massive volcanic upwellings.
- The greenhouse effect produced by the atmosphere means that surface temperatures are greater than those on Mercury, though Venus is more than twice as distant from the Sun.
- Ishtar Terra and Aphrodite Terra are two continent-sized highlands.

Orbit and rotation

- It has a very slow, retrograde rotation on its axis (rotates east to west).
- It always presents the same face to Earth when at its closest approach.

Composition

- Venus' composition is very similar to Earth.

Venus

Earth

Key words

atmosphere
core
crust
greenhouse gas
impact crater

mantle
rotational period
sidereal period

Atmosphere

- Earth has a thick atmosphere composed of nitrogen, oxygen, argon, and traces of other gases.
- The composition of the atmosphere is significantly influenced by the presence of life on the planet.
- Greenhouse gases in the atmosphere produce warming that allows Earth to have liquid water on its surface.

Surface

- Earth is the only planet known to have liquid water on its surface (covering about 70 percent of its total area).
- There are very few visible impact craters due to highly active erosion processes and frequent volcanic activity.
- Unlike any other planet the surface is composed of tectonic plates, which are in constant motion.

Composition

- Earth is the densest planet in the solar system.
- It is composed of a large iron-rich core, a semi-molten iron and magnesium mantle, and a thin silicon-rich crust.

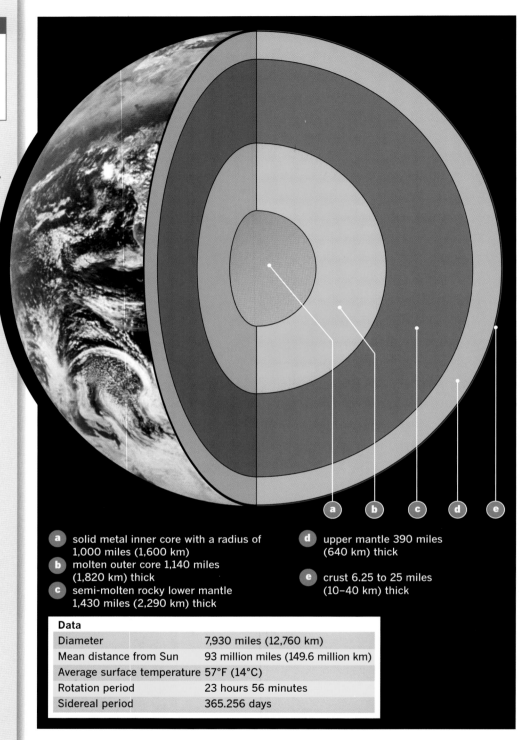

a solid metal inner core with a radius of 1,000 miles (1,600 km)

b molten outer core 1,140 miles (1,820 km) thick

c semi-molten rocky lower mantle 1,430 miles (2,290 km) thick

d upper mantle 390 miles (640 km) thick

e crust 6.25 to 25 miles (10–40 km) thick

Data	
Diameter	7,930 miles (12,760 km)
Mean distance from Sun	93 million miles (149.6 million km)
Average surface temperature	57°F (14°C)
Rotation period	23 hours 56 minutes
Sidereal period	365.256 days

Earth

The Moon

Comparative sizes of Earth and the Moon

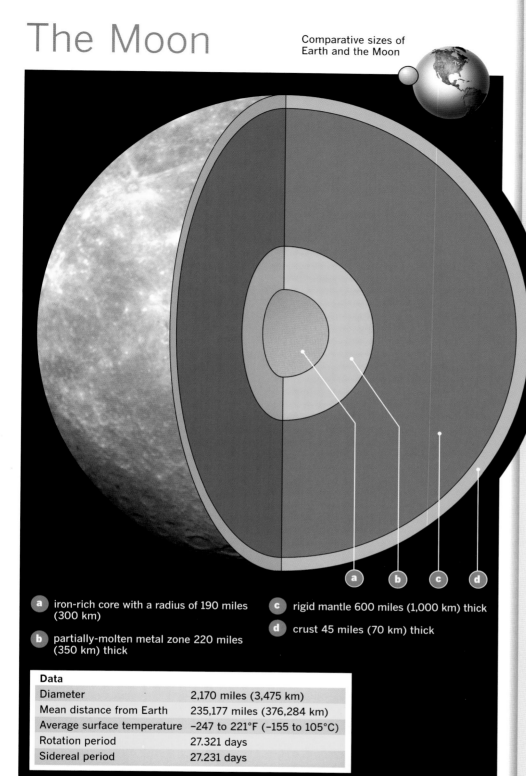

Key words

atmosphere	rotational period
core	sidereal period
crust	solar eclipse
impact crater	solar wind
mantle	terrae
mare	tidally locked

Atmosphere

- A very thin atmosphere composed of gases vented from the Moon's interior and particles of solar wind.

Surface

- Flat plains, known as *maria* (seas; singular: *mare*), are the result of ancient lava flows that filled giant impact craters.
- Highlands, known as *terrae*, are very irregular mountainous regions created by the crowding together of large impact craters.
- Almost all maria are found on the side of the Moon facing Earth (the near side).
- Terrae dominate the far side of the Moon (the "dark side").

Composition

- The thickness of the crust is greater on the far side (60 miles, 100 km) than on the near side (37 miles, 60 km).
- The composition of the Moon is thought to be identical to Earth's (though in different proportions).

Orbit and rotation

- The Moon is tidally locked to Earth.
- The relative distances of the Moon and the Sun from Earth mean that the Moon appears to be the same size in the sky as the Sun. This is why total solar eclipses are possible.

a iron-rich core with a radius of 190 miles (300 km)

b partially-molten metal zone 220 miles (350 km) thick

c rigid mantle 600 miles (1,000 km) thick

d crust 45 miles (70 km) thick

Data

Diameter	2,170 miles (3,475 km)
Mean distance from Earth	235,177 miles (376,284 km)
Average surface temperature	–247 to 221°F (–155 to 105°C)
Rotation period	27.321 days
Sidereal period	27.231 days

Earth

The Moon

Key words

equator	orbit
full Moon	tide
gravitational	
attraction	
new Moon	

Tides

- A *tide* is the regular rise and fall of the ocean's surface.
- Bodies of water are influenced by the gravitational effects of the Moon and the Sun.
- In large bodies of water, such as the oceans, these effects become evident as tides.
- At any point in the ocean there are usually two high tides and two low tides each day.

Simple equilibrium model

- A simplified model that assumes that Earth is covered by water at a uniform depth, and that the Moon remains directly above the equator, illustrates the Moon's influence on Earth's tides:
- The gravitational attraction of the Moon draws Earth's water toward it, creating a bulge of water on the Moon side of Earth.
- On the opposite side of Earth the Moon's gravitational attraction is correspondingly less, and an opposite bulge is formed.
- As Earth rotates every 24 hours, a point on the surface passes through the two bulges and the troughs in between them. These bulges are the high and low tides.
- In fact the Moon does not remain over the equator: its overhead position shifts between 28.5° N and 28.5° S, so the tidal bulges and troughs are rarely of equal size.
- Since the Moon advances in its orbit around Earth as Earth rotates, a full tidal cycle actually occurs every 24 hours and 50 minutes.

Earth's tides

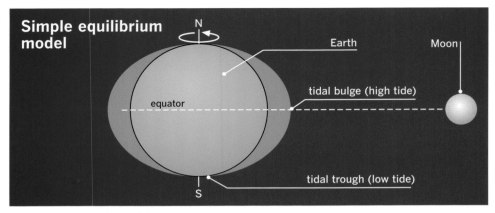

Simple equilibrium model

N

Earth

Moon

equator

tidal bulge (high tide)

tidal trough (low tide)

S

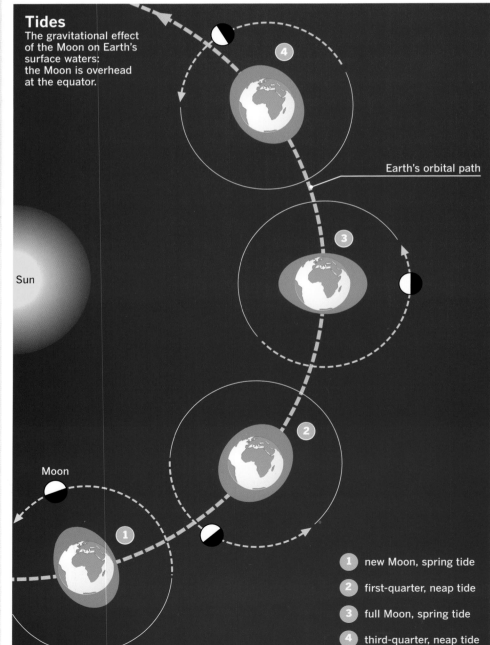

Tides
The gravitational effect of the Moon on Earth's surface waters: the Moon is overhead at the equator.

4

Earth's orbital path

3

Sun

2

Moon

1

1. new Moon, spring tide
2. first-quarter, neap tide
3. full Moon, spring tide
4. third-quarter, neap tide

Lunar phases

a Sun's light

b Earth

c Moon: half lit by Sun's light as it orbits Earth

d appearance of the Moon as seen from Earth

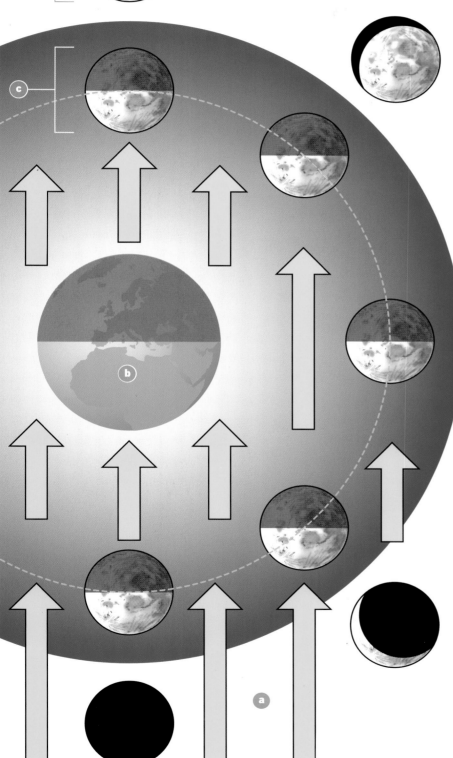

Key words

full Moon	orbit
lunar cycle	
lunar eclipse	
lunar phase	
new Moon	

Lunar phases

- *Lunar phases* refer to the regular cycle during which the appearance of the Moon changes as seen from Earth.

- Half of the Moon's surface is constantly illuminated by the Sun (except during a lunar eclipse).

- As the illuminated portion is very bright compared to the non-illuminated portion, only the illuminated portion is visible to the naked eye from Earth.

- At different times, varying amounts of the illuminated portion of the Moon's surface are visible from Earth.

- Lunar phases are a result of the constantly changing relative positions of Earth, the Moon, and the Sun.

- At times only a small crescent of the illuminated area of the Moon can be seen. At other times the entire illuminated area is facing Earth and is clearly visible.

- The amount of the illuminated area of the Moon that is visible increases until a full Moon is visible, and then decreases again until nothing of the Moon is visible.

- A *full Moon* is when the entire illuminated area is visible.

- A *new Moon* is when none of the illuminated area is visible.

- One *lunar cycle*, from new Moon to new Moon, takes 29.5 days.

Key words

annular solar eclipse	orbit
central duration	partial solar eclipse
eclipse magnitude	perigee
hybrid solar eclipse	solar eclipse
new Moon	total solar eclipse

Solar eclipse

- A *solar eclipse* occurs when the Moon passes in front of the Sun from the point of view of an observer.
- From the point of view of an observer on Earth, the Moon at perigee is slightly larger than the Sun in the sky. This means that the Moon can completely obscure the Sun.
- A *partial solar eclipse* is when only part of the Sun is obscured by the Moon.
- A *total solar eclipse* is when the entire Sun is obscured by the Moon.
- Observers may see a total solar eclipse, a partial solar eclipse, or no eclipse at all depending on their locations on Earth.
- An *annular solar eclipse* occurs when the Moon moves directly in front of the Sun and the Moon is at perigee. A thin ring of the Sun can still be seen around the Moon.
- A *hybrid solar eclipse* is when a total eclipse is visible from some locations on Earth and an annular eclipse is visible from other locations.
- *Eclipse magnitude* is a measure of how much of the Sun is covered by the Moon at the height of an eclipse. Any value greater than 1.0 is a total eclipse.
- *Central duration* is the length of time of the total or annular phase of an eclipse.
- A solar eclipse can only occur on the occasion of a new Moon. This is the only time when the Moon's shadow can fall on Earth.

Solar eclipses

Total eclipse

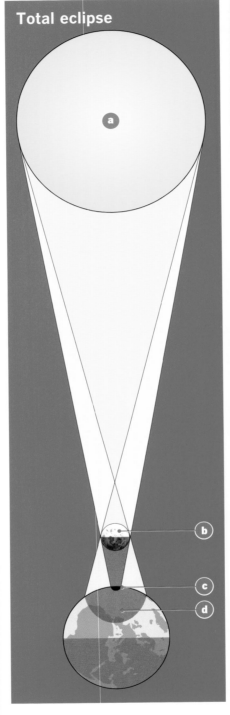

Partial eclipse

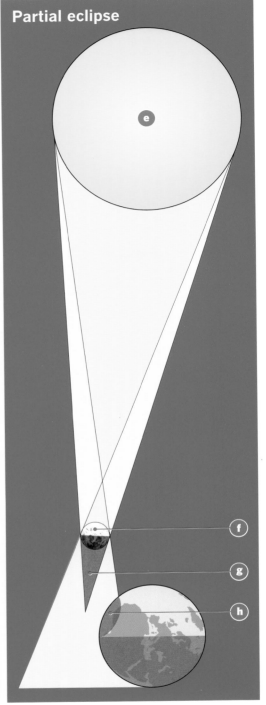

a Sun

b Moon at perigee of orbit

c area of totality—sunlight is completely blocked by Moon

d area of partial eclipse—sunlight is partially blocked by Moon

e Sun

f Moon

g total eclipse shadow misses Earth

h area of partial eclipse

Lunar eclipses

Total eclipse

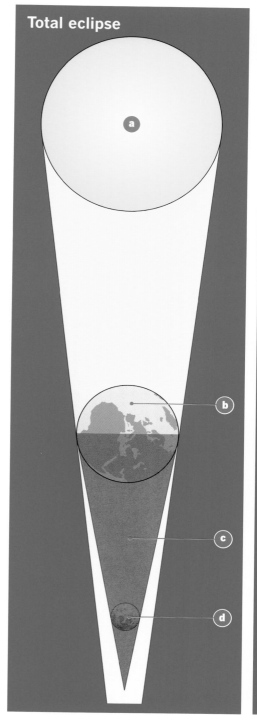

Partial eclipse

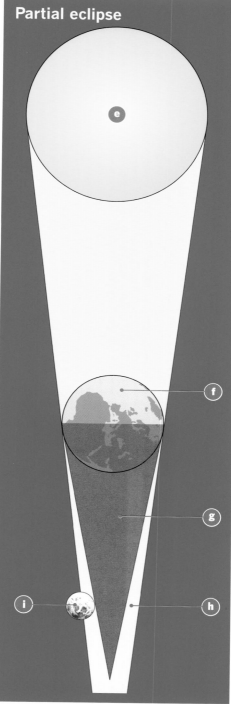

Key words

full Moon	total duration
lunar eclipse	total lunar
orbit	eclipse
partial lunar	umbral
eclipse	magnitude

Lunar eclipse

- A *lunar eclipse* occurs when Earth passes between the Sun and the Moon and stops the Sun's light from illuminating the Moon. In other words, when the Earth's shadow falls on the Moon.
- A *partial lunar eclipse* is when Earth's shadow obscures only part of the Moon.
- A *total lunar eclipse* is when Earth's shadow obscures the whole Moon.
- Lunar eclipses can only occur when the Moon is full. This is the only time when Earth is positioned directly between the Moon and the Sun.
- Lunar eclipses do not occur at every full Moon because the Moon's orbit around Earth is tipped by about five degrees from the plane of Earth's orbit around the Sun. The Moon usually passes above or below Earth's shadow.
- During a total lunar eclipse the Moon is not completely dark. Some light is refracted by Earth's atmosphere and cast on the Moon.
- *Umbral magnitude* is the portion of the Moon's visible surface obscured by Earth's shadow. Values greater than 0 but less than 1 indicate a partial lunar eclipse. Values of 1 or greater indicate a total lunar eclipse.
- *Total duration* is the length of time that a total lunar eclipse persists.

a Sun

b Earth

c total shadow cast by Earth

d Moon enters Earth's total shadow

e Sun

f Earth

g total shadow cast by Earth

h partial shadow cast by Earth

i Moon enters Earth's partial shadow

Lunar features

© Diagram Visual Information Ltd.

Key words

impact crater
lunar sea
mare

Impact craters

- An *impact crater* is a depression in the surface of a celestial body formed by the impact of another body.
- Impact craters once completely covered the Moon's surface before the formation of the lunar seas.
- Most of the Moon's craters are believed to have been formed between three and four billion years ago.
- Craters located in the lunar seas are more recent.

Seas

- A lunar sea, or *mare*, is a large, smooth, dark-colored area on the surface of the Moon.
- The lunar seas do not, and have never, contained water.
- They are flat areas created by huge lava flows in the Moon's distant past.
- Lunar seas are only found on the side of the Moon facing Earth (the near side).

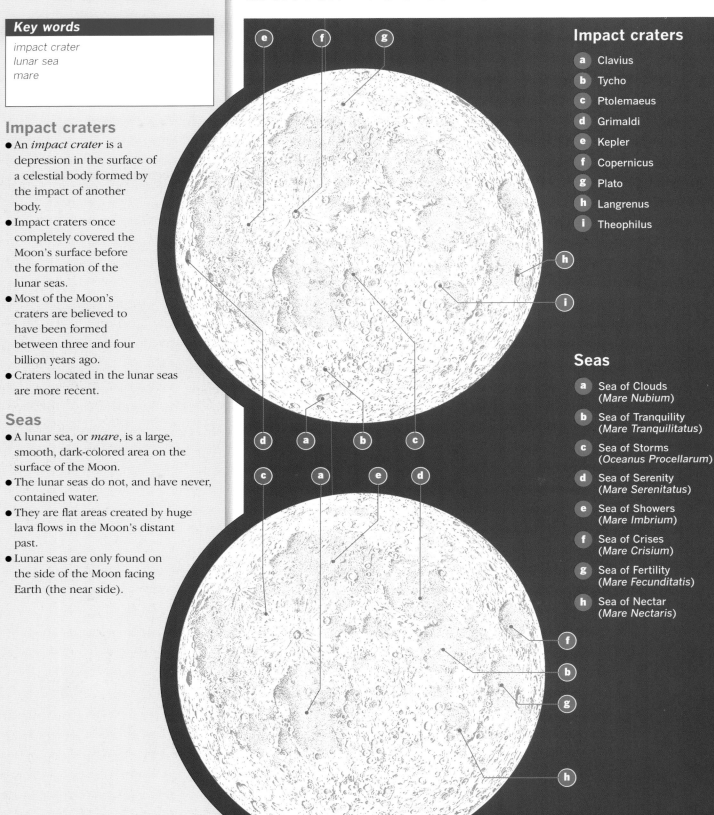

Impact craters

- **a** Clavius
- **b** Tycho
- **c** Ptolemaeus
- **d** Grimaldi
- **e** Kepler
- **f** Copernicus
- **g** Plato
- **h** Langrenus
- **i** Theophilus

Seas

- **a** Sea of Clouds (*Mare Nubium*)
- **b** Sea of Tranquility (*Mare Tranquilitatus*)
- **c** Sea of Storms (*Oceanus Procellarum*)
- **d** Sea of Serenity (*Mare Serenitatis*)
- **e** Sea of Showers (*Mare Imbrium*)
- **f** Sea of Crises (*Mare Crisium*)
- **g** Sea of Fertility (*Mare Fecunditatis*)
- **h** Sea of Nectar (*Mare Nectaris*)

Meteoroids

Meteorite

a enters Earth's atmospheric at 30 miles per second (50 kmps)

b friction with atmospheric gases heats surface to several thousand degrees Fahrenheit

c bright tail of vaporized material given off by heated meteorite

d meteorite slows and cools; bright tail fades by altitude of about 10–15 miles (16–24 km)

e meteorite free falls at about 150–200 miles per hour (240–320 kmph)

f cooled meteorite coated with "sooty" crust impacts ground

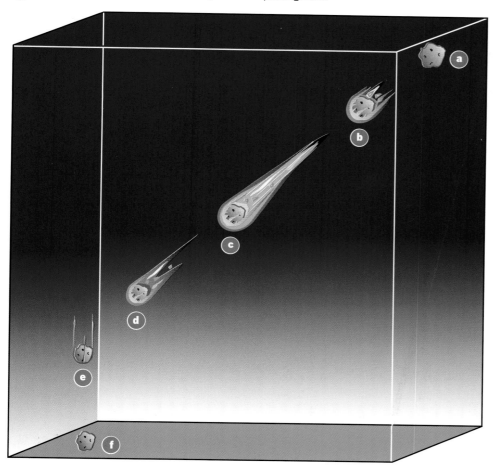

Key words

aerodynamic heating	meteorite
atmosphere	meteoroid
impact crater	micrometeoroid
meteor	orbital velocity
	planet

Classification

- *Meteoroid* is a general term for a lump of material in space that is larger than a molecule but smaller than about 160 feet (50 m) in diameter.
- *Micrometeoroid* is a general term for a meteoroid that is between five microns and six inches (15 cm) in diameter.

Meteors

- *Meteor* is a general term for a meteorite that enters the atmosphere of a planet (usually Earth) but is vaporized by aerodynamic heating before it reaches the surface.
- *Meteorite* is a general term for a meteorite that enters the atmosphere of a planet (usually Earth) and impacts the surface.
- The vast majority of meteorites are slowed from their orbital speeds by the atmosphere and impact the surface traveling no faster than a rock dropped from a tall building.
- Very few meteorites are large enough to still be traveling at a significant percentage of their orbital velocities when they impact the surface. These large meteorites can create impact craters many miles in diameter.
- About 500 small meteorites reach Earth's surface every year.
- Most fall in the ocean and very few of the rest land near inhabited areas.

Meteor showers

- Meteors enter the atmosphere at an average rate of about six per hour.
- At certain regular times of the year large numbers of meteors enter the atmosphere. These are known as meteor showers.
- Meteor showers occur when Earth passes through trails of dust and debris left by comets or asteroids (known as parent comets).

Regular meteor showers

Shower	Date of peak activity	Parent comet	Meteor frequency (maximum no. per hour)
Quadrantids	January 4	unknown	110
Lyrids	April 22	Thatcher	8
Eta Aquarids	May 5	Halley	18
Delta Aquarids	July 3	unknown	30
Perseids	August 12	Swift-Tuttle	65
Orionids	October 21	Halley	25
Taurids	November 8	Encke	10
Leonids	November 17	Temple-Tuttle	15
Geminids	December 14	Asteroid 3200 Phaeton	55
Ursids	December 23	Tuttle	20

Key words

atmosphere	mantle
core	pole
crust	rotational period
hemisphere	sidereal period
impact crater	solar system

Atmosphere

- Mars has a thin atmosphere composed of carbon dioxide (95 percent), nitrogen, and argon.
- Atmospheric pressure at the surface is about 0.75 percent of that on Earth.

Surface

- The northern hemisphere of the planet is mostly flat and dominated by smooth lava flows.
- The southern hemisphere is dominated by highland with many ancient impact craters.
- Recent exploration suggests that large amounts of liquid water may have flowed on the surface in the distant past.
- The northern and southern polar regions contain frozen carbon dioxide and some frozen water.
- Olympus Mons is an extinct volcano 17 miles (27 km) tall. It is the highest mountain in the solar system.
- Valles Marineris is a 4.5 mile (7 km) deep canyon that stretches for 2,500 miles (4,000 km).

Composition

- Mars is composed of a small iron-rich core, a thick silicate mantle, and a thick crust.
- Unlike Earth, it is thought that the interior of Mars has cooled and no longer produces volcanic activity.

Mars

Comparative sizes of Mars and Earth

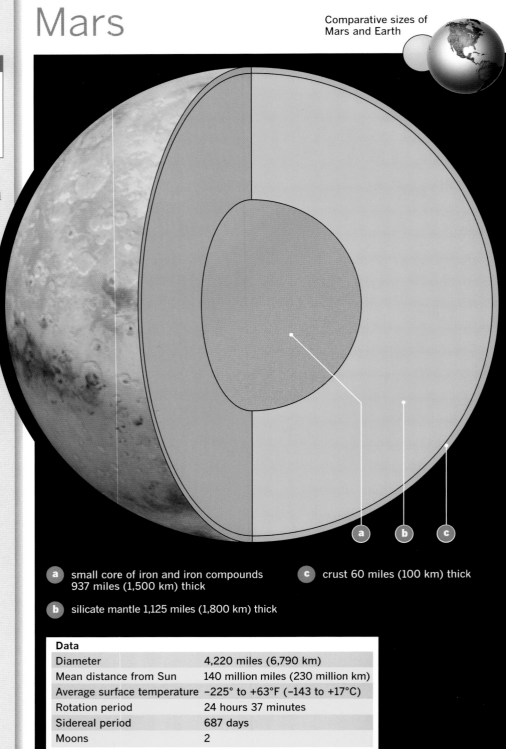

a small core of iron and iron compounds 937 miles (1,500 km) thick

b silicate mantle 1,125 miles (1,800 km) thick

c crust 60 miles (100 km) thick

Data	
Diameter	4,220 miles (6,790 km)
Mean distance from Sun	140 million miles (230 million km)
Average surface temperature	−225° to +63°F (−143 to +17°C)
Rotation period	24 hours 37 minutes
Sidereal period	687 days
Moons	2

Mars

Jupiter

Comparative sizes of Jupiter and Earth

Key words

atmosphere	pole
axis	rotational period
core	sidereal period
equator	
gas giant	

Composition

- Jupiter is a *gas giant*, which means that it is mostly composed of elements that are usually gases on Earth.
  - The atmosphere consists of about 86 percent hydrogen and 14 percent helium.
    - There is no clear distinction between atmosphere and surface. Closer to the planet's center, pressure causes the gases of the atmosphere to become a liquid and eventually a metallic solid.
    - There may be a solid rocky core at Jupiter's center that is about ten to 15 times the size of Earth.

Upper atmosphere

- In the upper "gaseous" part of the atmosphere bands of clouds circle the planet.
- Adjacent bands may be traveling in the opposite direction, which causes swirling vortices to form at their boundaries.
- These vortices are similar to hurricane and typhoon storms on Earth but are many times more powerful.
- The "great red spot" is a giant storm system (about three times the diameter of Earth) that has persisted in Jupiter's atmosphere for at least 300 years.

Orbit and rotation

- Jupiter rotates on its axis more rapidly than any other planet.
- This rapid rotation distorts the shape of the planet, flattening its poles and fattening its equator.

a compact iron-silicate core

b zone of liquid/metallic hydrogen 28,125 miles (45,000 km) thick

c layer of liquid molecular hydrogen 15,652 miles (25,000 km) thick

d hydrogen-rich atmosphere 600 miles (1,000 km) thick

Data

Diameter	89,350 miles (142,980 km)
Mean distance from Sun	483 million miles (778 million km)
Average surface temperature	−250°F (−157°C)
Rotation period	9 hours 55 minutes
Sidereal period	11.86 years
Moons	63

Jupiter

Key words

interplanetary
  dust
orbit
retrograde

Inner moons

- Jupiter's inner moons orbit within 124,000 miles (200,000 km).
- They all have diameters smaller than 125 miles (200 km).

Galilean moons

- The Galilean moons were all discovered by Italian astronomer Galileo Galilei (1564–1642).
- They orbit between 250,000 and 1.2 million miles (400,000–2 million km) from Jupiter.
- They include the largest moons in the solar system.

Outer moons

- The outer moons orbit between 6.8 million and 7.5 million miles (11–12 million km) from Jupiter.

Retrograde moons

- The retrograde moons all have retrograde orbits.
- They orbit between 13 million and 15 million miles (21–24 million km) from Jupiter.
- All have diameters of less than 30 miles (50 km).

Rings

- Jupiter has four faint rings. The three inner rings are thought to be composed of dust-sized fragments from the planet's moons. The fourth and most distant ring has a retrograde orbit and may consist of captured fragments of interplanetary dust.

Jupiter's moons

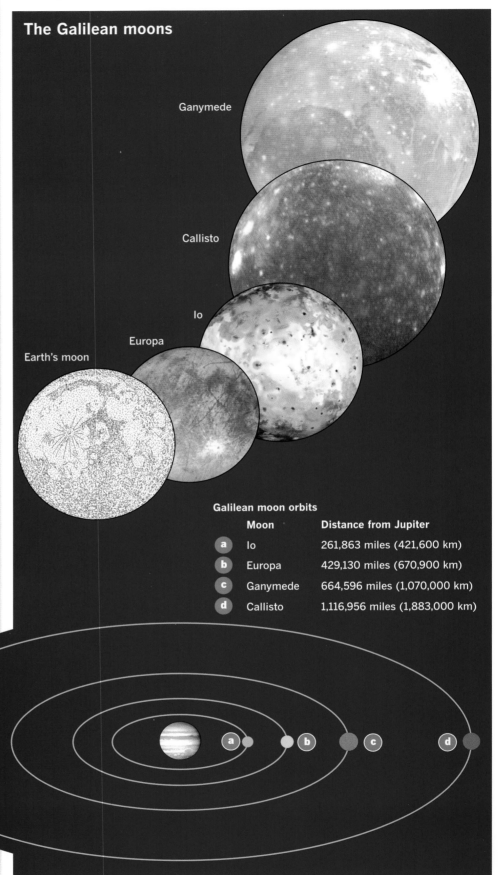

The Galilean moons

Ganymede

Callisto

Io

Europa

Earth's moon

Galilean moon orbits

	Moon	Distance from Jupiter
a	Io	261,863 miles (421,600 km)
b	Europa	429,130 miles (670,900 km)
c	Ganymede	664,596 miles (1,070,000 km)
d	Callisto	1,116,956 miles (1,883,000 km)

Asteroids

Main belt asteroids		Trojans	
Name	**Diameter**	Hector	111 miles (179 km)
Ceres	622 miles (1,003 km)	Patroclus	91 miles (147 km)
Pallas	377 miles (608 km)	**Near Earth Asteroids**	
Vesta	334 miles (538 km)	Icarus	0.9 miles (1.4 km)
Hygeia	279 miles (450 km)	Eros	8.1 x 20.5 miles (13 x 33 km)
		Apollo	1.1 miles (1.7 km)

Orbits of some major asteroids

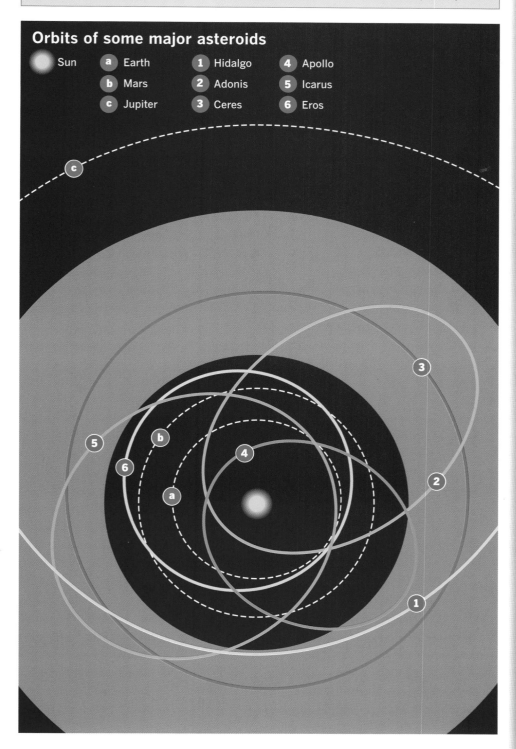

- Sun
- **a** Earth
- **b** Mars
- **c** Jupiter
- **1** Hidalgo
- **2** Adonis
- **3** Ceres
- **4** Apollo
- **5** Icarus
- **6** Eros

Key words

albedo	Near Earth
asteroid	Asteroid (NEA)
main belt	orbit
asteroid	Trojan

Classification

- *Asteroid* is a general term for a body in space that is larger than about 160 feet (50 m) in diameter, but smaller than a moon and mostly composed of rock rather than icy material.
- Asteroids may be classified according to the composition of their surfaces. Compositions are measured by observing the color, albedo, and spectral lines of reflected light.
- "C-type" asteroids have predominantly carbonaceous surfaces.
- "S-type" asteroids have predominantly silicaceous surfaces.
- "M-type" asteroids have predominantly metallic surfaces.
- There are other more detailed schemes for asteroid classification.
- Asteroids are not necessarily spherical and can be irregularly shaped; for example, Eros is an oblong object measuring 8.1 by 20.5 miles (13 by 33 km) across.

Asteroid belts

- There are three main concentrations of asteroids in the solar system.
- The majority of asteroids orbit the Sun in a broad belt between Mars and Jupiter. This is known as the *main belt*.
- Two clusters of asteroids exist one sixth of an orbit in front of and behind Jupiter in a gravitational "trap." These are known as the *Trojans*.
- Several groups of asteroids are found in orbits that approach or fall inside the orbits of Mars and Earth. These are known as *Near Earth Asteroids*.

© Diagram Visual Information Ltd.

Key words

Amor	Near Earth
Apollo	Object (NEO)
asteroid	orbit
Aten	potentially
comet	hazardous
meteoroid	object (PHO)
Near Earth	solar system
Asteroid (NEA)	

Near Earth Objects

- A *Near Earth Object* (*NEO*) is any object in the solar system with an orbit that approaches Earth's orbit to within 0.3 au (28 million miles, 45 million km).
- A *Potentially Hazardous Object* (*PHO*) is an NEO with an orbit that approaches Earth's orbit to within 0.025 au (2.3 million miles, 3.7 million km).
- NEOs may be meteoroids, asteroids, or comets.
- The vast majority of NEOs are only a few feet in diameter, but some can be 25 miles (40 km) or more across.
- NEOs have been studied intensively in recent years because they represent unaltered examples of material from the formation of the solar system within easy reach of Earth, and because of the potential risk of Earth impacts.

Near Earth Asteroids

- A *Near Earth Asteroid* (*NEA*) is an asteroid that is also an NEO.
- NEAs originate in the asteroid belt between Mars and Jupiter. They become NEAs when their orbits are perturbed by Jupiter.
- There are thought to be between 1,000 and 10,000 NEAs with diameters of 0.6 miles (1 km) or more.
- *Amors* are NEAs with orbits that approach or cross the orbit of Mars.
- *Apollos* are NEAs with orbits that approach the orbit of Earth.
- *Atens* are NEAs with orbits that are closer to the Sun than Earth's orbit most or all of the time.
- Apophis is a 1,280-foot (390 m) wide NEA that is predicted to pass very close to Earth in 2029, with an impact risk in 2036 dependent on how Earth's gravity alters its orbit at its first pass.

Near Earth Objects

Near Earth Objects (NEOs)

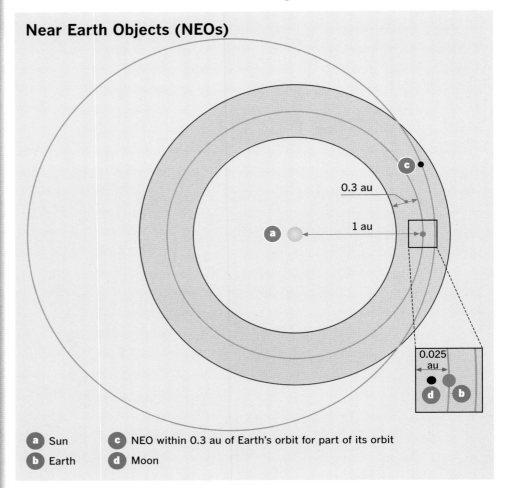

0.3 au

1 au

0.025 au

a Sun	**c** NEO within 0.3 au of Earth's orbit for part of its orbit
b Earth	**d** Moon

Near Earth Asteroids (NEA)

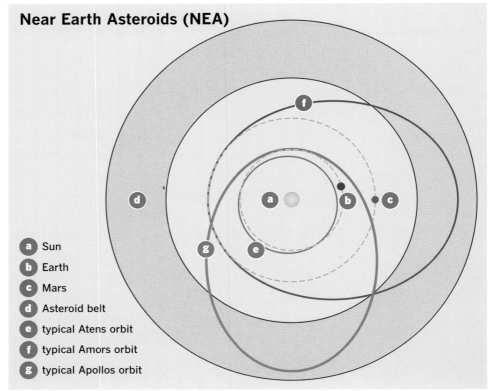

- **a** Sun
- **b** Earth
- **c** Mars
- **d** Asteroid belt
- **e** typical Atens orbit
- **f** typical Amors orbit
- **g** typical Apollos orbit

Saturn

Comparative sizes of Saturn and Earth

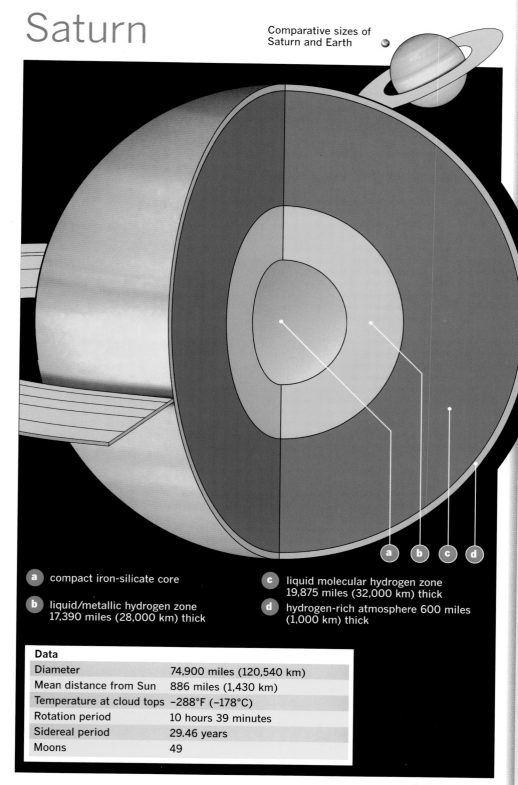

Key words

atmosphere	pole
axis	rotational period
core	sidereal period
equator	
gas giant	

Composition

- Like Jupiter, Saturn is a gas giant, with no clear distinction between its atmosphere and surface. Closer to the planet's center, pressure causes the gases of the atmosphere to become a liquid and eventually a metallic solid.
  - There may be a solid rocky core at Saturn's center that is about ten to 15 times the size of Earth.
  - Saturn has the lowest average density of any planet.

Upper atmosphere

- The clouds of the upper atmosphere form bands that circle the planet. These bands are paler in color than Jupiter's cloud bands.
- Long-lived oval storms similar to the "great red spot" on Jupiter have been observed.

Orbit and rotation

- Like Jupiter, Saturn rotates very rapidly on its axis. This rapid rotation distorts the shape of the planet, flattening its poles and widening its equator.

a compact iron-silicate core

b liquid/metallic hydrogen zone 17,390 miles (28,000 km) thick

c liquid molecular hydrogen zone 19,875 miles (32,000 km) thick

d hydrogen-rich atmosphere 600 miles (1,000 km) thick

Data

Diameter	74,900 miles (120,540 km)
Mean distance from Sun	886 miles (1,430 km)
Temperature at cloud tops	−288°F (−178°C)
Rotation period	10 hours 39 minutes
Sidereal period	29.46 years
Moons	49

Saturn

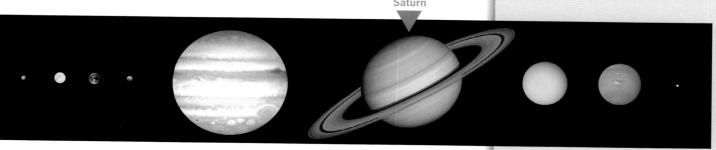

Key words

Cassini Division
flyby

Rings

- Saturn's rings were first observed by Galileo in 1610, though his telescope was not powerful enough for him to identify them as rings.
- In 1665 Dutch astronomer Christian Huygens (1629–95) described observing a thin solid ring around Saturn.
- French astronomer Jacques Cassini (1677–1756) was able to discern an apparent gap in the rings known today as the Cassini Division.
- Saturn's rings are named for the order in which they were discovered. The A Ring is the densest and most easily observed from Earth.
- With the *Pioneer 11* and *Voyager 1* and *2* flybys of Saturn (1979–81), astronomers discovered that the rings have an extremely complex structure.
- Each of the main named rings contain hundreds of "ringlets" and apparently empty regions, such as the Cassini Division, also contain fine ringlike structures.
- The rings are made up of particles ranging in size from dust to large boulders.
- Although it stretches for about 300,000 miles (480,000 km) from the surface of Saturn, the ring structure is rarely more than 30 feet (9 m) thick.

Saturn's rings

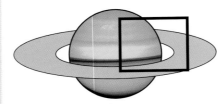

Ring name	Distance from center of Saturn miles (km)	Span of ring miles (km)	Particle size (approx.)
1 D ring	37,450 (60,300)	5,750 (14,100)	fine grains
2 C ring	46,200 (74,400)	10,870 (17,500)	4 inches–7 feet (10 cm–2 m)
3 B ring	57,070 (91,900)	15,840 (25,500)	1 inch–7 feet + (3 cm–2 m +)
4 Cassini Division	72,900 (117,400)	2,800 (4,500)	4 inches–26 feet (10 cm–8 m)
5 A ring	75,700 (121,900)	9,130 (14,700)	fine grains to several feet
6 Encke Division	82,820 (133,370)	170 (270)	4 inches–7 feet (10 cm–2 m)
7 F ring	87,310 (140,600)	310 (500)	4 inches–3 feet + (10 cm–1 m +)
8 G ring	105,570 (170,000)	310 (500)	fine grains to several feet
9 E ring	111,780 (180,000)	186,300 (300,000)	fine grains to boulders

Uranus

Comparative sizes of
Uranus and Earth

Composition

- Uranus is a gas giant, like Jupiter and Saturn, with no clear distinction between its atmosphere and surface. Closer to the planet's center, pressure causes the gases of the atmosphere to become a liquid and eventually a metallic solid.

Upper atmosphere

- There may be extreme seasonal variations in Uranus' weather due to the planet's axial tilt.
- The first close observations of Uranus made by *Voyager 2* revealed very faint cloud bands. Recent observations made by the *Hubble Space Telescope* show much more marked bands.

Orbit and rotation

- Uranus has a more extreme axial tilt than any other planet.
- Depending on which end of the planet is considered the north pole, the tilt is slightly more or slightly less than 90 degrees.
- This means that for one part of its orbit the planet's north pole faces directly toward the Sun. On the other side of its orbit the south pole faces directly toward the Sun.

Rings

- Uranus has a single ring made up of dust-sized particles of dark material.

a iron silicate core

b mantle of water, ammonia, and methane

c deep atmosphere of hydrogen, methane, and helium

Data	
Diameter	31,760 miles (51,120 km)
Mean distance from Sun	1,780 million miles (2,870 million km)
Temperature at cloud tops	−357°F (−216°C)
Rotation period	17 hours 8 minutes
Sidereal period	84.01 years
Moons	27

Uranus

Neptune

Comparative sizes of
Neptune and Earth

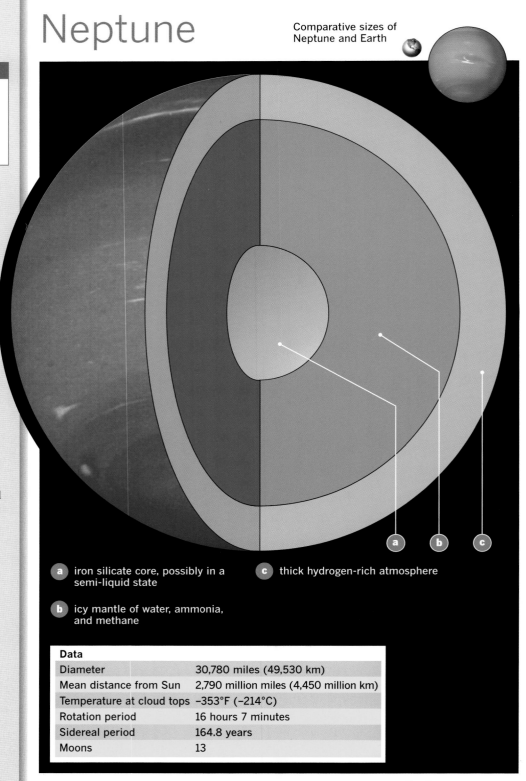

Key words

atmosphere	solar system
core	
gas giant	
rotational period	
sidereal period	

Composition

- Like the other outer planets, Neptune is a gas giant.

Upper atmosphere

- Evidence of 1,200-mile-per-hour (2,000 kmph) winds has been observed in Neptune's upper atmosphere. This is the fastest wind speed observed anywhere in the solar system.
- The high wind speeds are thought to be a result of a heat source inside the planet. This heat is probably left over from energy produced when the planet first coalesced.
- Neptune also has a giant long-term storm known as the "great dark spot" similar to the "great red spot" on Jupiter. The storm has been observed to disappear and then reappear a few years later.
- The planet's blue color is thought to be a result of methane in its upper atmosphere.

Rings

- Neptune has a faint ring system first confirmed by *Voyager 2*.
- Some of the rings seem to be incomplete arcs rather than complete ellipses.

a iron silicate core, possibly in a semi-liquid state

b icy mantle of water, ammonia, and methane

c thick hydrogen-rich atmosphere

Data	
Diameter	30,780 miles (49,530 km)
Mean distance from Sun	2,790 million miles (4,450 million km)
Temperature at cloud tops	–353°F (–214°C)
Rotation period	16 hours 7 minutes
Sidereal period	164.8 years
Moons	13

Neptune

Pluto

Comparative sizes of
Pluto and Earth

Key words

atmosphere	mantle
core	orbit
crust	rotational period
ecliptic	sidereal period
Jovian planet	tidally locked

Composition

- Pluto is the smallest and least massive planet. It is even smaller and less massive than several of the moons of the Jovian planets.
  - It is thought to be mostly composed of water ice with a rocky core. The crust probably contains frozen ammonia and methane as well as water ice.

Atmosphere

- Pluto probably has a thin atmosphere of nitrogen and methane only when it is at its closest to the Sun.
- When the planet is farther from the Sun, its atmosphere probably freezes and becomes part of the surface layers.

Orbit and rotation

- Pluto's orbit is also unique because it is much more elliptical than those of any of the other planets.
- For about 20 years of each of its 248-year orbits Pluto is closer to the Sun than Neptune.
- Pluto's orbit also has a greater inclination to the plane of the ecliptic than any other planet.
- Pluto and its moon Charon are tidally locked to one another—a feature unique to this solar system member.

a rocky core

b ice mantle of mainly water ice

c icy surface of water, ammonia, and methane

d thin nitrogen atmosphere

Data

Diameter	1,420 miles (2,280 km)
Mean distance from Sun	3,700 million miles (5,900 million km)
Surface temperature	−387° to −369°F (−233° to −223°C)
Rotation period	6 days
Sidereal period	248.54 years
Moons	3

Pluto

© Diagram Visual Information Ltd.

Key words

apparition	Kuiper belt
coma	long period
comet	comet
comet nucleus	Near Earth
dust tail	Object (NEO)
inner solar	Oort cloud
system	short period
ion tail	comet

Comets

- Comets are irregular agglomerations of water ice, frozen gases, and small amounts of rocky material.
- Comets are thought to have been formed from material left over from the formation of the solar system.
- Millions of them orbit the Sun in the Kuiper belt and Oort cloud.
- Occasionally a comet's orbit is perturbed so that it enters a highly elliptical orbit that takes it through the inner solar system.
- When a comet enters the inner solar system, radiation from the Sun causes material from its surface to boil off.
- This material forms a tail behind the comet that is millions of miles long.
- Because comets lose material each time they approach the Sun, they cannot remain active for more than about a million years.
- Many Near Earth Objects may be the rocky remains of comets that have lost all of their volatile material.
- *Apparition* is the period of time when a comet is observable.
- The *nucleus* is the solid body of the comet.
- The *coma* is the haze of material that surrounds the nucleus.
- The *dust tail* is the visible trail of dust particles driven off the comet nucleus by escaping gases.
- The *ion tail* is the trail of plasma driven off the comet by interactions with the solar wind.
- A *long period comet* is a comet with an orbital period of more than 200 years.
- A *short period comet* is a comet with an orbital period of fewer than 200 years.

Comets

Orbits of Halley's comet and Encke's comet

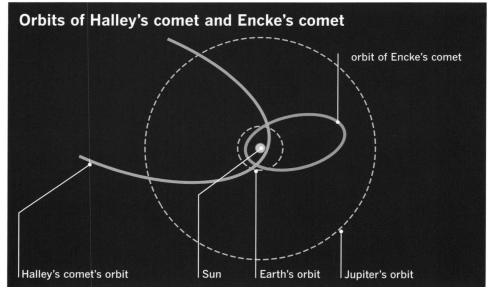

orbit of Encke's comet

Halley's comet's orbit | Sun | Earth's orbit | Jupiter's orbit

Nucleus of a comet

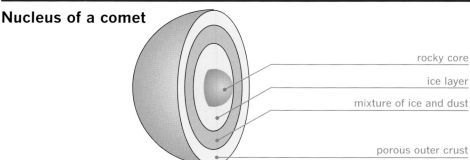

rocky core

ice layer

mixture of ice and dust

porous outer crust

A comet's tail

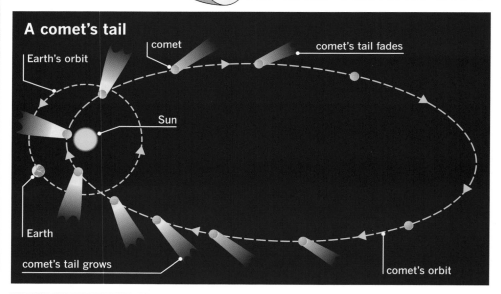

comet

comet's tail fades

Earth's orbit

Sun

Earth

comet's tail grows

comet's orbit

Comet frequency

- The most famous comet is named for British astronomer Edmund Halley (1656–1742) who, in 1706, correctly predicted its return in 1758. It has an orbital period of 76 years.
- Some comets have much shorter orbital periods. Comet Encke has an orbital period of just 3.3 years.
- Comets Hyakutake and Hale-Bopp, which were highly visible in 1996 and 1997, have orbital periods of 40,000 and 4,000 years respectively.

Trans-Neptunian objects

Mean distance from the Sun

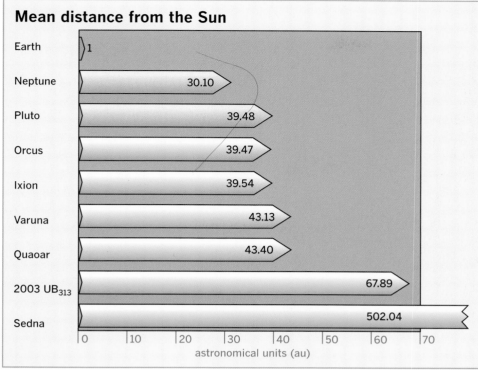

Earth	1
Neptune	30.10
Pluto	39.48
Orcus	39.47
Ixion	39.54
Varuna	43.13
Quaoar	43.40
2003 UB$_{313}$	67.89
Sedna	502.04

astronomical units (au)

Size of Kuiper belt objects relative to Earth
Diameter miles (km)

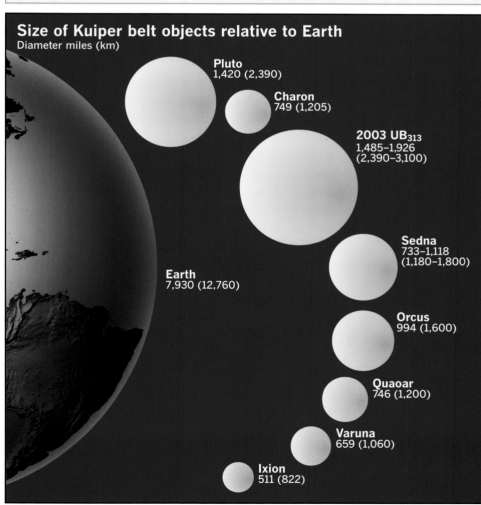

Pluto
1,420 (2,390)

Charon
749 (1,205)

2003 UB$_{313}$
1,485–1,926
(2,390–3,100)

Sedna
733–1,118
(1,180–1,800)

Earth
7,930 (12,760)

Orcus
994 (1,600)

Quaoar
746 (1,200)

Varuna
659 (1,060)

Ixion
511 (822)

Key words

Kuiper belt object
(KBO)
Oort cloud object
orbit
planet
solar system
trans-Neptunian
object (TNO)

Trans-Neptunian objects

- A *trans-Neptunian object* (TNO) is any object that orbits the Sun at a greater average distance than the planet Neptune.
- The region of the solar system beyond the orbit of Neptune is little understood and is thought to contain thousands of as yet unknown Sun-orbiting bodies. Pluto and its moon Charon, discovered in 1930 and 1978 respectively, are TNOs.
- The last decade of the twentieth century and the early years of the twenty-first have seen a rapid increase in the number of newly-discovered TNOs.
- At least one TNO, designated 2003 UB$_{313}$ (discovered in 2003), is thought to be larger than Pluto, and several others are nearly as large. It is likely that if Pluto were discovered today it would not be accorded special status as a planet since it resembles many other TNOs in both its size and orbit.
- TNOs may be classified as *Kuiper belt objects* (KBOs) or *Oort cloud objects*, depending on their orbits.

Notable TNOs

- There are currently more than 900 known TNOs and more are discovered monthly. Apart from Pluto and Charon only nine have been named. In order of discovery with the most recent first, they are 90482 Orcus, 90377 Sedna, 53311 Deucalion, 50000 Quaoar, 38628 Huya, 38083 Rhadamanthus, 28978 Ixion, and 20000 Varuna.
- The two largest named TNOs are Orcus, with a diameter of about 1,000 miles (1,600 km), and Sedna with a diameter of 733–1,118 miles (1,180–1,800 km). Pluto's diameter is 1,420 miles (2,390 km) and the currently unnamed object 2003 UB$_{313}$ may have a diameter of 1,485–1,926 miles (2,390–3,100 km).

Kuiper belt objects

Key words

cubewano	plutino
ecliptic	solar system
Kuiper belt	trans-Neptunian
Kuiper belt object	object (TNO)
(KBO)	twotino

Kuiper belt objects

- A *Kuiper belt object* (*KBO*) is any Sun-orbiting object within the *Kuiper belt*. The Kuiper belt is a thin disc of space beyond the orbit of Neptune. It is occupied by hundreds, possibly thousands, of Sun-orbiting objects.
- The Kuiper belt stretches from 30 to 50 au from the Sun and is limited to a few degrees either side of the plane of the ecliptic.
- To date, more than 800 objects have been found orbiting in this region and there may be tens of thousands more.
- Pluto and its moon Charon are KBOs.
- The belt is thought to have formed because of the gravitational influence of Jupiter, which may have caused many small bodies to be ejected from the inner solar system. The small bodies that were not projected out of the solar system altogether by this process would have ended up in orbits consistent with KBOs.
- KBOs are a subset of *trans-Neptunian objects* (TNOs).

Types of KBO

- A *cubewano* is a large KBO in an orbit that is more than 41 au from the Sun and not in resonance with the orbits of the outer planets (does not have an orbital period that is in a simple ratio to that of an outer planet). Cubewanos are named for the first TNO to be discovered which had the initial designation 1992 QB$_1$.
- A *plutino* is a KBO with an orbit that has the same resonance to the orbit of Neptune as Pluto. Like Pluto, a plutino completes two solar orbits in the time it takes Neptune to complete three (a simple ratio of 2:3). About 25 percent of KBOs are plutinos.
- A *twotino* is a KBO that completes one solar orbit in the time it takes Neptune to complete two (a simple ratio of 1:2). Twotinos are rarer than plutinos.

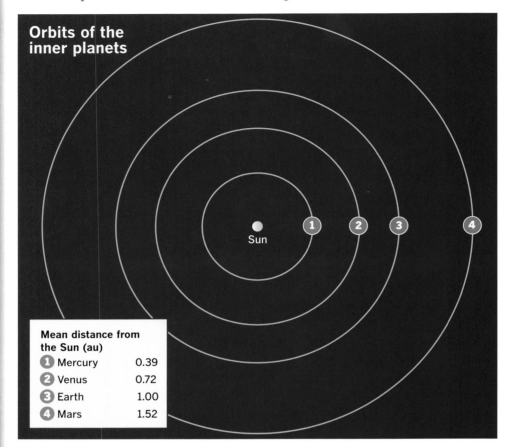

Orbits of the inner planets

Sun

Mean distance from the Sun (au)	
1 Mercury	0.39
2 Venus	0.72
3 Earth	1.00
4 Mars	1.52

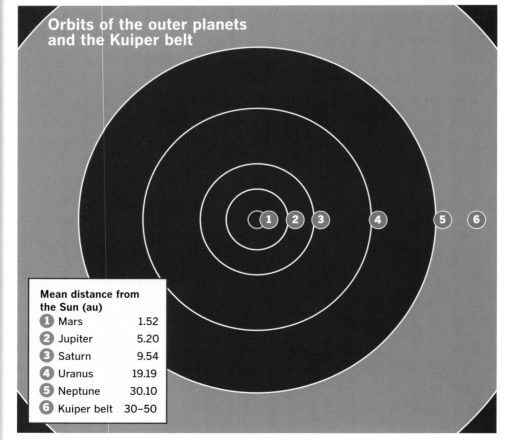

Orbits of the outer planets and the Kuiper belt

Mean distance from the Sun (au)	
1 Mars	1.52
2 Jupiter	5.20
3 Saturn	9.54
4 Uranus	19.19
5 Neptune	30.10
6 Kuiper belt	30–50

Oort cloud objects

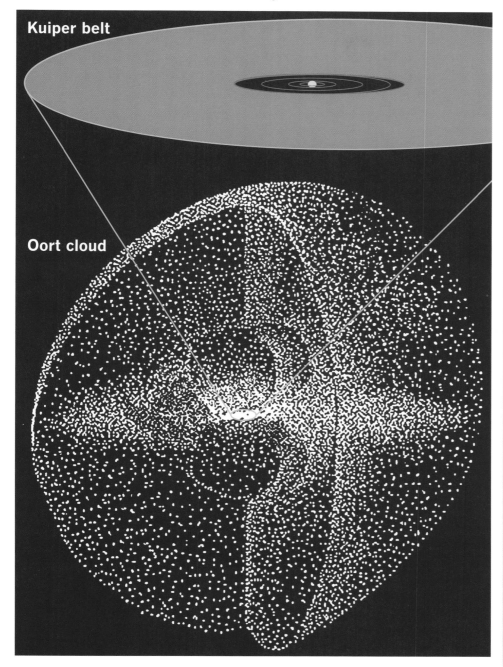

Kuiper belt

Oort cloud

Orbit of Sedna

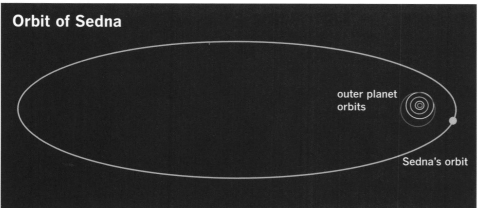

outer planet orbits

Sedna's orbit

Key words

aphelion   solar system
comet   trans-Neptunian
  nucleus   object (TNO)
Oort cloud
Oort cloud object
perihelion

Oort cloud objects

- An *Oort cloud object* is any Sun-orbiting object within the *Oort cloud*. The Oort cloud is a postulated spherical shell of space extending from about 50,000 to 100,000 au from the Sun.

- The Oort cloud is thought to be the origin of comets. Its existence was suggested by astronomers who noted that comets lose material every time they pass through the inner solar system and are heated by the Sun. Over time comets must be destroyed by repeated passes through the inner solar system. However, the fact that comets are still observed today some five billion years after the formation of the solar system suggests that new comets continue to be formed. The Oort cloud is thought to be populated by thousands of icy bodies that may become comet nuclei when their orbits are perturbed enough for them to travel in toward the Sun.

- At a distance of 100,000 au, the outer limits of the Oort cloud would lie one quarter of the distance to Proxima Centauri, the closest star to the Sun.

- Astronomers speculate that Oort clouds around neighboring stars may sometimes overlap and that this is the process that causes the orbits of some Oort cloud objects to be perturbed enough to become comets.

- The trans-Neptunian object (TNO) 90377 Sedna may be an Oort cloud object. With an orbit that extends between 76 au at perihelion and 928 au at aphelion, it is much closer to the Sun that the predicted inner edge of the Oort cloud. Some astronomers speculate that Sedna may belong to a separate "inner" Oort cloud. Others believe that the Oort cloud may be much denser and more compact than previously thought.

Sky watching

Key words

celestial equator	Northern
celestial north	Hemisphere
pole	North Pole
celestial south	orbit
pole	season
celestial sphere	Southern
equator	Hemisphere
latitude	South Pole
	star

Movement of the stars

- Earth rotates from west to east.
- The Sun and the stars appear to move across the sky from east to west.
- The angle of the path that the stars appear to take across the sky depends on the location of the observer.

Movement of Earth

- Earth's axis is tilted at an angle of 23.5° to the plane of its orbit around the Sun.
- This tilt means that different areas of Earth's surface receive varying amounts of sunlight through the year.
- This is the source of the seasons and seasonal variation between the Northern and Southern hemispheres.
- This tilt also means that there is a seasonal variation to the stars that are visible from the Northern and Southern hemispheres.

The movement of the stars

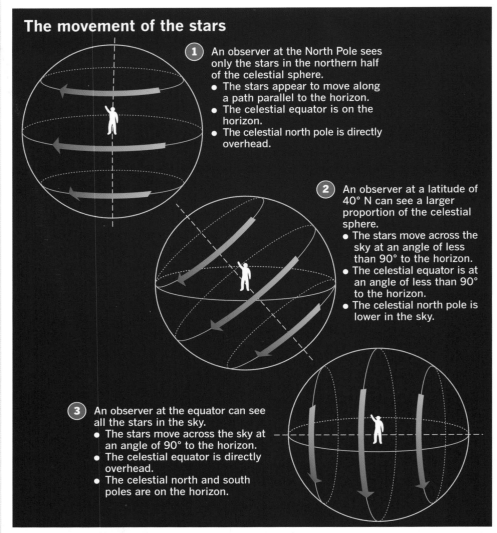

1. An observer at the North Pole sees only the stars in the northern half of the celestial sphere.
   - The stars appear to move along a path parallel to the horizon.
   - The celestial equator is on the horizon.
   - The celestial north pole is directly overhead.

2. An observer at a latitude of 40° N can see a larger proportion of the celestial sphere.
   - The stars move across the sky at an angle of less than 90° to the horizon.
   - The celestial equator is at an angle of less than 90° to the horizon.
   - The celestial north pole is lower in the sky.

3. An observer at the equator can see all the stars in the sky.
   - The stars move across the sky at an angle of 90° to the horizon.
   - The celestial equator is directly overhead.
   - The celestial north and south poles are on the horizon.

The movement of Earth

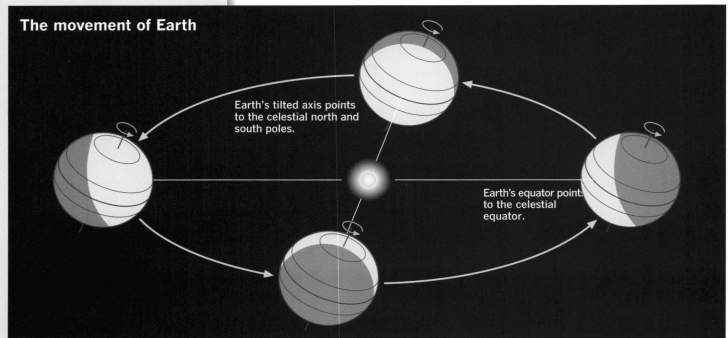

Earth's tilted axis points to the celestial north and south poles.

Earth's equator points to the celestial equator.

Early astronomy

Key words

calendar	summer solstice
comet	
conjunction	
eclipse	
planet	

Stonehenge

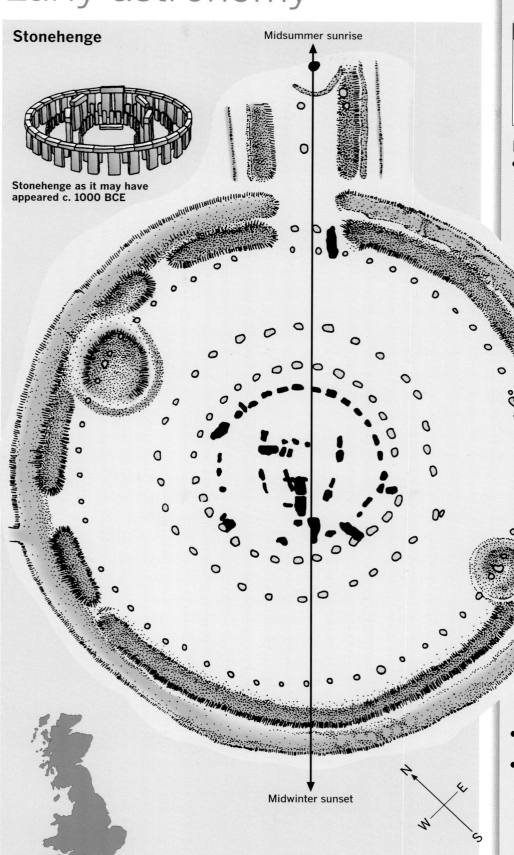

Stonehenge as it may have appeared c. 1000 BCE

Midsummer sunrise

Midwinter sunset

N E S W

Early astronomy

- Around 2500 BCE Akkadians (ancestors of the Babylonians) made some of the first astronomical observations and records. Chinese astronomers were recording the conjunction of bright planets at about the same time.

- Circa 1800 BCE work began on the erection of stone circles at an already ancient site in southern Britain (now Wiltshire, England). Over 400 years the structures known today as Stonehenge were built. The circle was used to mark the summer solstice and other astronomical events important to an agrarian culture.

- By c. 1800 BCE the Babylonians, Chinese, and Egyptians had developed the first accurate calendars from astronomical observations. Egyptians used the first appearance of the star Sirius to predict the annual flood of the river Nile accurately—a vital event in their calendar.

- By c. 1300 BCE Chinese astronomers were charting star positions and recording eclipses of the Sun and the Moon.

- By c. 700 BCE Babylonians were able to predict the positions of planets.

- Circa 400 BCE Chinese astronomers produced the earliest known atlas of comets.

First astronomers

Aristarchus

- From c. 280–260 BCE, a Greek astronomer called Aristarchus calculated the relative sizes of Earth, the Moon, and the Sun.
- He also measured the relative distances of Earth from the Moon and the Sun. He showed that the Sun must be much larger than Earth.
- Aristarchus proposed that objects in the sky revolve around the Sun, rather than Earth.
- His concept of a heliocentric (Sun-centered) universe was confirmed in part by Copernicus more than a thousand years later.

Hipparchus

- Hipparchus, a Greek astronomer from Nicaea, is considered to be the greatest figure of ancient astronomy. His work spanned the period c. 146–127 BCE.
- From his observations of the regular shift between the positions of the stars, Hipparchus concluded that Earth spins like a top and wobbles slightly. This process is known today as the *precession of the equinoxes*.
- He measured the length of a year to an accuracy of six minutes.
- Hipparchus is perhaps most famous for his catalogue of 850 stars completed in 129 BCE.
- He divided the stars into six classes of brightness.

The universe according to Ptolemaic theory

Sun · Venus · Mercury · Earth · Moon · Mars · Jupiter · Saturn

Ptolemy

- Claudius Ptolemaeus of Alexandria (Ptolemy, c. 90–168 CE), was an astronomer, geographer, and mathematician, now considered to be the last great astronomer of the ancient world.
- In his work, later known as the *Almagest*, he proposed a universe centered around Earth.
- To explain the phenomenon of retrograde motion—the occasional reversal of the motion of planets across the sky—he envisaged small, additional circular movements of the planets.
- Ptolemy's view became the accepted standard until the sixteenth century CE.

Renaissance astronomers

The universe according to Copernican theory

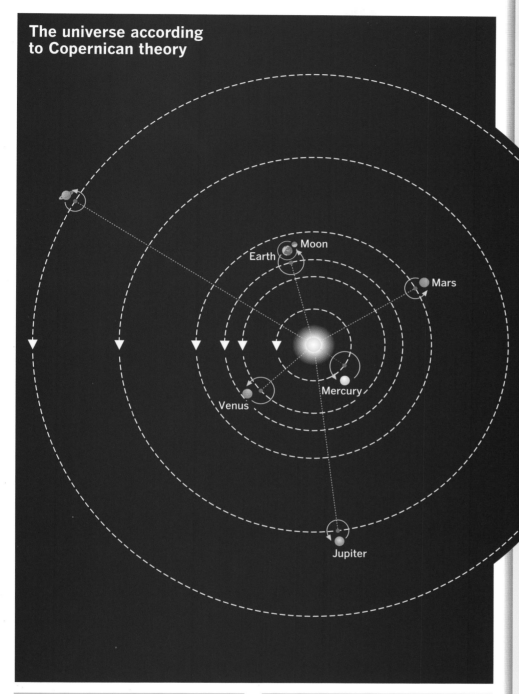

Key words

gravity
Kepler's laws
orbit
reflecting
  telescope
telescope

Nicolaus Copernicus

- Copernicus (1473–1543) was a Polish cleric who became an astronomer. His *On the Revolution of Celestial Spheres* (1543) stated that Earth and the other known planets orbited the Sun, and that the universe was much larger than had previously been thought.
- His work eventually overturned the Ptolemaic view of an Earth-centered universe, which had been accepted since the first century CE.
- His theories had profound religious and moral implications for the place of humans in the universe and they were vigorously attacked by the Christian church.

Galileo Galilei

- An Italian scientist, Galileo (1564–1642) was the first astronomer to make systematic observations of the night sky with a telescope.
- Using a telescope that he had built, Galileo saw the mountains of the Moon, the phases of Venus, and the four major moons of Jupiter.
- His discoveries convinced him that Copernicus was right. His support for the new theory led to his persecution by the Church.

Johannes Kepler

- Kepler (1571–1630) was a German astronomer who read Copernicus and studied orbital mechanics.
- He devised three laws of planetary motion (Kepler's laws), which describe the elliptical shape of orbits.

Sir Issac Newton

- Newton (1642–1727) was an English scientist most famous for his discovery of the law of gravity at the age of 22.
- His understanding of gravity enabled him to explain why Kepler's laws are true: he explained how the combination of gravity, mass, and inertia keeps bodies in elliptical orbits.
- Newton also built the first reflecting telescope.

Sir William Herschel

- Herschel (1738–1822) was born in Germany but went to England in 1757.
- Herschel built the largest telescope in the world in 1789. It was a reflector with a 48-inch (122 cm) diameter mirror.
- In 1791, he became the first person to discover a new planet using a telescope. The planet was Uranus.

Electromagnetic radiation

- Energy is emitted by objects such as stars and galaxies, and transmitted through space as electromagnetic radiation.
- Electromagnetic radiation can be emitted along a range of wavelengths from a few picometers to tens of kilometers.
- Sensing these radiations with instruments such as telescopes allows scientists to learn about the objects that emit them.
- Visible light is just one part of the spectrum of electromagnetic radiation.
- Visible light, short wavelength radio waves, and some infrared light waves are able to penetrate Earth's atmosphere. This means that they can be observed from the ground.
- Gamma rays, X-rays, ultraviolet light, long wavelength radio waves, and most infrared light waves cannot penetrate Earth's atmosphere. This means that they can only be observed by space-based instruments above Earth's atmosphere.

Electromagnetic spectrum

Wavelengths

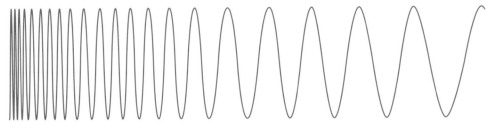

| picometers | nanometers | microns | millimeters | meters | kilometers |

1   100 1   100 1   100 1   100 1   100 1   100

Radiation reaching Earth's surface

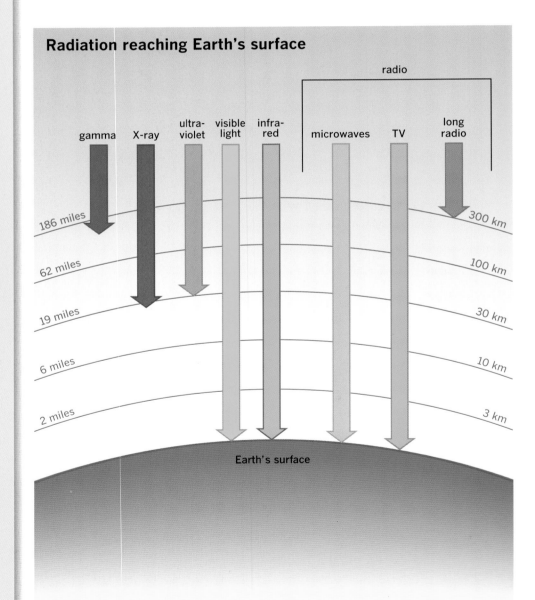

First telescopes

Key words

moon	telescope
reflecting	
telescope	
refracting	
telescope	

How refracting telescopes work

Light from an object passes through the objective lens (**a**) at the front of the telescope. The light is "bent" or refracted by the objective lens and is brought together at a point known as the focal point (**b**). A second lens called the eyepiece lens (**c**) magnifies and inverts the image produced by the objective lens.

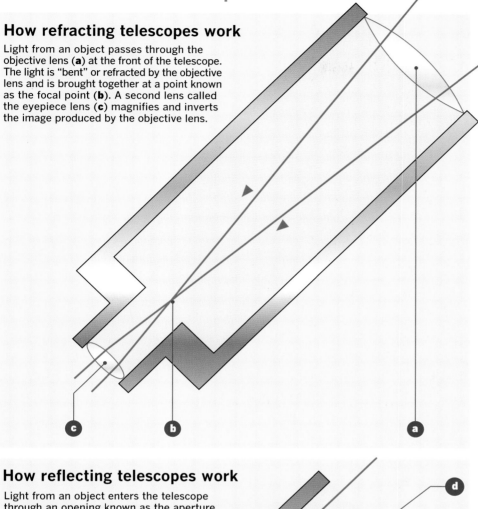

Refracting telescopes

- The first refracting telescope is thought to have been invented in 1608 by Hans Lippershey, who lived in Zeeland, Holland.
- Italian scientist Galileo Galilei is credited with making the first astronomical observations using a telescope in 1610.
- Galileo used a refracting telescope to discover craters on the Moon, the phases of Venus, and the four major moons of Jupiter.
- Because different components (wavelengths) of light are refracted differently, refracting telescopes tend to produce images with color distortions.

Reflecting telescopes

- English scientist Isaac Newton built the first reflecting telescope in 1671.
- Isaac Newton's reflecting telescope solved the problem of color distortion because all wavelengths of light are reflected equally.
- They can also be made with much larger apertures than refractors and the large mirrors used are easier to manufacture than accurate lenses of the same size.
- Reflecting telescopes became the standard form of modern optical telescopes.

How reflecting telescopes work

Light from an object enters the telescope through an opening known as the aperture (**d**). A concave mirror, known as the objective mirror (**e**), reflects the light back up the body of the telescope and brings it together. The reflected light strikes a secondary, flat mirror (**f**) that is angled to reflect it at 90°. An eyepiece lens (**g**) magnifies the image.

© Diagram Visual Information Ltd.

18th-century telescopes

Key words

atmosphere	refracting
moon	telescope
planet	telescope
reflecting	
telescope	

Herschel's refractors

- Herschel built his own telescopes and also manufactured his own mirrors and lenses. In his day he was recognized as the world's leading expert on optics.
- His 7-foot (2.13 m) long reflector with a 6.5-inch (16.5 cm) mirror provided a magnification of 200 times.
- It is similar to the instrument used by Herschel when, on March 13, 1781, he discovered the planet Uranus.
- In August 1798, Herschel completed the assembly of a 40-foot (12.18 m) long telescope, with a 48-inch (122 cm) diameter mirror. It weighed 2,118 pounds (960 kg) and was then the largest telescope in the world.
- Using this instrument he discovered two new moons orbiting Saturn.
- The telescope was clumsy to use and sensitive to movements in Earth's atmosphere, which blurred the image.
- Attempts by other astronomers to build very long refracting telescopes to increase magnification further were failures since even the slightest movement, such as someone walking close by, caused the telescope to vibrate, spoiling observations.

Herschel's reflector

- Herschel designed a new kind of reflecting telescope that removed the need for a second mirror.
- The main mirror was tilted so that an image could be formed at the end of a tube projecting from the main telescope tube.
- It proved very difficult to align the primary mirror without creating distortions and Herschel's reflector design is rarely used today.

Herschel's 7-foot refractor

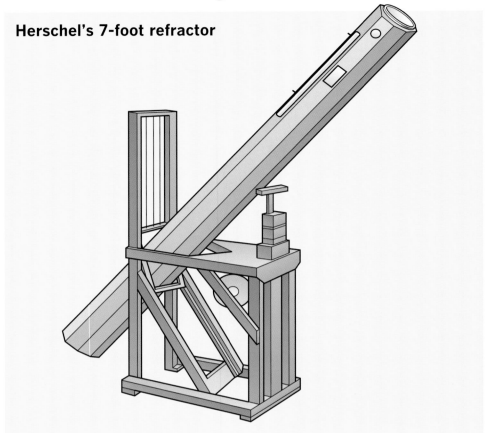

Herschel's reflector

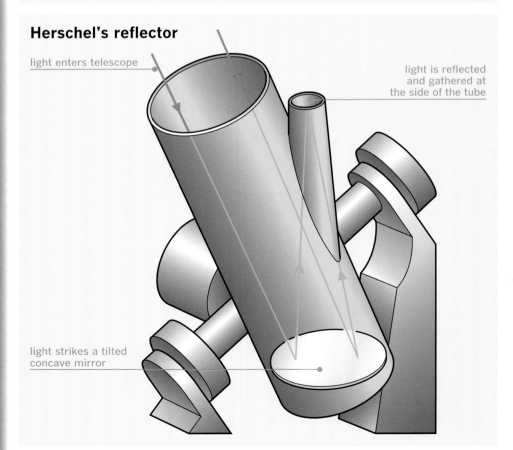

light enters telescope

light is reflected and gathered at the side of the tube

light strikes a tilted concave mirror

Radio astronomy

Radio telescope components

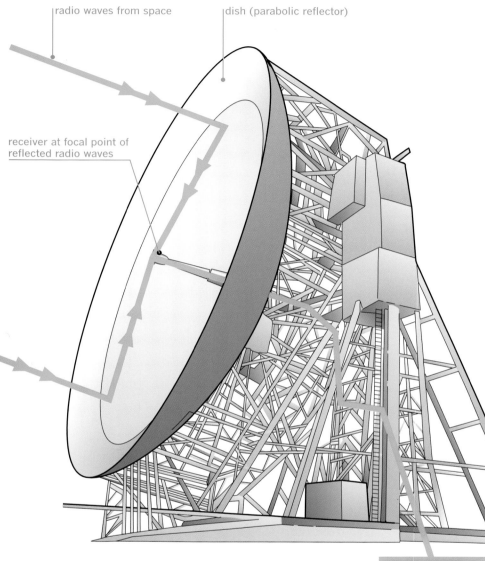

radio waves from space

dish (parabolic reflector)

receiver at focal point of reflected radio waves

received radio waves converted into electrical signals and displayed

Key words

atmosphere	*pulsar*
Doppler effect	*quasar*
electromagnetic	*radio telescope*
spectrum	*radio wave*
interstellar dust	

History

- Radio astronomy is the collection and analysis of radio waves emitted by objects in space.
- The first radio waves from space were detected by American engineer Karl G. Jansky (1905–50) in 1931.
- The first radio telescope was built in 1936 and the first giant radio telescope —with a 250-foot (76 m) dish—was built in 1957 by British astronomer Bernard Lovell (born 1913) at the Jodrell Bank Observatory in Manchester, England. This telescope was responsible for many of the early discoveries made by radio astronomers.

Advantages

- Radio telescopes can detect much weaker electromagnetic waves than optical telescopes so radio astronomers can examine objects much further away.
- Radio waves are emitted by some objects that emit little or no visible light and are therefore invisible to optical telescopes.
- Radio waves can travel through dust clouds in space without being diffused, so radio astronomers can study objects obscured from optical and other wavelength telescopes.

Disadvantages

- Long radio waves cannot penetrate Earth's atmosphere so satellites must be used to study them.
- Very large dishes are needed to focus radio waves.

Principal discoveries of radio astronomy

- Constituents of *interstellar dust* and gas invisible to optical telescopes.
- Background radiation: believed to be energy left over from the beginnings of the universe.
- Pulsars: regularly pulsing radio sources too distant to be observed optically.
- *Quasars*: very strong radio sources too distant to be observed optically.
- The velocity and direction of movement of very distant galaxies and dust clouds using *Doppler effect* analysis.

Key words

atmosphere
interferometry
telescope

Big mirrors

- Earth's atmosphere limits the resolution of any image that can be obtained with a ground-based telescope no matter how large its mirror.
- The advantage of a larger mirror is that it collects more light and allows the imaging of fainter, and therefore more distant, sources.
- Telescope designers have developed new techniques and technologies to overcome the difficulties of using very large mirrors.
- Traditional mirrors cannot be made to maintain their shape beyond a certain diameter. Their mass makes them sag. Very large traditional mirrors are also extremely heavy making them difficult and expensive to mount and point.

Segmented mirrors

- Recent and proposed designs for very large optical telescopes have tended to favor the use of segmented mirrors.
- The Keck Telescope has a main mirror 33 feet (10 m) in diameter that is made up of 36 hexagonal segments.
- Each segment is individually mounted and has an electric motor to keep it in exact alignment with its neighbors.
- The proposed California Extremely Large Telescope (CELT) will have a main mirror 98 feet (30 m) in diameter made up of 1,080 hexagonal segments.

Modern telescopes

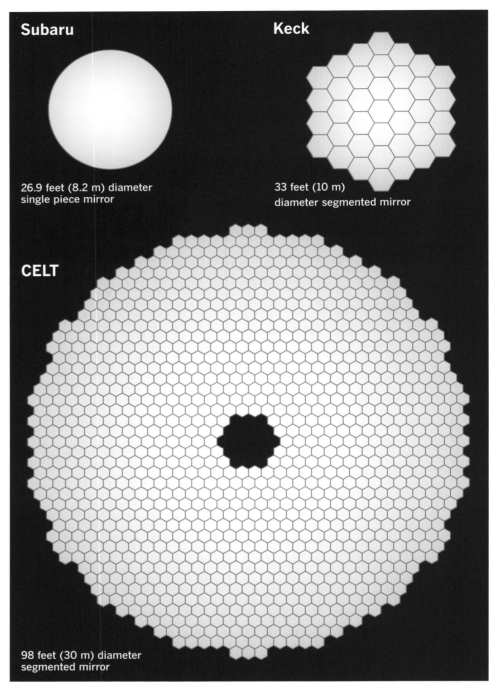

Subaru

26.9 feet (8.2 m) diameter single piece mirror

Keck

33 feet (10 m) diameter segmented mirror

CELT

98 feet (30 m) diameter segmented mirror

Largest telescopes

Name	Aperture feet (m)	Location
Keck	33 (10)	Mauna Kea, Hawaii
Keck II	33 (10)	Mauna Kea, Hawaii
Hobby-Eberly	30 (9.2)	Mount Fowlkes, Texas
Subaru	27 (8.3)	Mauna Kea, Hawaii
Very Large Telescope	54 (16.4)	Cerro Paranal, Chile
(comprised of)		(four telescopes linked by
Antu	27 (8.2)	interferometry)
Kueyen	27 (8.2)	
Melipan	27 (8.2)	
Yepun	27 (8.2)	

Infrared astronomy

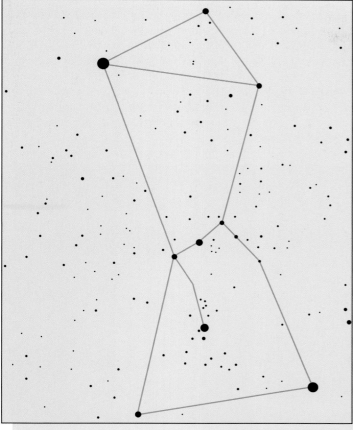

View of the constellation Orion from an optical telescope: the black dots are point sources of light.

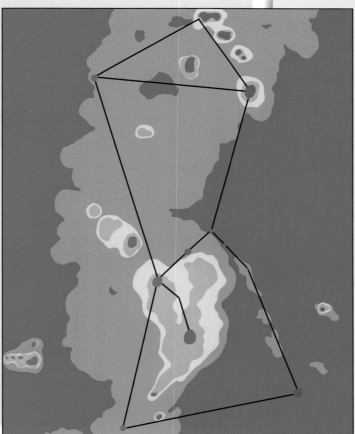

The same field of view from an infared telescope: darker areas indicate higher levels of infrared radiation.

Key words

dust cloud
galaxy
infrared
planet
star

Infrared radiation

- Infrared radiation is essentially heat.
- It has wavelengths a little greater than the extreme red limit of visible light.
- Almost all objects emit some heat radiation, even if they are close to absolute zero (−459.67°F, −273.15°C).
- Cool objects, such as dust clouds and dead stars, emit some heat but no light.

Advantages

- Infrared instruments can detect cool objects that emit little or no visible light or other high-energy wavelengths.
- Infrared radiation is capable of penetrating gas and dust clouds, which obscure observations by optical telescopes.
- Infrared observations provide more information about objects that are already visible to optical telescopes.

Disadvantages

- Little infrared radiation reaches Earth's surface from distant objects.
- Instruments for detecting infrared radiation must be kept super-cool to allow them to detect very low levels of heat radiation from very distant objects.
- Great care is needed to prevent contamination of observations by other heat sources.

Principal discoveries

- The universe contains a lot more water than had been supposed by theorists; the total water in our galaxy is millions of times the mass of the Sun.
- There are significant quantities of water vapor in the atmosphere of Titan, Saturn's largest moon.
- Planets have been observed forming around old cold stars.
- Remnants of supernovas have been observed thousands of years after they exploded.
- Pre-stellar cores (the beginnings of new stars) have been observed within large dust clouds.
- The space between galaxies contains far more dust than had previously been supposed by theorists.

Ultraviolet astronomy

Key words

big bang	*ozone layer*
dust cloud	*quasar*
galaxy	*satellite*
gas cloud	*star*
interstellar medium	*ultraviolet*

Ultraviolet radiation

- *Ultraviolet* radiation is harmful to living organisms on Earth, but much of it is filtered out by Earth's ozone layer.
- Ultraviolet radiation has wavelengths a little shorter than the extreme blue limit of visible light.
- Almost all objects emit ultraviolet radiation.

Advantages

- Ultraviolet observations are usually of the area surrounding objects rather than of objects themselves. Material in these areas is usually invisible to optical telescopes. The space between stars is known as the *interstellar medium*.
- Ultraviolet observations are an excellent source of information about the chemical makeup of objects or dust and gas clouds.
- Ultraviolet observations add more information about objects that are already visible to optical telescopes.

Disadvantages

- Very little ultraviolet radiation reaches Earth's surface; most observations must be made by satellites at more than 150 miles (250 km) above the surface.

Ultraviolet observations

- Astronomers use ultraviolet observations to study regions of space that emit little or no visible light.
- Ultraviolet radiation from bright ultraviolet sources, such as stars or quasars, passes through galactic halos and gas clouds before it reaches Earth. By analyzing this radiation astronomers are able to learn about the regions that it has passed through.

Principal discoveries of ultraviolet astronomy

Ultraviolet astronomy has investigated:
- Properties of interstellar gas clouds.
- Properties of haloes of gas around galaxies.
- Properties of the atmospheres of young hot stars active during the creation of galaxies.
- Properties of regions surrounding quasars.

- An abundance of deuterium was observed in the interstellar medium by the Orbiting Astronomical Observatory Copernicus in 1972. Deuterium is thought to have been formed during the big bang and its relative abundance may help answer questions about the first few minutes of the universe.

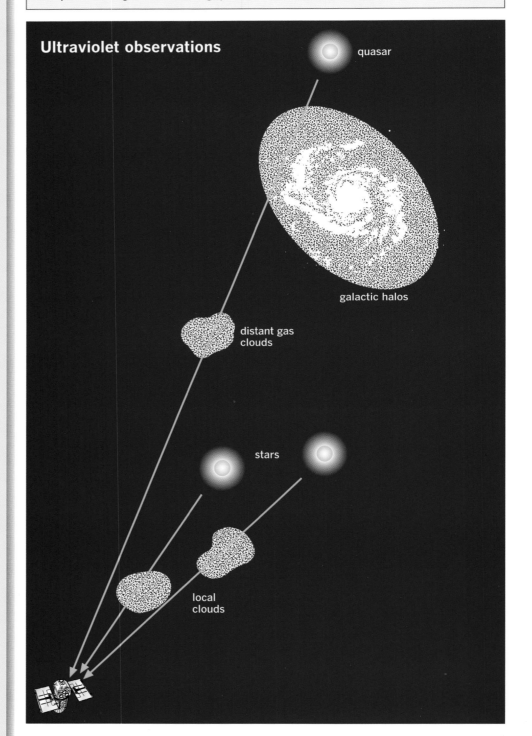

Ultraviolet observations

quasar

galactic halos

distant gas clouds

stars

local clouds

X-ray astronomy

Optical observations
An optical image of a cluster of galaxies known as A 1367 (galaxies appear as elongated white objects such as **a**).

Optical

X-ray observations
An X-ray telescope image of the same field of view reveals large clouds of hot gas that contain more mass than all the galaxies in this region put together.

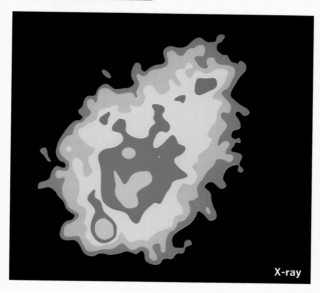

X-ray

Key words

atmosphere	neutron star
black hole	satellite
galaxy	X-ray
infrared	
interstellar medium	

Advantages
- Very energetic bodies emit large quantities of X-rays that reveal information about their structure and composition.
- X-ray observations may be the only way to locate black holes. Theories suggest that material being drawn into a black hole may emit X-rays.
- Neutron stars, galactic cores, the outer atmosphere of the Sun and other very hot objects can be studied with X-ray astronomy.

Disadvantages
- X-rays are very difficult to focus using mirrors because they pass through most solids or are absorbed by them.
- X-rays cannot penetrate Earth's atmosphere, so observations must be made from satellites.
- All known bodies in the universe emit fewer high-energy waves, such as X-rays, than lower-energy waves, such as visible light or infrared radiation.
- X-rays at some wavelengths are absorbed by interstellar gas and dust before they reach Earth.

Observing X-rays

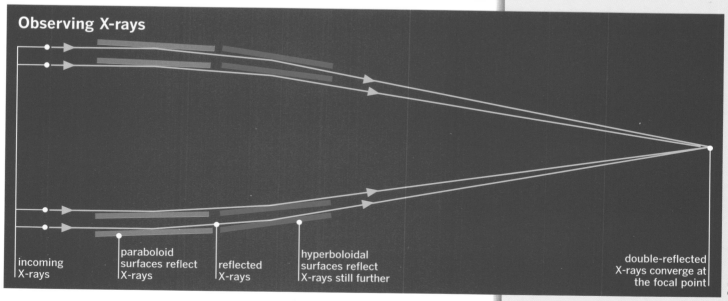

incoming X-rays

paraboloid surfaces reflect X-rays

reflected X-rays

hyperboloidal surfaces reflect X-rays still further

double-reflected X-rays converge at the focal point

© Diagram Visual Information Ltd.

© Diagram Visual Information Ltd.

Key words

atmosphere	quasar
gamma ray	supernova
interstellar medium	
pulsar	

Gamma ray radiation

- Gamma rays are harmful to life on Earth, but they are absorbed by Earth's atmosphere.
- A gamma ray photon has more than one million times the energy of a visible light photon.
- Gamma rays have wavelengths much shorter than those of visible light.

Advantages

- Because gamma rays penetrate interstellar gas and dust they can provide information about very distant objects.
- Although gamma rays cannot be observed directly from the ground they do produce measurable effects in the atmosphere.
- Gamma rays that strike the atmosphere at very high velocities can give rise to Cerenkov radiation, which can be detected by ground-based observatories. Cerenkov radiation is generated when a charged particle travels through a medium (such as the atmosphere) at a speed greater than the speed of light in that medium.
- Gamma rays provide information about high energy events and bodies.

Disadvantages

- Gamma rays cannot be observed directly by ground-based observers.
- Gamma rays are difficult to detect because of their ability to pass through many materials.

Principal discoveries of gamma ray astronomy

- The first source of gamma rays outside our solar system was detected in the Crab nebula by the ground-based Whipple Observatory in 1989.
- Gamma ray astronomy is also important in establishing the properties of supernovas, pulsars, and quasars.

Gamma ray astronomy

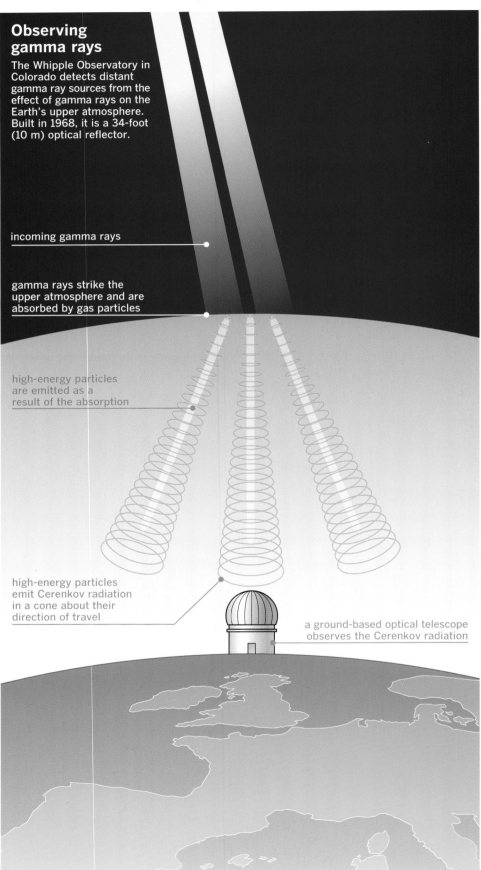

Observing gamma rays

The Whipple Observatory in Colorado detects distant gamma ray sources from the effect of gamma rays on the Earth's upper atmosphere. Built in 1968, it is a 34-foot (10 m) optical reflector.

incoming gamma rays

gamma rays strike the upper atmosphere and are absorbed by gas particles

high-energy particles are emitted as a result of the absorption

high-energy particles emit Cerenkov radiation in a cone about their direction of travel

a ground-based optical telescope observes the Cerenkov radiation

Cosmic ray astronomy

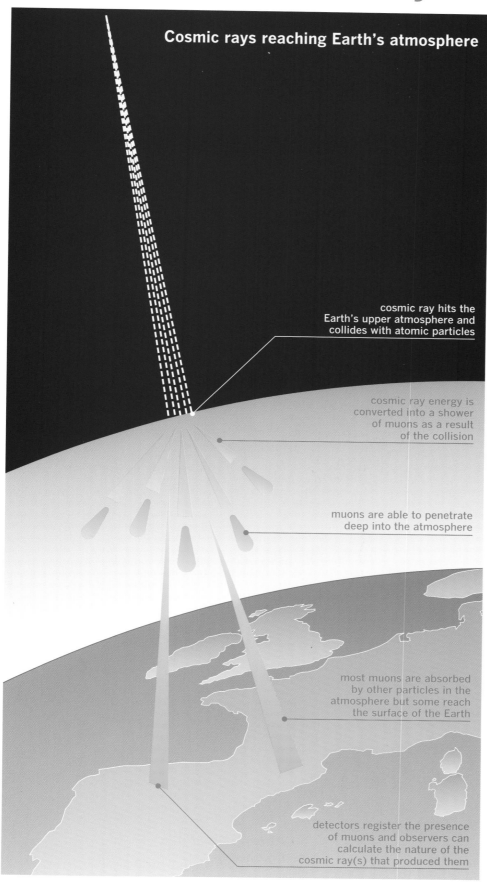

Cosmic rays reaching Earth's atmosphere

cosmic ray hits the Earth's upper atmosphere and collides with atomic particles

cosmic ray energy is converted into a shower of muons as a result of the collision

muons are able to penetrate deep into the atmosphere

most muons are absorbed by other particles in the atmosphere but some reach the surface of the Earth

detectors register the presence of muons and observers can calculate the nature of the cosmic ray(s) that produced them

Key words

atmosphere   supernova
cosmic ray
galaxy
heliosphere
solar flare

Cosmic rays

- Cosmic rays are the most powerful form of energy in the electromagnetic spectrum.
- They can have energies a billion times greater than those produced in particle accelerators.
- The direction of their origin and acceleration processes are often difficult to assess.
- They are harmful to life on Earth, but their energy is absorbed by Earth's atmosphere.

Sources of cosmic rays

- The sources of cosmic rays include:
- Distant galactic sources such as supernova explosions.
- Solar flares and other energetic solar events.
- Anomolous rays from a region at the edge of the Sun's influence known as the heliosphere.

Detecting cosmic rays

- Because of their very high energy levels and the shielding effect of Earth's atmosphere, cosmic rays are difficult to observe.
- When cosmic rays are absorbed by Earth's atmosphere however, their energy is converted into a shower of subatomic particles called muons. Some of the resulting muons reach Earth's surface where they can be detected.

Key words

celestial north pole	magnitude
celestial south pole	North Pole
hemisphere	South Pole
	star

Northern celestial hemisphere

- For an observer standing at the North Pole, Polaris—the Pole Star—is directly overhead.
- It is the closest star to the celestial north pole that is visible with the naked eye.

Southern celestial hemisphere

- For an observer standing at the South Pole, Sigma Octanis is almost directly overhead.
- It is the closest star to the celestial south pole that is visible with the naked eye—though with a magnitude of 5.4, it is only barely visible.

Sky map

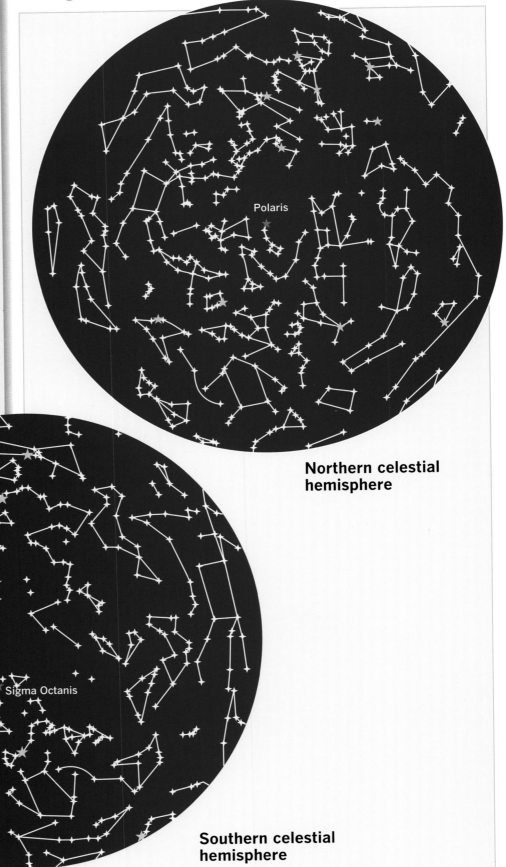

Polaris

Northern celestial hemisphere

Sigma Octanis

Southern celestial hemisphere

Constellations

Name	Common name	Notable stars
Andromeda	Andromeda	
Aquila	The Eagle	Altair
Aries	The Ram	
Auriga	The Charioteer	Capella
Boötes	The Bear Driver	Arcturus
Camelopardalis	The Giraffe	
Cancer	The Crab	
Canes Venatici	The Hunting Dogs	
Canis Major	The Great Dog	Sirius
Canis Minor	The Little Dog	Procyon
Cassiopeia	Cassiopeia	
Cepheus	Cepheus	
Cetus	The Whale	
Coma Berenices	Berenice's Hair	
Corona Borealis	The Northern Crown	
Cygnus	The Swan	Deneb
Delphinus	The Dolphin	
Draco	The Dragon	
Equuleus	The Foal	
Eridanus	The River	Achernar
Gemini	The Twins	Castor, Pollux
Hercules	Hercules	
Lacerta	The Lizard	
Leo	The Lion	Regulus
Leo Minor	The Lion Cub	
Lynx	The Lynx	
Lyra	The Lyre	Vega
Orion	The Hunter	Rigel, Betelgeuse
Pegasus	The Winged Horse	
Perseus	Perseus	
Pisces	The Fishes	
Sagitta	The Arrow	
Scutum	The Shield	
Serpens	The Serpent	
Taurus	The Bull	Aldebaran
Triangulum	The Triangle	
Ursa Major	The Great Bear/ The Big Dipper	Polaris
Ursa Minor	Polaris	
Virgo	The Virgin	Spica
Vulpecula	The Fox	

Key words

constellation
hemisphere
star

Constellations

- There are about 2,500 stars visible to the naked eye in the northern celestial hemisphere.
- Only the brightest or most highly-colored stars are named.
- All visible stars in the northern and southern celestial hemispheres fall into one of 88 named constellations or star groupings.

Star names

- Some stars have individual names.
- Sirius, also known as the Dog Star, is the brightest star in the sky.
- The brightest stars visible to the naked eye are also named according to the constellation they belong to:
- This naming system, devised by Johann Bayer in 1603, attempted to name the stars visible to the naked eye in order of magnitude within each constellation: so Betelgeuse and Rigel were designated α *Orionis* and β *Orionis*; and Castor and Pollux α *Geminorum* and β *Geminorum* respectively.
- With the technological advance of telescopes however, this naming convention rapidly became obsolete, since far more stars were revealed to exist than could be usefully named, and the designated orders of magnitude within a constellation were later proven to be incorrect after all.

Key words

atmosphere	planet
escape velocity	spacecraft
gravity	space station
moon	star
orbit	

Orbit

- An *orbit* is the path that a body takes around another, usually more massive, body. It is determined by the gravity of the massive body and the velocity of the orbiting body.
- In the context of space travel, an orbit is the path that a spacecraft or space station takes around a planet, moon, star, or other massive body.

Achieving Earth orbit

- For a spacecraft to leave the surface of Earth and go into orbit around Earth, it must achieve sufficient altitude to take it out of the atmosphere.
- At an altitude of about 100 miles (160 km) above Earth's surface the atmosphere is thin enough for it not to cause significant frictional drag.
- A planet's *escape velocity* is the minimum speed that an object must be traveling at to escape the gravity of that planet.
- Earth has an escape velocity of about seven miles per second (25,000 miles per hour, 40,200 kmph). An object traveling straight upwards at that speed would never fall back down to Earth. It would continue into space forever, or until another force intervened.
- An object does not have to be traveling at escape velocity to enter orbit. At about half of escape velocity, an object will fall into a continuous orbit around Earth.

Getting into orbit

Entering orbit

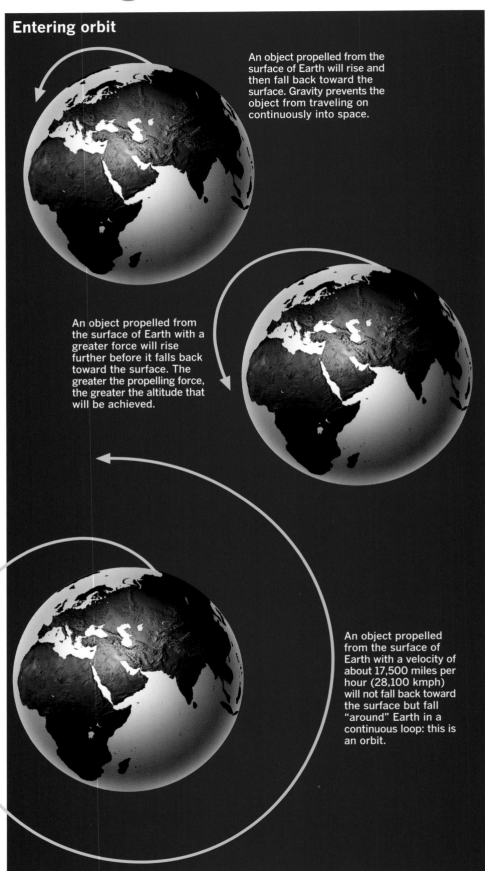

An object propelled from the surface of Earth will rise and then fall back toward the surface. Gravity prevents the object from traveling on continuously into space.

An object propelled from the surface of Earth with a greater force will rise further before it falls back toward the surface. The greater the propelling force, the greater the altitude that will be achieved.

An object propelled from the surface of Earth with a velocity of about 17,500 miles per hour (28,100 kmph) will not fall back toward the surface but fall "around" Earth in a continuous loop: this is an orbit.

Changing orbits

Apogee and perigee

satellite's orbit

Earth

apogee of satellite orbit

perigee of satellite orbit

Key words

apastron
aphelion
apoapsis
apogee
apolune
orbit
periapsis

periastron
perigee
perihelion
perilune
satellite
spacecraft

Elliptical orbits

- All orbits are elliptical. A perfectly circular orbit is only theoretically possible.
- In every elliptical orbit there is a point at which the orbiting object makes its closest approach to the body it is orbiting, and a point at which it reaches its maximum distance from that body.
- *Periapsis* is the point of closest approach.
- *Apoapsis* is the point of maximum distance.
- At periapsis the object is moving at its greatest speed; at apoapsis it is moving at its lowest speed.
- When an object is in orbit around Earth periapsis is known as *perigee* and apoapsis is known as *apogee*. For the Sun the terms are *perihelion* and *aphelion* respectively. For the Moon the terms are *perilune* and *apolune* respectively. For any star (including, but not specifically, the Sun) the terms are *periastron* and *apastron* respectively.

Changing orbit

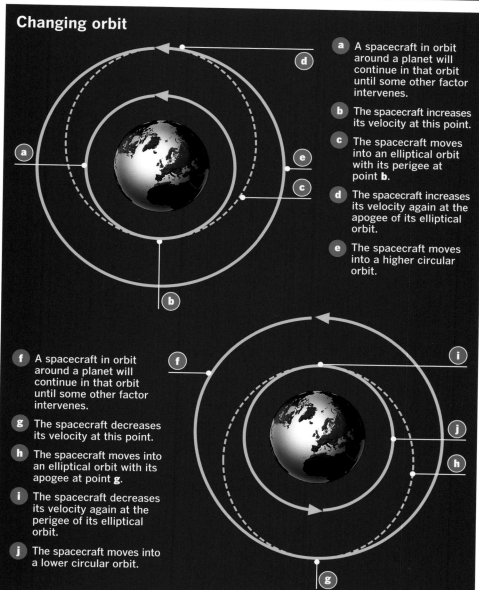

a A spacecraft in orbit around a planet will continue in that orbit until some other factor intervenes.

b The spacecraft increases its velocity at this point.

c The spacecraft moves into an elliptical orbit with its perigee at point **b**.

d The spacecraft increases its velocity again at the apogee of its elliptical orbit.

e The spacecraft moves into a higher circular orbit.

f A spacecraft in orbit around a planet will continue in that orbit until some other factor intervenes.

g The spacecraft decreases its velocity at this point.

h The spacecraft moves into an elliptical orbit with its apogee at point **g**.

i The spacecraft decreases its velocity again at the perigee of its elliptical orbit.

j The spacecraft moves into a lower circular orbit.

Orbits and velocity

- In order to change its orbit an object must change its velocity.
- By increasing its speed in the direction of its orbit an object will enter a more elliptical orbit with a more distant apoapsis.
- By decreasing its speed in the direction of its orbit an object will enter a more elliptical orbit with a lower periapsis.
- Spacecraft are often launched into low orbits that are then raised by firing orbital maneuvering engines.
- The shape of a spacecraft's orbit can also be changed by adding or subtracting speed.

Getting to planets

Key words

gravitational	orbit
slingshot	outer planet
Hohmann	planet
transfer orbit	solar system
Lagrange point	spacecraft
launch window	

Hohmann transfer orbit

- A *Hohmann transfer orbit* is an orbit that takes a spacecraft from a starting orbit around one body to a final orbit around another using as little fuel as possible.
- Hohmann transfer orbits are highly elliptical, touching the starting orbit and the desired final orbit.
- The transfer orbit is achieved by firing the spacecraft's engine so that it is propelled along the desired ellipse. When the spacecraft reaches the point on the transfer orbit that touches its desired final orbit, its engine is fired again to slow it into that final orbit.
- Timing is crucial for a Hohmann transfer orbit. The spacecraft must arrive at the correct point in space at the same time as the body it is finally intended to orbit. The relatively short time period during which the spacecraft must begin its transfer orbit is known as the *launch window*.

Gravitational slingshot

- Hohmann transfer orbits are impractical for reaching the outer planets from Earth because of the great velocity changes (and therefore large fuel loads) required.
- A *gravitational slingshot* is a method of increasing a spacecraft's velocity by propelling it past a planet in such a way that the spacecraft acquires some of the orbital velocity of that planet.
- As a spacecraft approaches a planet the planet's gravity speeds the spacecraft up. As it moves away from the planet its gravity slows the spacecraft down again. Because the planet is in motion however, the spacecraft is slowed by less than it was initially speeded up. The net result is an increase in the spacecraft's speed.
- Gravitational slingshots rely on accurate timing.

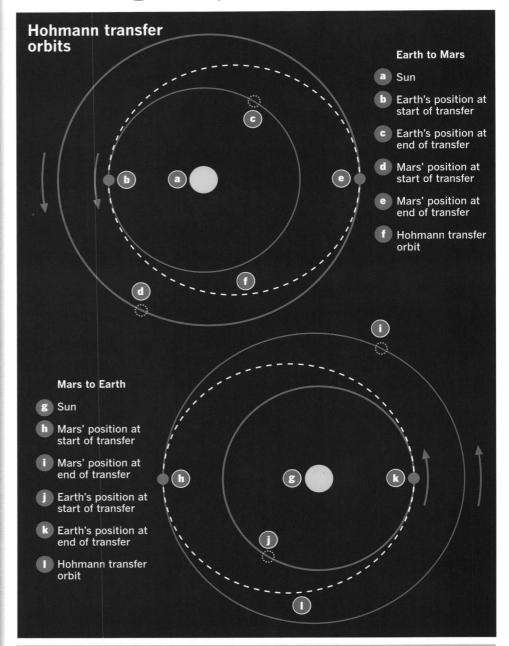

Hohmann transfer orbits

Earth to Mars

- **a** Sun
- **b** Earth's position at start of transfer
- **c** Earth's position at end of transfer
- **d** Mars' position at start of transfer
- **e** Mars' position at end of transfer
- **f** Hohmann transfer orbit

Mars to Earth

- **g** Sun
- **h** Mars' position at start of transfer
- **i** Mars' position at end of transfer
- **j** Earth's position at start of transfer
- **k** Earth's position at end of transfer
- **l** Hohmann transfer orbit

Interplanetary superhighway

- The "interplanetary superhighway" is a set of orbits that provide low-energy transfers between bodies within the solar system.
- The orbits lead to and from the Lagrange points via all of the major bodies that orbit the Sun.
- Lagrange points exist where the gravitational attractions of two neighboring bodies cancel each other out. For example, there is a point in space between the Moon and Earth where the gravitational attraction of one is no stronger than that of the other.
- A very small velocity change to a spacecraft at a Lagrange point can tip it into the region of space where the gravitational attraction of one neighboring body is just greater than the other. The spacecraft will gradually move toward that body and eventually settle into an orbit around it.
- Interplanetary superhighway orbits require very little energy to achieve, but transfer times can be very slow.

Orbital inclination

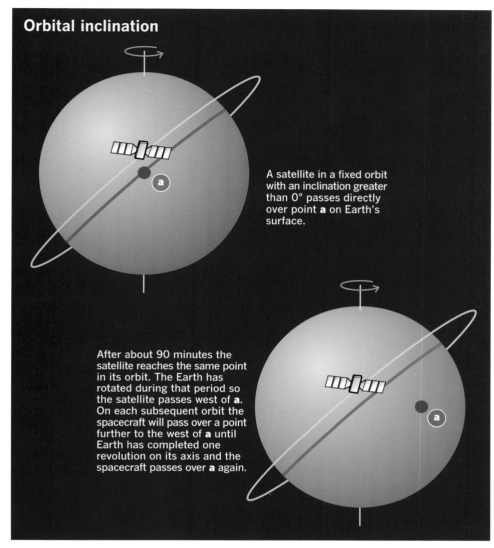

Orbital inclination

A satellite in a fixed orbit with an inclination greater than 0° passes directly over point **a** on Earth's surface.

After about 90 minutes the satellite reaches the same point in its orbit. The Earth has rotated during that period so the satellite passes west of **a**. On each subsequent orbit the spacecraft will pass over a point further to the west of **a** until Earth has completed one revolution on its axis and the spacecraft passes over **a** again.

Key words

axis	orbit
ecliptic	pole
equator	satellite
ground track	spacecraft
inclination	

Inclination

- An orbit's *inclination* is the angle between the plane of that orbit and a reference plane.
- For a spacecraft in Earth orbit the reference plane is usually the plane of Earth's equator.
- For an object orbiting in the solar system the reference plane is usually the plane of the ecliptic.

Earth orbits

- An inclination of zero degrees means that a spacecraft is orbiting in the same plane as the equator and in the same direction as Earth's rotation around its axis.
- An inclination of 90° means that a spacecraft is orbiting at a right angle to the equator and therefore passes over both the North and South poles.
- An inclination of 180° means a spacecraft is orbiting in the same plane as the equator but in the opposite direction to Earth's rotation around its axis.

Coverage

- A spacecraft in an orbit with an inclination of 0° follows a ground track that is the same as Earth's equator.
- A spacecraft in an orbit with an inclination of 30° follows a ground track that curves between 30° N and 30° S.
- A spacecraft in an orbit with an inclination of 90° follows a ground track that curves between 90° N and 90° S. It passes over every region of the planet from the equator to both poles.

Sputnik 1 **orbital coverage (first 24 hours)**
Orbital inclination 65°
Orbital period 96 minutes

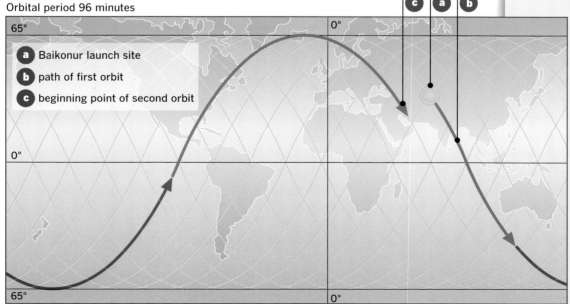

- **a** Baikonur launch site
- **b** path of first orbit
- **c** beginning point of second orbit

Key words

axis	geosynchronous
equator	orbit (GEO)
geostationary	Hohmann
orbit (GSO)	transfer orbit
geostationary	low Earth orbit
transfer orbit	(LEO)
(GTO)	orbit

Low Earth orbit

- A *low Earth orbit* (LEO) lies within about 220 to 870 miles (350–1,400 km) of Earth's surface.
- This is the lowest altitude at which a stable Earth orbit can be maintained. Any lower and atmospheric gases tend to cause drag that would quickly cause an orbit to decay.
- Communications satellites are often placed in LEO because they require less energy to achieve and because transmission to and from the satellite requires less power.
- Every crewed spaceflight apart from nine of the Apollo missions and *Gemini 11* have been to LEO.
- An object in LEO takes about 90 minutes to complete one Earth orbit.

Geosynchronous orbit

- A *geosynchronous orbit* (GEO) is an Earth orbit that has the same orbital period as Earth's rotational period. An object in GEO completes one orbit of Earth in exactly the same time that it takes for Earth to revolve once on its axis.
- A *geostationary orbit* (GSO) is a circular GEO above Earth's equator with the same direction of travel as Earth's rotation.
- GSO lies at an altitude of about 22,240 miles (35,786 km) above Earth.
- An object in GSO remains in a fixed position relative to a point on Earth's surface.

Geostationary transfer orbit

- A *geostationary transfer orbit* (GTO) is a transitional orbit between LEO and GSO. It is a class of Hohmann transfer orbit.
- Most satellites bound for GSO are launched into LEO and later boosted into GSO via GTO.

Common Earth orbits

Low Earth orbit (LEO)

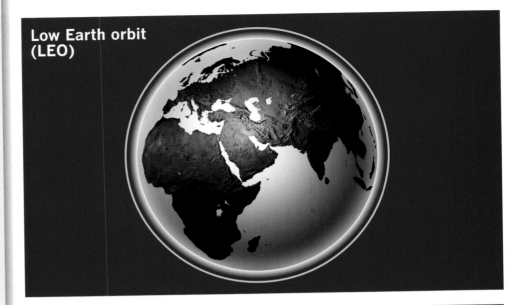

Geosynchronous orbit (GEO)

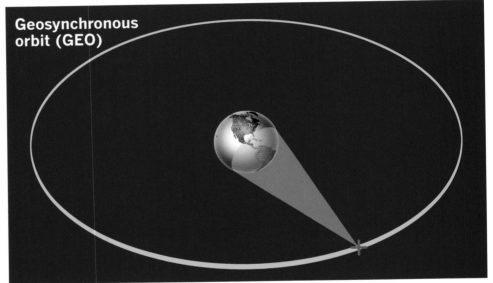

Geostationary transfer orbit (GTO)

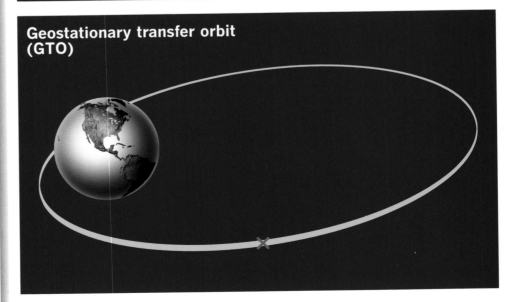

Uncommon Earth orbits

Polar orbit

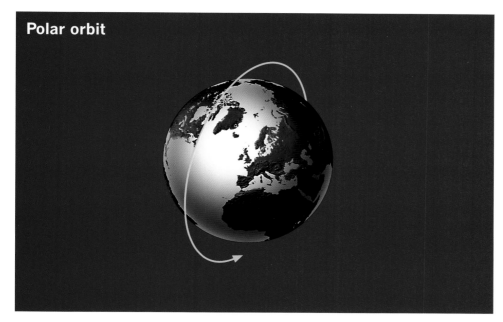

Molniya orbit

Key words

geostationary orbit (GSO)	longitude
geosynchronous orbit (GEO)	low Earth orbit (LEO)
high Earth orbit (HEO)	medium Earth orbit (MEO)
inclination	Molniya orbit
intermediate circular orbit (ICO)	orbit
	polar orbit
	pole

Polar orbit

- A *polar orbit* passes over or close to both poles of a planet.
- A polar orbit has an inclination of exactly or close to 90°.
- A spacecraft or satellite in a polar orbit will pass over an area with a different longitude on each orbit. Observation satellites are often placed in polar orbits because they provide complete coverage of a planet.

High Earth Orbit

- A *high Earth orbit* (HEO) is an Earth orbit above geosynchronous orbit (GEO).
- Satellites in a geostationary orbit (GSO) that have reached the end of their operational life are often boosted into HEO to clear GSO space.

Intermediate circular orbit

- An *intermediate circular orbit* (ICO) is an Earth orbit that is higher than low Earth orbit (LEO) but not as high as GEO.
- ICO is also known as *medium Earth orbit* (MEO).
- The Global Positioning System constellation of satellites orbit in ICOs.

Molniya orbit

- A *Molniya orbit* is a highly elliptical Earth orbit that allows a spacecraft to remain in sight from the north or south polar region for a large part of its orbital period.
- It is named for the Molniya class of Soviet military communications satellites that were the first to be placed in this kind of orbit.
- Satellites in Molniya orbits allow communications with polar sites that cannot see satellites in GSO.

Key words
gravity
propellant
rocket

Newton's laws

- Newton's third law of motion states that "for every action, there is an equal and opposite reaction."
- When rocket fuel is burned it produces a large volume of hot gas.
- This gas tends to expand rapidly and, in a rocket engine, is directed through a narrow nozzle that accelerates it further.
- In accordance with Newton's third law of motion the body of the rocket moves in the opposite direction to that of the expanding exhaust gases.
- A rocket's fuel, which becomes its exhaust gases, is known as reaction mass.
- Rockets are used both to accelerate vehicles out of Earth's atmosphere and to provide propulsion in space.

Atmospheric propulsion

- All launch vehicles to date have used rockets to provide the thrust necessary to overcome Earth's gravity.
- To overcome Earth's gravity, launch vehicle rockets must provide great acceleration in a short period of time.
- Even in the most efficient modern launch vehicles 95 percent of the mass of the vehicle consists of reaction mass (fuel) with only five percent accounted for by the vehicle's structure and payload.

Space propulsion

- In space, rockets that produce far lower accelerations over longer periods of time can be used because they do not have to counteract Earth's gravity.
- Rockets used to maneuver spacecraft in orbit, or to boost them into new orbits, are much smaller than those initially needed to accelerate the vehicle into space.

How rockets work

Balloon propulsion

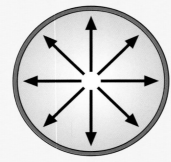

Compressed air or gas keeps the balloon's surface expanded.

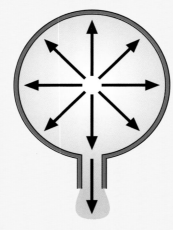

Air or gas escapes through an exit hole.

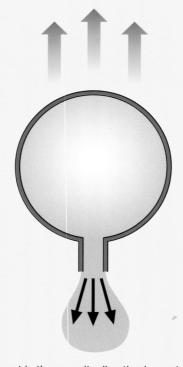

Thrust in the opposite direction is created by the motion of the escaping gas.

Rocket propulsion

Propellants are burned in a thrust chamber.

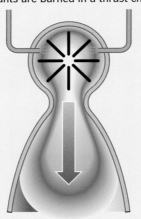

Expanding hot gases from the burning propellants are accelerated as they pass through a narrow exit.

The hot gases pass through a shaped nozzle, creating thrust in the opposite direction.

Liquid rocket fuel

Third stage Saturn V

To save space and weight the liquid oxygen tank of a Saturn V's third stage was contained within the liquid hydrogen tank.

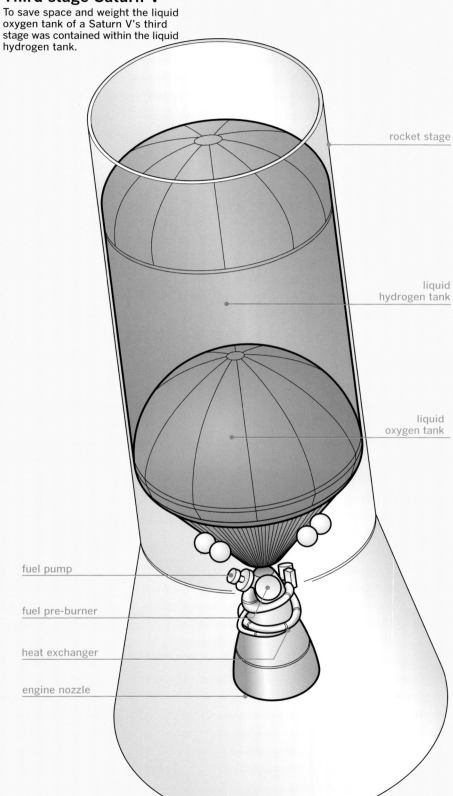

rocket stage

liquid hydrogen tank

liquid oxygen tank

fuel pump

fuel pre-burner

heat exchanger

engine nozzle

Key words

cryogenic liquid propellant
hypergolic liquid propellant
liquid propellant
oxidizer
propellant
rocket
stage

Ignitable liquid propellants

- The U.S. Atlas III and Delta III rockets, among others, use ignitable *liquid propellants*.
- An oxidizer, commonly liquid oxygen, and a fuel such as kerosene are mixed and ignited in a combustion chamber.

Cryogenic liquid propellants

- In *cryogenic liquid propellants*, the oxidizer is liquid oxygen and the fuel is liquid hydrogen.
- Oxygen and hydrogen must be kept at very low temperatures to remain liquid, hence the term "cryogenic."
- The fuel and the oxidizer must be mixed and ignited in a combustion chamber.
- Cryogenic propellants produce better thrust than kerosene.
- The European Ariane main stage rocket and the Space Shuttle main engines use these propellants.

Hypergolic liquid propellants

- *Hypergolic liquid propellants* are two liquids that spontaneously ignite when they are mixed.
- Nitric oxide and hydrazine are common hypergolic propellants.
- The U.S. Titan V rocket uses these propellants.

Combinations

- A number of modern launch systems use a combination of solid and liquid propellant engines.
- The Space Shuttle's main engines burn cryogenic liquid fuel supplied by the large disposable External Tank that it is mated to for launch.
- The Shuttle's External Tank holds 1,360,000 pounds (616,500 kg) of liquid oxygen and 226,000 pounds (102,500 kg) of liquid hydrogen in separate internal tanks.

Solid rocket fuel

Key words

booster
liquid propellant
oxidizer
propellant
rocket

solid propellant

Solid propellants

- Solid propellants are precisely mixed combinations of chemicals including fuels, oxidizers, and binding agents.
- Unlike liquid propellant engines, solid propellant engines cannot be turned off once they have been ignited.
- A number of modern launch systems, such as Ariane and the Space Shuttle, use liquid propellant main engines supplemented by "strap-on" solid propellant boosters.

Space Shuttle Solid Rocket Booster (SRB)

- The Space Shuttle employs two SRBs during launch.
- An empty core shaft through the solid propellant inside the SRB produces a greater burning area.
- Once all the propellant in the SRBs has burned, they are detached from the rest of the craft.
- Unlike most solid propellant boosters, the Shuttle's SRBs are reusable.

Data

Thrust: 2,650,000 pounds
(11,790 kilonewtons)
Weight: 1,300,000 pounds (589,670 kg)

Propellant

1,107,000 pounds (502,125 kg)
16% atomized aluminum powder fuel
69.83% ammonium perchlorate oxidizer
0.17% iron oxide catalyst
12% polybutadiene acrylic powder binder
2% epoxy curing agent

Components

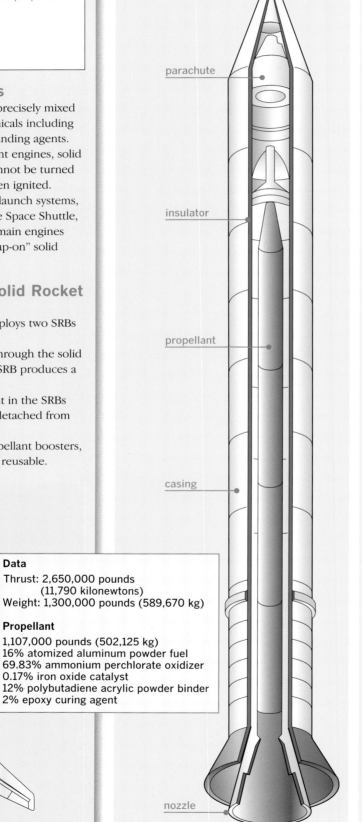

parachute

insulator

propellant

casing

nozzle

Propellant segments

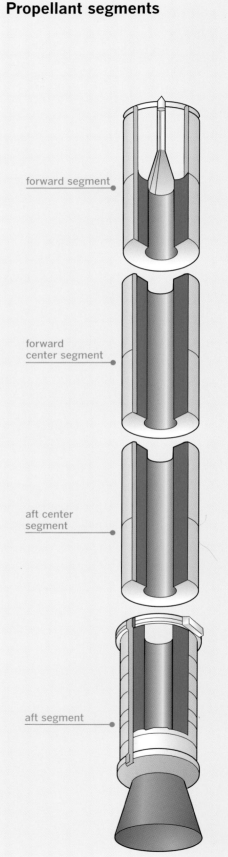

forward segment

forward
center segment

aft center
segment

aft segment

Rocket stages

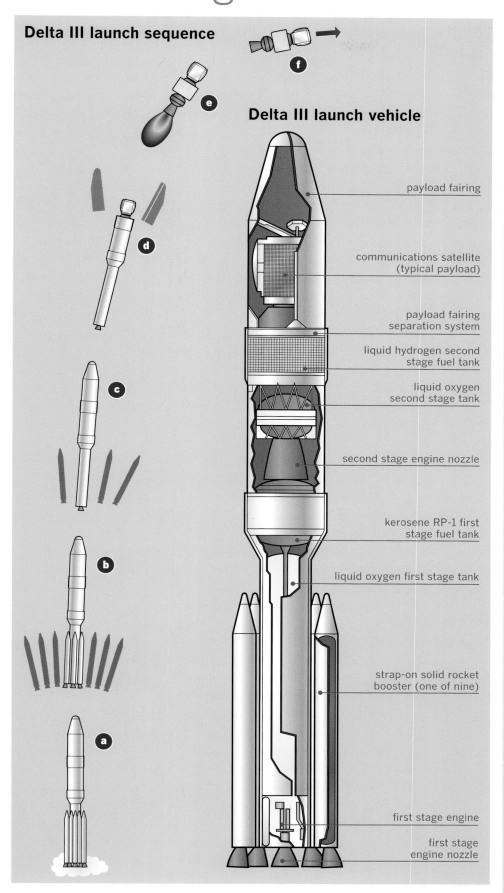

Delta III launch sequence

Delta III launch vehicle

- payload fairing
- communications satellite (typical payload)
- payload fairing separation system
- liquid hydrogen second stage fuel tank
- liquid oxygen second stage tank
- second stage engine nozzle
- kerosene RP-1 first stage fuel tank
- liquid oxygen first stage tank
- strap-on solid rocket booster (one of nine)
- first stage engine
- first stage engine nozzle

Stages ascent

- Satellites are placed into orbit using launch vehicles with a number of stages, usually three.
- The stages fall away when their propellants are depleted and the next stage engine fires to continue the ascent.
- Some launchers are also equipped with solid propellant strap-on boosters to augment thrust.

Delta III launch vehicle

- The Delta III is a U.S. launch vehicle used to propel payloads to geosynchronous orbit or lower altitudes.
- Like almost all launch vehicles it has stages. It also utilizes solid propellant strap-on boosters.
- Delta IIIs have been in use since 1999. They were a development of the successful Delta I and Delta II vehicles.

Delta III launch sequence

T+ refers to time after launch.

a Launch T+0

b Six solid rocket boosters jettisoned T+81s at 14.2 miles (23 km)

c Three solid rocket boosters jettisoned T+159s at 44 miles (71 km)

d Payload fairing jettisoned T+225s at 75 miles (121 km)

e First stage jettisoned and second stage engine ignites T+281s at 105 miles (170 km)

f Second stage shutdown, initial orbit achieved T+804s at 121 miles (196 km)

Key words

accelerometer	*satellite*
attitude	
gyroscope	
orbit	
rocket	

Rocket steering

Guidance and control system

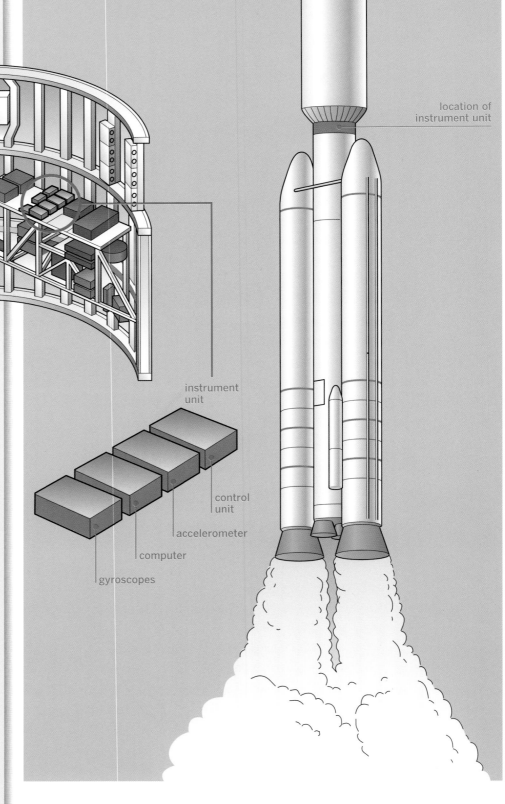

location of instrument unit

instrument unit

control unit

accelerometer

computer

gyroscopes

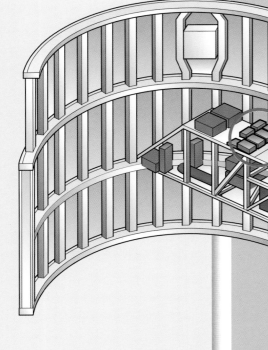

Typical rocket systems

- Launching a satellite and placing it in the correct orbit depends on the direction and speed of the rocket being accurately controlled throughout the flight.
- Guiding the rocket to follow the determined course in the correct time frame is achieved by the guidance control system.
- The rocket's speed is calculated using the law of inertia: launch vehicles use inertial guidance systems, which are mounted in the instrument unit.
- *Gyroscopes* sense the altitude of the rocket.
- Data from the *accelerometers* is used to calculate speed and position.
- The data is compared with the scheduled flight path stored on the rocket's computer.
- The flight control unit adjusts the course of the rocket if required.

Ion engines

Xenon Ion Propulsion System (XIPS)

propellant supply (xenon)

direction
of thrust

electrical power unit

ionization chamber

accelerated ion streams

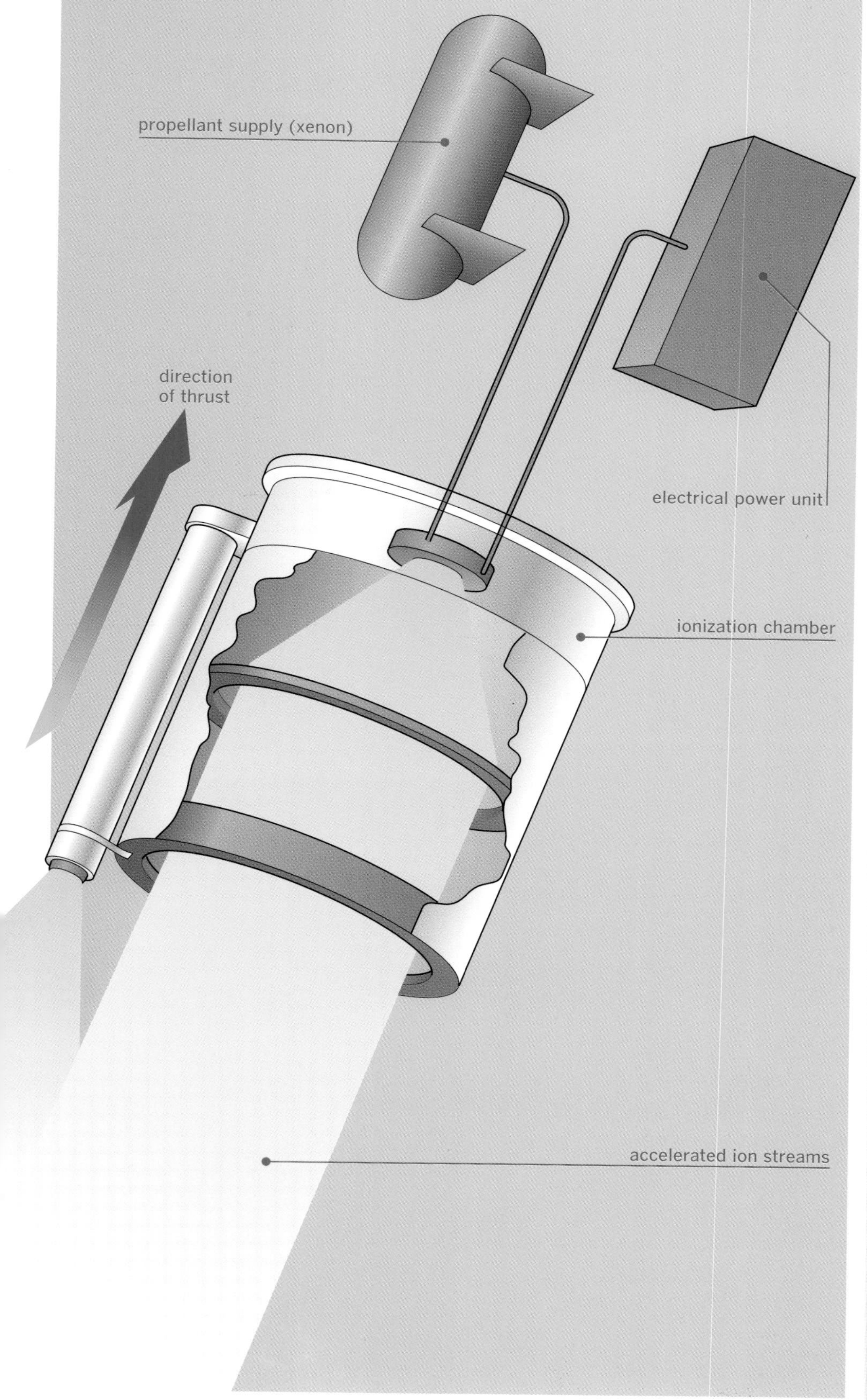

Key words

asteroid
chemical rocket
comet
geostationary
  orbit (GSO)
ion engine
orbit

probe
propellant
satellite
spacecraft

Ion engines

- In space, most satellites and other spacecraft use chemical rockets to maneuver.
- Chemical rockets require heavy propellant tanks and are inefficient in their use of that propellant.
- An ion engine uses a gas, such as xenon, and a power processor.
- Thrust is created by accelerating positive ions through a series of electrodes in a thrust chamber.
- The thrust produced is less powerful than that of a chemical rocket of comparable size, but it can be maintained for long periods and is far more efficient in the use of its gas propellant.

Deep Space 1

- NASA's *Deep Space 1* probe is the first operational spacecraft to make use of an ion propulsion system.
- *Deep Space 1* is an uncrewed probe designed to rendezvous with asteroid Braille and Comet Borelly.
- The *Xenon Ion Propulsion System* (XIPS)—a form of ion engine—fired continuously for 678 days to accelerate *Deep Space 1* to 9,600 miles per hour (15,450 kmph).

PAS 5

- The first commercial satellite to use XIPS was the *PAS 5* communications satellite (launched 1997).
- Satellites use their propulsion systems to achieve their operation orbits and to maintain those orbits.
- The lifetime of a satellite is usually limited by the amount of fuel it can carry for its maneuvering systems: the more fuel it carries the more expensive it is to launch.
- XIPS reduces fuel requirements by up to 90 percent.

Key words

apogee	perigee
astronaut	re-entry
docking	rendezvous
orbit	spacecraft
orbital mechanics	space station

Orbital maneuvers

- Rendezvous and docking is the close approach and joining together of spacecraft, or of a spacecraft and a space station, in orbit.
- The first space rendezvous was achieved by *Gemini 6* and *Gemini 7* on December 16, 1965.
- The first docking was made by *Gemini 8* with an Agena target vehicle on March 16, 1966.
- Rendezvous and docking was a vital maneuver during the Apollo missions because the modules of the Apollo spacecraft had to be joined together in their correct configuration in Earth orbit.
- Astronauts returning from the surface of the Moon in the landing module also had to perform a rendezvous and docking in order to return to the command and service modules of the Apollo spacecraft.
- Rendezvous is a highly complicated series of maneuvers based on orbital mechanics.
- Today, rendezvous and docking is a routine maneuver that is part of many spaceflights, especially those involving the *International Space Station*.

Meeting in space

Gemini 6's rendezvous with *Gemini 7*
Gemini 7 was already in orbit when *Gemini 6* was launched

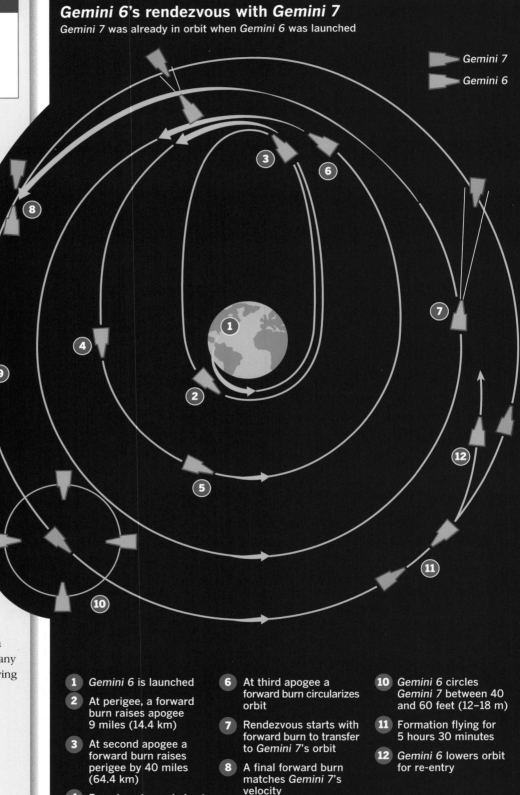

1. *Gemini 6* is launched
2. At perigee, a forward burn raises apogee 9 miles (14.4 km)
3. At second apogee a forward burn raises perigee by 40 miles (64.4 km)
4. Experiments carried out
5. Tweak burn raises apogee 0.5 mile (0.8 km)
6. At third apogee a forward burn circularizes orbit
7. Rendezvous starts with forward burn to transfer to *Gemini 7*'s orbit
8. A final forward burn matches *Gemini 7*'s velocity
9. Approach to within 10 feet (3 m) of *Gemini 7*
10. *Gemini 6* circles *Gemini 7* between 40 and 60 feet (12–18 m)
11. Formation flying for 5 hours 30 minutes
12. *Gemini 6* lowers orbit for re-entry

Walking in space

Voskhod 2 EVA: March 18, 1965

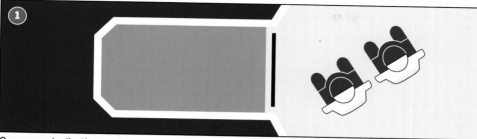

Cosmonauts (both wearing spacesuits) deploy and pressurize inflatable airlock.

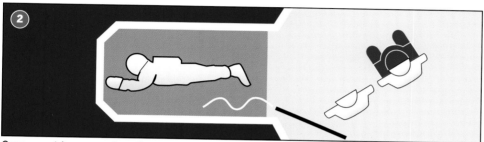

Cosmonaut Leonov enters the airlock and seals the Voskhod hatch behind him.

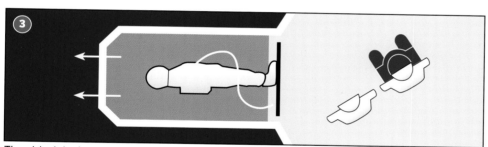

The airlock is depressurized and Leonov secures himself with a tether.

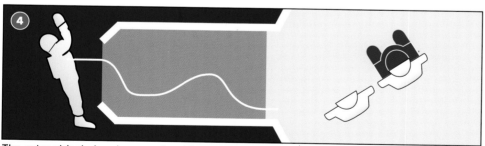

The outer airlock door is opened and Leonov emerges for his EVA supplied with oxygen bottles on his back.

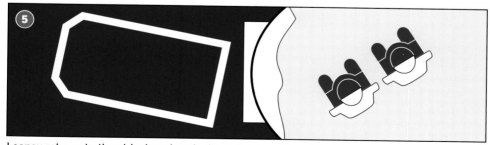

Leonov returns to the airlock and seals the outer door. The airlock is repressurized and the Voskhod hatch is opened. Once Voskhod is resealed the airlock is jettisoned.

Key words

astronaut	satellite
extravehicular activity (EVA)	spacecraft
	space station
life support	spacesuit
orbit	spacewalk

Spacewalking

- *Spacewalking* is any activity carried out by an astronaut in space outside the pressurized part of a spacecraft or space station. It is also known as *extravehicular activity* (EVA).
- EVAs are an essential part of many space missions.
- EVAs have been made to repair or service satellites in orbit such as the *Hubble Space Telescope*.
- EVAs are an essential part of the construction of the *International Space Station*.
- Most EVAs are conducted using tethers to ensure that the astronaut does not become separated from the spacecraft.
- EVA spacesuits are self-contained units containing air and life support systems in a backpack.
- There have been over 245 EVAs in Earth orbit.

EVA chronology

- In March 1965 Soviet cosmonaut Alexei Leonov became the first person to walk in space during a 22-minute EVA from *Voskhod 2*.
- In July 1969 U.S. astronaut Neil Armstrong became the first person to carry out a Lunar Extravehicular Activity (LEVA).
- In August 1971 U.S. astronaut Alfred Worden became the first person to walk in deep space in transit between the Moon and Earth.
- In August 1982 Soviet cosmonaut Svetlana Savitskaya became the first woman to walk in space.
- In February 1984 U.S. Space Shuttle astronaut Bruce McCandless became the first person to make an untethered EVA using a self-propelled maneuvering unit.
- In 1992 Pierre Thuot, Rick Hieb, and Tom Akers made the longest ever spacewalk lasting 8 hours 29 minutes.

Key words

aerodynamic heating	orbit
atmosphere	re-entry
de-orbit	spacecraft
heat shield	splashdown

Return to Earth

- To return to Earth a spacecraft must be able to reduce its velocity so that it leaves orbit. It must also be able to withstand the extreme heating caused by friction with the air as it passes through the atmosphere at high speeds (aerodynamic heating), and it must be able to slow its descent so that it impacts the surface at a safe speed.

De-orbiting

- In order to leave orbit, a spacecraft must change its velocity.
- The spacecraft burns its main or orbital manuevering engines in the direction of travel until the vehicle no longer has the velocity necessary to maintain orbit and begins to fall toward Earth.

Re-entry

- On re-entry, spacecraft are still traveling at very high speeds as they encounter the denser layers of Earth's atmosphere.
- *Aerodynamic heating* is the heating caused by friction between the fabric of the spacecraft and the air.
- A *heat shield* is the protective layer on the outside of a spacecraft that protects the rest of the vehicle from aerodynamic heating.
- An "ablative" heat shield dissipates heat by vaporizing. It can only be used once.
- A "reusable" heat shield is not destroyed during re-entry and can be used many times.

Returning to Earth

Apollo 15 landing and recovery

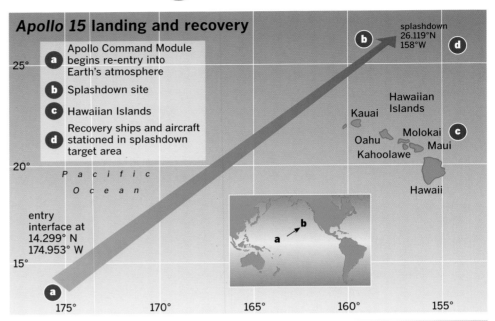

- **a** Apollo Command Module begins re-entry into Earth's atmosphere
- **b** Splashdown site
- **c** Hawaiian Islands
- **d** Recovery ships and aircraft stationed in splashdown target area

splashdown 26.119°N 158°W

Kauai · Hawaiian Islands · Oahu · Molokai · Maui · Kahoolawe · Hawaii

Pacific Ocean

entry interface at 14.299° N 174.953° W

25° · 20° · 15°

175° · 170° · 165° · 160° · 155°

Apollo landing sequence

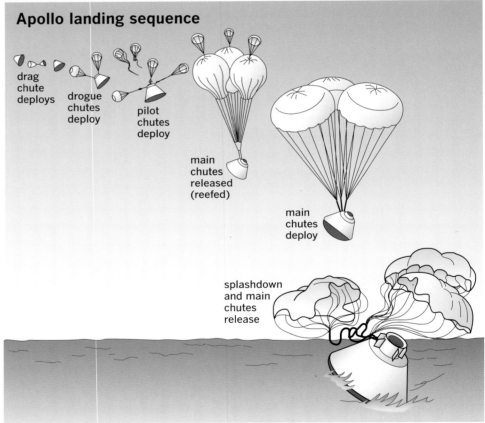

drag chute deploys

drogue chutes deploy

pilot chutes deploy

main chutes released (reefed)

main chutes deploy

splashdown and main chutes release

Landing methods

- Vostok cosmonauts left their capsules and landed by parachute on land.
- Mercury, Gemini, Apollo, and Skylab astronauts stayed inside their capsules and landed by parachute in the ocean (known as *splashdown*).
- Voskhod and Soyuz cosmonauts stay inside their capsules and land by parachute on land.
- The Space Shuttle makes a controlled glide and then lands on a runway.

Space junk

Debris

13%

other items such as tools lost by spacewalkers

17%

spent rocket stages

22%

ejected payload shrouds and covers

fragments of exploded rocket stages

41%

Key words

extravehicular activity (EVA)	space junk
rocket	space station
satellite	stage
spacecraft	

Orbital hazard

- *Space junk* is any man-made object in space that is no longer serving a useful function. It is also known as "space debris" or "orbital debris."
  - Space junk consists of used rocket stages, inactive satellites, tools, and other equipment lost or discarded by astronauts during EVAs, garbage from spacecraft or space stations, and fragments of all of these created by collisions between them.
  - Because many pieces of space junk are traveling at orbital velocities, they pose a serious threat to operational satellites crewed spacecraft, and space stations.
  - A collision with a 0.5-inch piece of space debris traveling at 17,400 miles per hour (28,000 kmph) could destroy a satellite or the Space Shuttle.
- About 8,700 man-made objects larger than a tennis ball can be tracked in Earth orbit. Only about 700 of these are operational satellites.
- There are also believed to be more than 150,000 smaller pieces of debris (down to about 0.5 inch, 1 cm) in orbit, and millions of even smaller particles.
- Space junk also interferes with astronomers' observations: a small object in Earth orbit can be mistaken for a distant star or other object.

Collisions

- The *Long Duration Exposed Facility*, a NASA experiments platform, was in space for 68 months. When it was returned to Earth, it was found to have been impacted by 34,000 micron-sized particles.
- In 1996 the French satellite *Cerise* had an antenna severed by a collision with a fragment from an Ariane 4 booster third stage: this was the first known space collision.
- A window of the Space Shuttle *Challenger* was chipped by a fleck of paint traveling at 4 miles per second (6.4 kmps).

Early rockets

Key words

Congreve rocket
propellant
rocket

Military origins

- Rockets are thought to have evolved from firecrackers used by the Chinese from at least 300 BCE.
- By 1045 CE, rockets fueled by gunpowder were an established part of military equipment in China.
- Rockets were first used in Europe by invading Mongols in the mid-thirteenth century.
- Military rocket technology spread throughout Europe in the following centuries.
- Rockets were used by the French against the English in 1492 during the Hundred Years' War.
- In the late eighteenth century the British and the French both encountered large and established rocket forces deployed by the armies of Mysore in South India.
- The British adopted a range of military rockets developed by Sir William Congreve (Congreve rockets) in the early nineteenth century.
- Congreve rockets were used by the British against U.S. forces during the War of 1812 and were soon adopted by U.S. forces for campaigns in Mexico.
- Rockets were first used in the Civil War on July 3, 1862 when Confederate troops deployed them against Union forces.
- Aircraft equipped with rockets were used during the First World War to shoot down observation balloons.

Early modern military rockets

1 Congreve rockets (1800s)
  a with shell warhead
  b bombardment type
2 Hale rocket (1840s–60s)
  a side view
  b rear view
3 French artillery rockets (1870s)
  a explosive warhead
  b incendiary warhead
  c solid shot warhead
  d grooved stick stabilizer
  e end view with exhaust vents

First western rockets

Robert Goddard's liquid propellant rocket

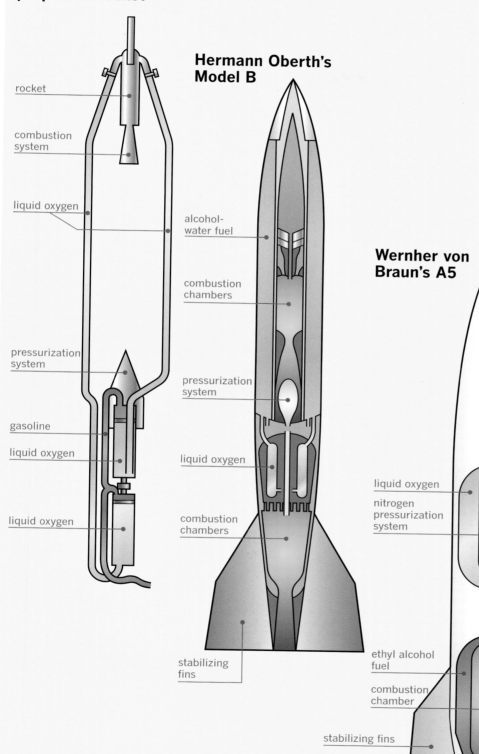

Hermann Oberth's Model B

Wernher von Braun's A5

rocket

combustion system

liquid oxygen

pressurization system

gasoline

liquid oxygen

liquid oxygen

alcohol-water fuel

combustion chambers

pressurization system

liquid oxygen

combustion chambers

stabilizing fins

liquid oxygen

nitrogen pressurization system

ethyl alcohol fuel

combustion chamber

stabilizing fins

steerable exhaust vanes

Key words

gyroscope
liquid propellant
payload
propellant
rocket

stage

Robert Goddard

- Robert Hutchings Goddard (1882–1945) was the first U.S. scientist to study the possibility of rocket flight in space seriously.
- He built and successfully fired the world's first liquid propellant rocket in 1926.
- He was the first to launch a scientific payload (a barometer and a camera) using a rocket.
- Goddard also developed the concepts of gyroscopic guidance control for rockets, the use of gimbals to pivot a rocket motor, and fuel pumps that could cope with liquid fuels.
- He received a U.S. patent for the concept of the multi-stage rocket.

Hermann Oberth

- Hermann Julius Oberth (1894–1989) was a Romanian-born German scientist who independently developed many of the same concepts about rocket travel as Robert Goddard.
- His doctoral thesis on rocketry was rejected by the University of Munich but he remained determined to show that his theories were correct.
- He was part of the team that developed the V2 rocket for Nazi Germany.
- After the Second World War he worked on U.S. rocket programs.

© Diagram Visual Information Ltd.

Key words

cosmonaut	satellite
liquid propellant	vacuum
orbit	
propellant	
rocket	

Tsiolkovsky

- Konstantin Tsiolkovsky (1857–1935) was a Russian scientist who was the first to publish theories about the possibility of rocket flight in space.
- He published his ideas about rocket propulsion in a vacuum in 1883.
- He predicted artificial satellites in Earth orbit in 1895.
- He designed practical crewed spacecraft and suggested the use of liquid propellants and engine nozzle gimballing for rocket guidance.

Semiliquid propellant rockets

- Soviet engineers began developing a series of liquid propellant rocket engines in 1929.
- The first engine, ORM 1, was test fired in 1931. It had a thrust of 44 pounds (19.9 kg).
- Prototype liquid propellant rockets called GIRD were then developed.
- The first Soviet semiliquid propellant rocket, the GIRD 9, was test fired on August 17, 1933. It reached an altitude of 4,920 feet (1,500 m).
- GIRD 9 was powered by liquid oxygen and "solid" gasoline: a solution of rosin in gasoline.
- Five more GIRD 9s were launched before May 1934.

Liquid propellant rockets

- The first fully liquid-powered rocket launched by the Soviet Union was GIRD 10.
- It was first launched on November 25, 1933 and reached 16,000 feet (4,880 m).
- The propellants were liquid oxygen and gasoline.

First eastern rockets

Tsiolkovsky's designs

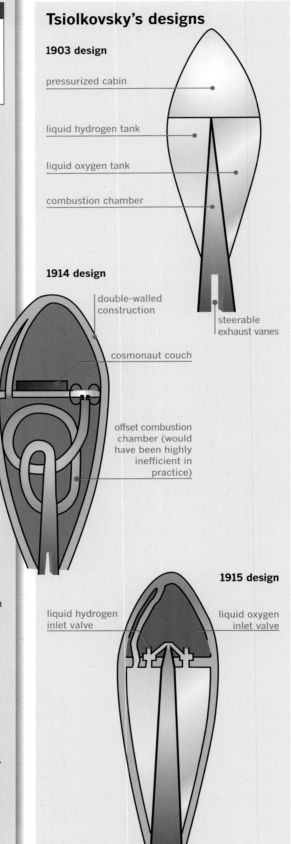

1903 design

- pressurized cabin
- liquid hydrogen tank
- liquid oxygen tank
- combustion chamber

1914 design

- double-walled construction
- cosmonaut couch
- offset combustion chamber (would have been highly inefficient in practice)
- steerable exhaust vanes

1915 design

- liquid hydrogen inlet valve
- liquid oxygen inlet valve

GIRD 10

Length 7.2 feet (2.2 m)
Weight 65 pounds (29 kg)

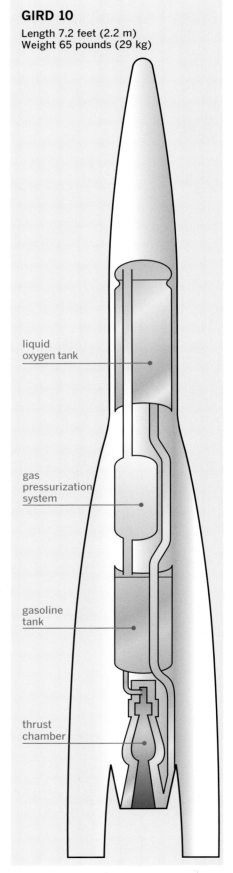

- liquid oxygen tank
- gas pressurization system
- gasoline tank
- thrust chamber

First military rockets

V2

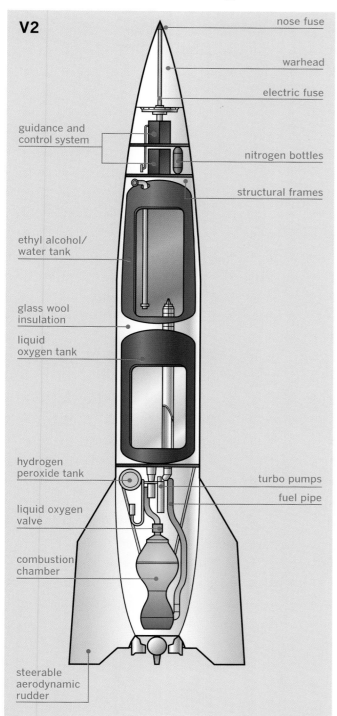

- nose fuse
- warhead
- electric fuse
- guidance and control system
- nitrogen bottles
- structural frames
- ethyl alcohol/ water tank
- glass wool insulation
- liquid oxygen tank
- hydrogen peroxide tank
- liquid oxygen valve
- combustion chamber
- steerable aerodynamic rudder
- turbo pumps
- fuel pipe

R7

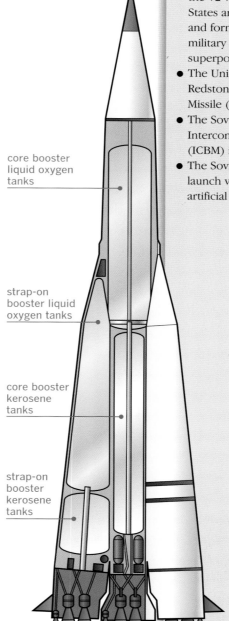

- core booster liquid oxygen tanks
- strap-on booster liquid oxygen tanks
- core booster kerosene tanks
- strap-on booster kerosene tanks

Key words

ballistic missile	rocket
ICBM	satellite
IRBM	
liquid propellant	
propellant	

First ballistic missiles

- The first large-scale liquid-propellant rocket developed as a military missile was the German A4, later called V2 (Vengeance Weapon 2) and used during the Second World War.
- The designs and some hardware for the V2 were captured by the United States and Soviet Union after the war and formed the basis for the first large military missiles developed by the superpowers.
- The United States developed the Redstone Intermediate Range Ballistic Missile (IRBM) launched in 1953.
- The Soviet Union developed the R7 Intercontinental Ballistic Missile (ICBM) in 1957.
- The Soviet R7 formed the basis of the launch vehicle for the world's first artificial satellite, *Sputnik 1*.

V2 milestones

Oct 3, 1942 First successful launch of a V2: travels 120 miles.

Feb 17, 1943 A V2 travels 121 miles (193 km) after launch.

Sep 8, 1944 First V2 fired in combat explodes in a Paris suburb; another strikes London a few hours later.

May 8, 1945 By the end of the war it is estimated that 1,115 V2s have been successfully fired against England and another 1,675 against targets in continental Europe.

Apr 16, 1946 First American-assembled V2 is launched from White Sands, New Mexico.

Oct 30, 1947 First Soviet-assembled V2 is launched.

Key words

aerodynamic	orbit
heating	re-entry
atmosphere	rocket
booster	satellite
ICBM	space
inclination	race
ionosphere	

Sputnik 1

- *Sputnik 1* was the first artificial satellite to be put into orbit around Earth.
- *Sputnik* means "satellite" in Russian. In official records the vehicle was also referred to as *PS 1*.
- It was launched by the Soviet Union on October 4, 1957.
- Its launch marked the beginning of the "space race": a period of intense rivalry between the United States and the Soviet Union over achievements in space technology.
- NASA was created in response to the launch of *Sputnik 1* when Congress passed the National Aeronautics and Space Act in July 1958.
- Two radio transmitters onboard emitted a signal that could be received all over the world for about 21 days.
- It also carried instruments to measure the properties of Earth's ionosphere and temperatures in space.
- Its orbit decayed after about three months and the vehicle was destroyed by aerodynamic heating as it re-entered the atmosphere

Launch vehicle

- *Sputnik 1* was launched with an adapted intercontinental ballistic misssile (ICBM) known as the R7.
- It consisted of a core rocket surrounded by four strap-on boosters.
- The core and the boosters fired for liftoff and the boosters were jettisoned after about two minutes while the core continued firing.

Sputnik 1

Sputnik 1 satellite

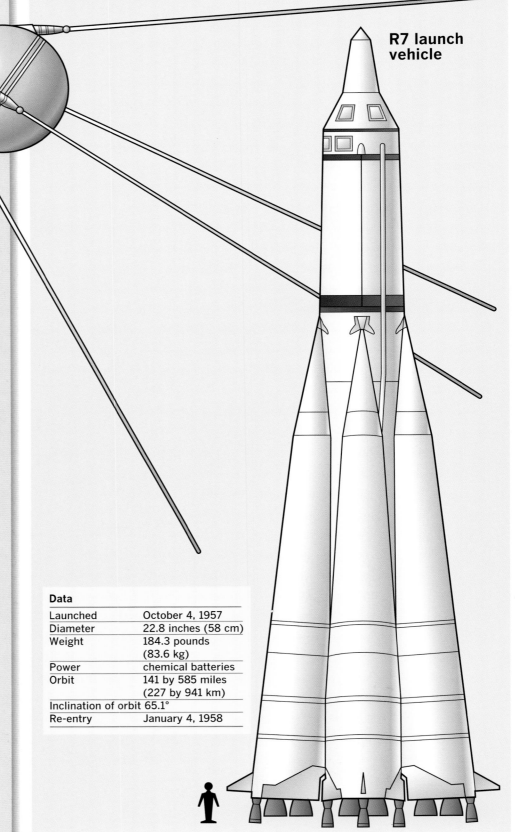

R7 launch vehicle

Data	
Launched	October 4, 1957
Diameter	22.8 inches (58 cm)
Weight	184.3 pounds (83.6 kg)
Power	chemical batteries
Orbit	141 by 585 miles (227 by 941 km)
Inclination of orbit 65.1°	
Re-entry	January 4, 1958

Sputnik 2 and 3

Sputnik 2

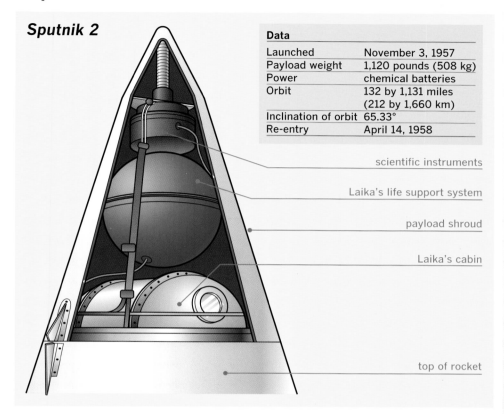

Data	
Launched	November 3, 1957
Payload weight	1,120 pounds (508 kg)
Power	chemical batteries
Orbit	132 by 1,131 miles (212 by 1,660 km)
Inclination of orbit	65.33°
Re-entry	April 14, 1958

scientific instruments

Laika's life support system

payload shroud

Laika's cabin

top of rocket

Sputnik 3

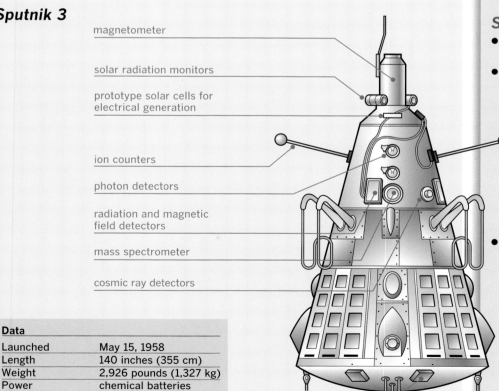

magnetometer

solar radiation monitors

prototype solar cells for electrical generation

ion counters

photon detectors

radiation and magnetic field detectors

mass spectrometer

cosmic ray detectors

micrometeorite detectors

Data	
Launched	May 15, 1958
Length	140 inches (355 cm)
Weight	2,926 pounds (1,327 kg)
Power	chemical batteries
Orbit	135 by 1,158 miles (217 by 1,864 km)
Inclination of orbit	65.18°
Re-entry	April 6, 1960

Key words	
atmosphere	payload
cosmic ray	re-entry
ICBM	satellite
inclination	solar cell
life support	telemetry
orbit	

Sputnik 2

- *Sputnik 2* was the second artificial satellite to be put into orbit around Earth.
- It was also the first spacecraft to carry a living creature into Earth orbit—a dog named Laika.
- The spacecraft carried radio transmitters, a telemetry system, life-support systems, and a pressurized cabin for Laika.
- No provision was made for returning Laika to Earth. She is believed to have died between five and seven hours after achieving orbit.
- *Sputnik 2* was launched with an R7 adapted intercontinental ballistic missile (ICBM).

Sputnik 3

- *Sputnik 3* was designed to be the Soviet Union's first satellite.
- Because the R7 launch vehicle was ready before the satellite had been completed, the much simpler *Sputnik 1* and *Sputnik 2* were launched first.
- *Sputnik 3* carried 12 scientific instruments that were designed to measure the concentrations of charged particles, cosmic rays, magnetic fields, and the composition of the upper atmosphere.
- It was also launched with an R7 ICBM.

Key words

cosmic ray	re-entry
ICBM	rocket
inclination	satellite
micrometeorite	solid propellant
orbit	stage
orbital period	Van Allen belt
propellant	

Explorer 1

Explorer 1

- *Explorer 1* was the third artificial satellite put into orbit around Earth.
- It was launched by the United States on February 1, 1958.
- The vehicle was officially designated as *Satellite 1958 Alpha*.
- The satellite carried instruments to measure cosmic rays and temperature, and to detect micrometeorite impacts.
- The instruments were contained in a nose cone and an empty fourth stage rocket casing.
- Results from instruments for detecting cosmic rays led to the discovery of the Van Allen radiation belt, named for Dr James Van Allen, the instrument's designer.

Launch vehicle

- *Explorer 1*'s launch vehicle was the Jupiter C rocket (also known as the Juno 1).
- The Jupiter C was an adaptation of the Redstone intercontinental ballistic missile (ICBM).
- It consisted of a Redstone first stage equipped with two clustered upper stages of solid propellant rocket motors about four feet (1.2 m) long and six inches (15.2 cm) in diameter. Eleven of the motors were clustered in a ring to form the second stage. Three identical rockets were fitted inside this ring as the third stage. A single, similar motor was attached to the *Explorer 1* satellite as the fourth stage.

Data	
Launched	January 31, 1958
Weight	10.5 pounds (4.8 kg)
Orbit	226 by 1,582 miles (356 by 2,548 km)
Inclination	33.3°
Orbital period	114.7 minutes
Re-entry	March 31, 1970

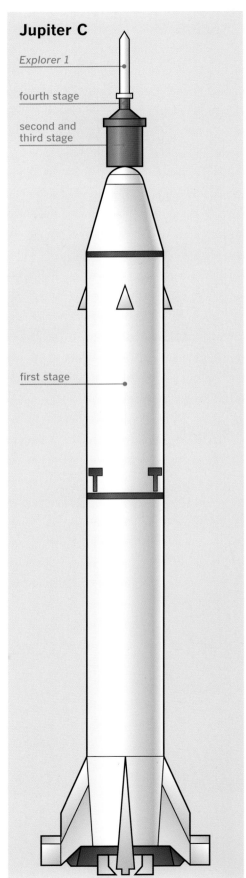

Redstone IRBM

Jupiter C

Explorer 1

fourth stage

second and third stage

first stage

Vanguard program

Vanguard 2

Launch attempts

December 6, 1957	TV-3	Failed on launch pad
February 5, 1958	TV-3BU	Failed at T+57sec
March 17, 1958	TV-4	*Vanguard 1* success
April 28, 1958	TV-5	Staging failure
May 27, 1958	SLV-1	Trajectory failure
June 26, 1958	SLV-2	Second stage failure
September 26, 1958	SLV-3	Failed to reach orbital velocity
February 17, 1959	SLV-4	*Vanguard 2* success
April 13, 1959	SLV-5	Control failure
June 22, 1959	SLV-6	Helium sphere explosion
September 18, 1959	TV-4BU	*Vanguard 3* success

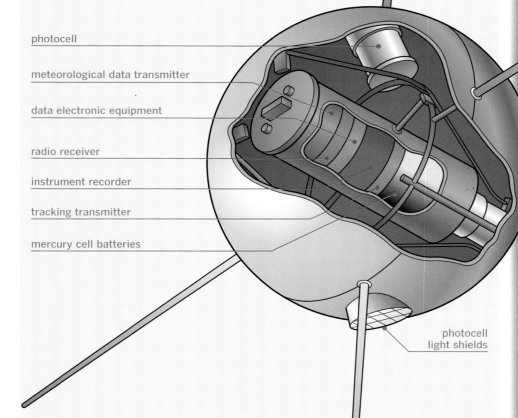

photocell

meteorological data transmitter

data electronic equipment

radio receiver

instrument recorder

tracking transmitter

mercury cell batteries

photocell light shields

Key words

atmosphere	solar radiation
orbit	upper
rocket	atmosphere
satellite	
solar power	

Vanguard

- Project Vanguard was a U.S. program that was intended to place the first artificial satellite into Earth orbit.
- It was proposed by the U.S. Naval Research Laboratory and chosen over proposals from both the Air Force and the Army in 1955.
- It failed to place the first satellite in orbit and also failed to place the first U.S. satellite in orbit (*Explorer 1* was the first).
- Three satellites were eventually placed in orbit by the program. Vanguard become the responsibility of NASA in 1958.

Vanguard 1

- The second satellite to be placed into Earth orbit by the United States was *Vanguard 1*.
- The satellite made discoveries about the precise shape of Earth and proved the effectiveness of solar power in space.
- Although now inactive, it has remained in Earth orbit for 47 years—longer than any other satellite.

Vanguard 2

- *Vanguard 2* carried instruments to measure Earth's cloud cover and was used to determine the density of the upper atmosphere.

Vanguard 3

- *Vanguard 3* carried instruments to measure Earth's magnetic field and the interaction between solar radiation and Earth's atmosphere.

Launch vehicle

- All three Vanguard satellites were launched with Vanguard rockets.
- The Vanguard rocket was based on the Viking and Aerobee rocket systems.

Explorer program

Explorer

- The Explorer program was responsible for placing the first U.S. satellite (*Explorer 1*) into Earth orbit.

- Since the launch of *Explorer 1* (February 1958), there have been 79 further successful Explorer missions (*Explorer 83 SWIFT* was launched in November 2004).

- *Explorer 50 Interplanetary Monitory Platform (IMP-J)*, a magnetosphere research satellite, has been operational for more than three decades.

- Sixteen Explorer spacecraft are still operational (*Explorer 50, 67–74, and 77–83*). They were launched on the following dates:
  Explorer 50 IMP-J, October 26, 1973
  Explorer 67 EXUV, June 7, 1992
  Explorer 68 SAMPEX, July 3, 1992
  Explorer 69 XTE, December 30, 1995
  Explorer 70 FAST, August 21, 1996
  Explorer 71 ACE, August 25, 1997
  Explorer 72 SNOE, February 26, 1998
  Explorer 73 TRACE, April 2, 1998
  Explorer 74 SWAS, December 6, 1998
  Explorer 77 FUSE, June 23, 1999
  Explorer 78 IMAGE, March 25, 2000
  Explorer 79 WMAP, June 30, 2001
  Explorer 80 RHESSI, February 5, 2002
  Explorer 81 CHIPSat, January 13, 2003
  Explorer 82 GALEX, April 28, 2003
  Explorer 83 SWIFT, November 20, 2004

Explorer 1958–62

Launch date	Designation	Comment
February 1, 1958	*Explorer 1*	Radiation study
March 5, 1958	*Explorer 2*	Launch failure
March 26, 1958	*Explorer 3*	Radiation, micrometeoroid study
July 26, 1958	*Explorer 4*	Radiation study
August 24, 1958	*Explorer 5*	Launch failure
October 23, 1958	*Beacon*	Launch failure
July 16, 1959	*Explorer S-1*	Launch failure
August 7, 1959	*Explorer 6*	Earth observation
August 14, 1959	*Beacon 2*	Launch failure
October 13, 1959	*Explorer 7*	Magnetic field, solar flare study
March 23, 1960	*Explorer S-46*	Launch failure
November 3, 1960	*Explorer 8*	Ionosphere study
December 4, 1960	*Explorer S-46*	Launch failure
February 16, 1961	*Explorer 9*	Atmosphere study
February 24, 1961	*Explorer S-45*	Launch failure
March 25, 1961	*Explorer 10*	Magnetic field study
April 27, 1961	*Explorer 11*	Gamma ray study
May 24, 1961	*Explorer S-45A*	Launch failure
June 30, 1961	*Explorer S-55*	Launch failure
August 16, 1961	*Explorer 12*	Radiation, solar wind study
August 25, 1961	*Explorer 13*	Micrometeoroid study
October 2, 1962	*Explorer 14*	Magnetosphere study
October 27, 1962	*Explorer 15*	Radiation study
December 16, 1962	*Explorer 16*	Micrometeoroid study

Explorer 10

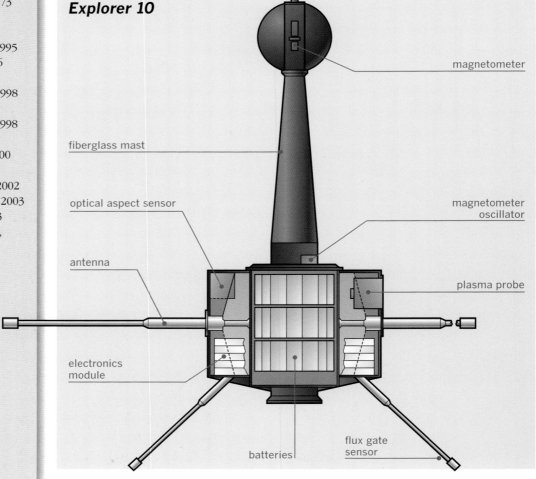

- magnetometer
- fiberglass mast
- optical aspect sensor
- magnetometer oscillator
- antenna
- plasma probe
- electronics module
- batteries
- flux gate sensor

Discoverer and Corona

Discoverer flights 1–14

Flight	Launch date	Comments
1	February 28, 1959	Test flight, no capsule
2	April 13, 1959	Capsule landed in Arctic, never found
3	June 3, 1959	Launch failure
4	June 25, 1959	Launch failure
5	August 13, 1959	Capsule lost
6	August 19, 1959	Capsule recovery failed
7	November 7, 1959	Capsule did not separate
8	November 20, 1959	Capsule not recovered
9	February 4, 1960	Launch failure
10	February 19, 1960	Launch failure
11	April 5, 1960	Recovery failed
12	June 29, 1960	Launch failure
13	August 10, 1960	Capsule recovered from sea
14	August 18, 1960	Capsule caught in midair, film recovered

Key words

atmosphere
re-entry
satellite
spy satellite

Discoverer program

- The Discoverer program was a cover for an early U.S. spy satellite program known as Corona.
- Corona satellites carried cameras to photograph the Soviet Union, China, and other parts of the world.
- The program ran from June 1959 until May 1972.
- During this period, 144 Corona satellites were launched, 102 of which returned usable film.

Corona satellites

- Corona satellites were designated as type KH-1, KH-2, KH-3, KH-4, KH-4A, or KH-4B, depending on the type of cameras they carried. "KH" stands for "keyhole."
- Each satellite carried 31,500 feet (9,600 m) of film.
- The earliest KH-1 satellites could resolve objects on the ground as small as 24.5 feet (7.5 m). The last KH-4A satellites could resolve objects as small as six feet (1.8 m).

Midair recovery

- Film taken by Corona satellites had to be physically returned to Earth for processing and evaluation.
- Re-entry capsules containing the exposed film detached from the satellite and re-entered Earth's atmosphere.
- In order to ensure the security of the film cannisters and to prevent damage on landing, they were intercepted in midair as they descended on parachutes.
- The first successful midair capture did not occur until the fourteenth Corona flight.

Corona

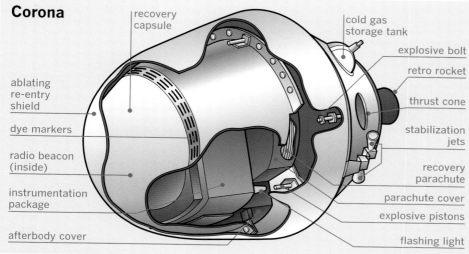

- recovery capsule
- cold gas storage tank
- explosive bolt
- retro rocket
- ablating re-entry shield
- thrust cone
- dye markers
- stabilization jets
- radio beacon (inside)
- recovery parachute
- instrumentation package
- parachute cover
- explosive pistons
- afterbody cover
- flashing light

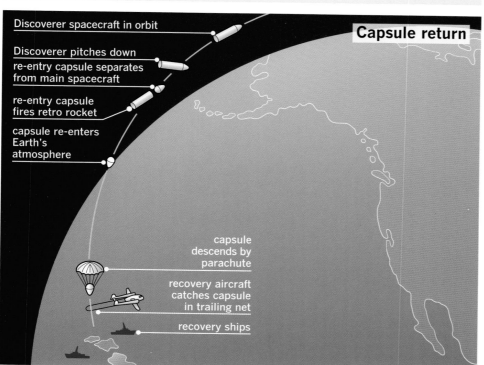

Capsule return

- Discoverer spacecraft in orbit
- Discoverer pitches down
- re-entry capsule separates from main spacecraft
- re-entry capsule fires retro rocket
- capsule re-enters Earth's atmosphere
- capsule descends by parachute
- recovery aircraft catches capsule in trailing net
- recovery ships

Communications satellite

- *Telstar 1* was the first dedicated communications satellite to be placed in Earth orbit.
- It was also the first satellite designed to transmit telephone traffic and television pictures, and the first privately-owned satellite.
- It was designed to facilitate the transmission of information between the United States and Europe.
- Unlike later communications satellites, *Telstar 1* was not placed in a geostationary orbit: it could only be used for communications during a 20 minute period of each of its 2 hour 37 minute orbits.
- *Telstar 1* was funded and developed under a joint agreement between AT&T, Bell Telephone Laboratories, NASA, the British General Post Office, and the French National Post and Telecom Office.

Telstars

- *Telstar 1* was essentially a test vehicle. It ceased operating in February 1963.
- Since then, numerous communications satellites have carried the name *Telstar*.
- *Telstar 5, 6, 7,* and *Telstar 10, 11, 12,* and *13* are currently in operation.

Telstar 1

Telstar 1

Data	
Launched	July 10, 1962
Weight	169 pounds (77 kg)
Diameter	2.6 feet (0.8 m)
Orbit	581 by 3,449 miles (936 by 5,553 km)
Inclination	44.8°

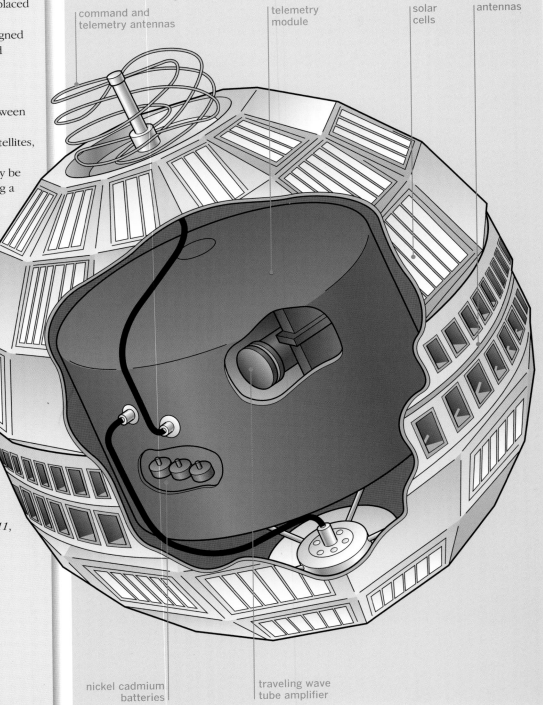

command and telemetry antennas

telemetry module

solar cells

antennas

nickel cadmium batteries

traveling wave tube amplifier

Exploring the Sun

Ulysses

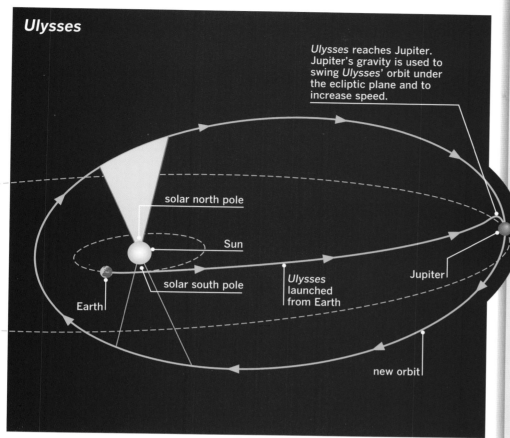

Ulysses reaches Jupiter. Jupiter's gravity is used to swing *Ulysses'* orbit under the ecliptic plane and to increase speed.

solar north pole

Sun

solar south pole

Earth

Ulysses launched from Earth

Jupiter

new orbit

SOHO

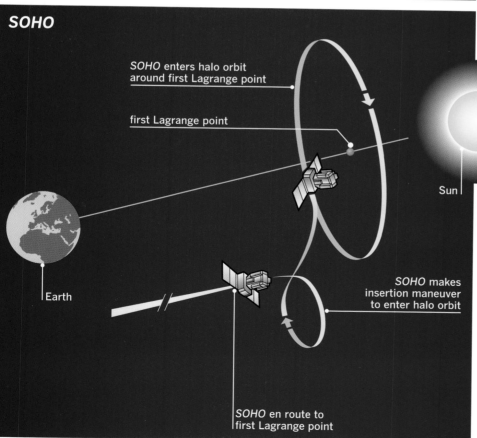

SOHO enters halo orbit around first Lagrange point

first Lagrange point

Sun

Earth

SOHO makes insertion maneuver to enter halo orbit

SOHO en route to first Lagrange point

Ulysses

- *Ulysses* is a joint NASA and ESA solar exploration spacecraft.
- It was the first spacecraft to enter a solar orbit that takes it over the Sun's poles.
- Its orbit was achieved after a gravitational slingshot maneuver around Jupiter in 1992.
- *Ulysses* has made two passes of both the north and south poles of the Sun, and is expected to make a third.
- It has provided new data about the output of the Sun at all latitudes and the nature of the heliosphere.

SOHO

- *SOHO* is an acronym for *Solar and Heliopheric Observatory*.
- It is also a joint NASA and ESA solar exploration spacecraft.
- The spacecraft is in a "halo" orbit around the first Lagrange point.
- It provides constant data about current conditions on the Sun and provides early warning of solar flares that may cause damage to satellites or interfere with communications.

Cluster 2

- The ESA's Cluster 2 program has placed four identical spacecraft in Earth orbit to investigate the interactions between Earth's magnetic field and solar radiation.
- The four spacecraft fly in formation to provide a unique three-dimensional picture of the region of space they are investigating.
- The spacecraft are separated by distances ranging from 370 miles (600 km) to 12,400 miles (20,000 km).
- The four Cluster 2 spacecraft are replacements for the original Cluster spacecraft, which were destroyed during launch in 1996.

Exploring Mercury

Key words

atmosphere	orbit
core	reaction control
crater	solar panel
flyby	spacecraft
gravitational	
slingshot	

Mariner 10

- *Mariner 10* was the first spacecraft to visit Mercury.
- It was also the first spacecraft to visit two planets (Venus and Mercury) and the first spacecraft to use a "gravitational slingshot" maneuver around one planet (Venus) in order to reach another (Mercury).
- It made three close approaches to Mercury between March 1974 and March 1975.
- About 45 percent of Mercury's surface was photographed and the planet was shown to be heavily cratered and Moonlike in appearance.
- *Mariner 10*'s instruments also confirmed that Mercury has no more than a trace of an atmosphere, and indicated that it has a disproportionately large iron core.

MESSENGER

- *MESSENGER* is a NASA spacecraft designed to orbit and investigate Mercury. *MESSENGER* is an acronym of *Mercury Surface, Space Environment, Geochemistry and Ranging*.
- Currently en route, it will become only the second spacecraft to visit Mercury.
- It will make three close approaches to the planet between January 2008 and September 2009 before entering orbit in 2011.
- The spacecraft's instruments will provide much more accurate and comprehensive information than that provided by *Mariner 10*.

Mariner 10

Three flybys of Mercury	March 29, 1974 closest approach 439 miles (703 km)
	September 21, 1974 closest approach 3,610 miles (48,069 km)
	March 16, 1975 closest approach 204 miles (327 km)

MESSENGER

Study objectives	• Origin of Mercury's high density • Composition and structure of crust • Tectonic history • Characteristics of atmosphere • Polar caps
October 2006	Venus flyby
June 2007	Venus flyby
January 2008	Mercury flyby
October 2008	Mercury flyby
September 2009	Mercury flyby
March 2011	Mercury orbit

Mariner 10

tiltable solar panel

ultraviolet spectrometer

TV cameras

low gain antenna

X-band transmitter

plasma science experiment

charged particle telescope

magnetometers

high gain antenna

Canopus star tracker

ultraviolet spectrometer

reaction control jets

acquisition Sun sensor

Exploring Venus

Mariner 2

Launched	August 27, 1962
Flyby	December 14, 1962
Major discoveries	Indicated surface temperatures of 797°F (425°C), little difference between day and night temperatures, cloud layer densest between 35 and 50 miles (56–80 km)

Key words

aerobraking	probe
atmosphere	retrograde
bus	solar orbit
flyby	solar panel
orbit	spacecraft
orbiter	

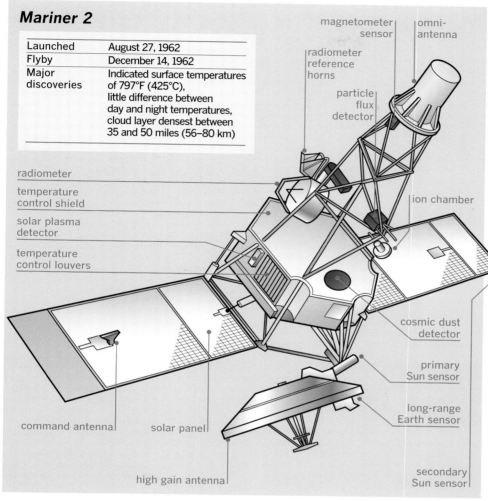

magnetometer sensor · omni-antenna · radiometer reference horns · particle flux detector · ion chamber · radiometer · temperature control shield · solar plasma detector · temperature control louvers · cosmic dust detector · primary Sun sensor · long-range Earth sensor · command antenna · solar panel · high gain antenna · secondary Sun sensor

Mariner 2

- *Mariner 2* was a NASA spacecraft. It was the first spacecraft to visit Venus and the first to investigate a planet other than Earth.
- *Mariner 2* was a replacement for *Mariner 1*, which failed after launch.
- The spacecraft made one close approach to Venus.
- *Mariner 2*'s instruments revealed the planet's slow retrograde rotation, its high surface pressure and temperature, and the predominance of carbon dioxide in its atmosphere.

Mariner 5

- *Mariner 5* was a NASA spacecraft that made one close approach to Venus.
- Its instruments provided more accurate and comprehensive data than that obtained by *Mariner 2*.

Pioneer Venus

- *Pioneer Venus* was a NASA spacecraft that consisted of a Venus orbiter (or "bus") and four probes designed to enter and parachute down into Venus' atmosphere.
- The orbiter also entered Venus' atmosphere and made measurements before it was destroyed.

Magellan

- *Magellan* was a NASA spacecraft that orbited Venus for about four years and mapped 98 percent of the planet's surface using cloud-penetrating radar.
- *Magellan* was the first spacecraft to use *aerobraking*. Its orbit was lowered until the spacecraft encountered the upper limits of the atmosphere during part of its orbit. This gradually slowed the spacecraft and circularized its orbit.
- At the end of its mission, *Magellan*'s orbit was deliberately lowered until it encountered the dense atmosphere and was destroyed.

Magellan's radar mapping

- A high gain antenna transmitted millions of radar pulses—microwave energy—each second toward the planet.
- Pulses penetrated the thick cloud cover.
- Radar pulses bounced off the surface and were picked up by the spacecraft.
- By measuring the differences in each radar signal, a physical profile was made of the surface.
- A technique known as Synthetic Aperture Radar was used to provide a resolution that would normally only be obtained by a larger antenna.

Launched	May 4, 1989
Entered Venus orbit	August 10, 1989
Objective achieved	Radar mapped 93% of the surface with a resolution down to 327 feet (100 m)

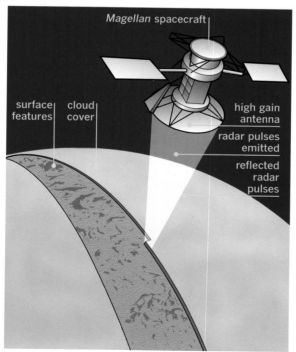

Magellan spacecraft · surface features · cloud cover · high gain antenna · radar pulses emitted · reflected radar pulses

Key words

atmosphere
bus
orbit
probe
spacecraft

Venera

- The Venera program consisted of 17 spacecraft launches by the USSR to explore all aspects of the planet Venus (*Venera* is Russian for "Venus").

- The program started in 1961 with *Venera 1*, and continued until October 1983, when *15* and *16* mapped Venus' northern hemisphere.

- Most of the Venera probes were launched in pairs with a second nearly identical craft being launched a week or two after the first of the pair.

- *Venera 3, 4, 5, 6, 7,* and *8* consisted of a cruise "bus" and a spherical probe, both of which entered Venus' atmosphere and transmitted data until they were destroyed.

- *Venera 9, 10, 11, 12, 13,* and *14* consisted of a bus that could decelerate into a Venus orbit and a probe that was designed to enter the atmosphere and make a landing on the surface.

- *Venera 15* and *16* were similar in design to Venera *13* and *14*, but they were built to remain in orbit and map the surface with radar.

- In October 1967, *Venera 4* became the first spacecraft to enter the atmosphere of another planet and return data.

- On December 15, 1970, *Venera 7* became the first spacecraft to land on another planet successfully. It remained operational for 23 minutes.

- *Venera 9* was the first spacecraft to transmit monochrome images from the surface of another planet (October 22, 1975).

- *Venera 13* was the first spacecraft to transmit color photographs of Venus' surface (March 1982).

Landing on Venus

Venera 11

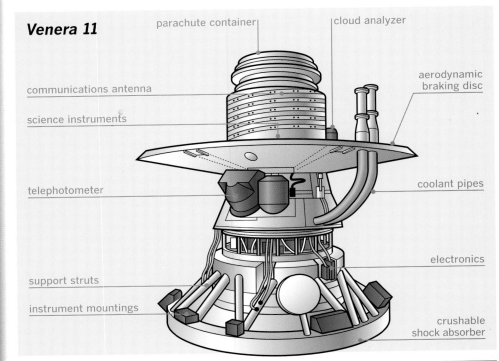

parachute container

cloud analyzer

communications antenna

aerodynamic braking disc

science instruments

telephotometer

coolant pipes

support struts

electronics

instrument mountings

crushable shock absorber

Venera 9 landing sequence

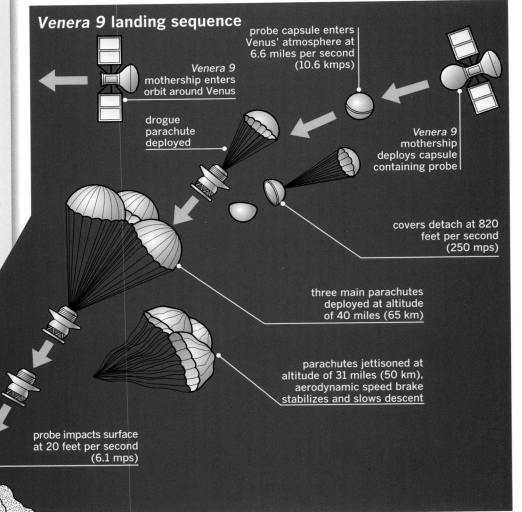

probe capsule enters Venus' atmosphere at 6.6 miles per second (10.6 kmps)

Venera 9 mothership enters orbit around Venus

Venera 9 mothership deploys capsule containing probe

drogue parachute deployed

covers detach at 820 feet per second (250 mps)

three main parachutes deployed at altitude of 40 miles (65 km)

parachutes jettisoned at altitude of 31 miles (50 km), aerodynamic speed brake stabilizes and slows descent

probe impacts surface at 20 feet per second (6.1 mps)

Exploring the Moon

Luna 2

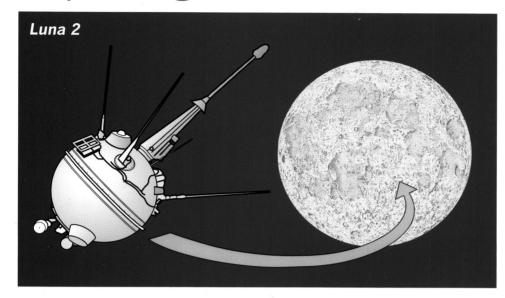

Pioneer 4

Ranger 9

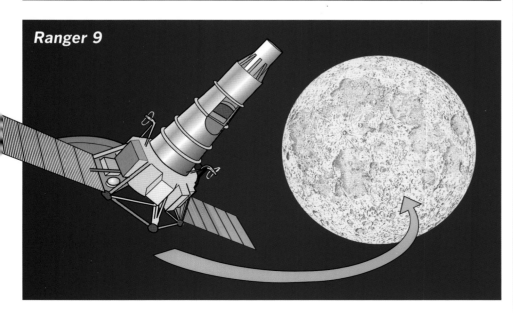

Key words
flyby
orbit
orbiter
spacecraft

Luna

- Beginning in 1958, the Luna program was the first attempt by the Soviet Union to orbit, impact, and land on the Moon.
- *Luna 1* was the first spacecraft to make a close flyby of the Moon, although it was probably intended to impact the surface.
- *Luna 2* was the first spacecraft to impact the Moon.
- *Luna 3* was the first spacecraft to fly around the Moon and return to Earth orbit. It was also the first spacecraft to transmit photographs of the far side of the Moon.
- The Luna program ended in 1976 with *Luna 24*.

Pioneer

- The Pioneer program was the first U.S. attempt to place spacecraft into orbit around the Moon, also in 1958.
- The first three spacecraft (known as *Able 1*, *2*, and *3*) failed to reach the Moon.
- *Pioneer 3* also failed and *Pioneer 4* passed the Moon at a much greater distance than had been planned.
- Three Pioneer orbiters also failed.

Ranger

- The Ranger program (1961–65) was the first U.S. effort to impact an uncrewed spacecraft on the Moon.
- *Ranger 1*, *2*, and *3* all failed in their missions.
- *Ranger 4* lost power on the way to the Moon but became the first U.S. spacecraft to reach the lunar surface. *Ranger 5* and *6* failed in transit.
- *Ranger 7*, *8*, and *9* all impacted the Moon and transmitted thousands of photographs of the surface as they approached.
- The Ranger program ended in 1965 with *Ranger 9*.

Landing on the Moon

Key words

orbit
rover
solar panel
spacecraft

Luna

- Launched in June 1965, *Luna 6* was the first spacecraft to attempt a controlled landing on the Moon, but it flew past it due to a miscalculation.
- *Luna 9* was the first spacecraft to make a successful controlled landing on the Moon and the first to transmit photographs taken on the surface.
- *Luna 13, 16, 17, 20, 21, 23,* and *24* also successfully landed on the Moon.
- In 1970, *Luna 16* was the first Soviet spacecraft to collect samples of material from the surface and return them to Earth.
- *Luna 17* and *21* landed surface rovers on the Moon (*Lunokhod 1* and *2*) that analyzed soil and transmitted photographs and television pictures.

Surveyor

- Starting in 1966, the Surveyor program was the first U.S. attempt to make a controlled landing on the Moon with uncrewed spacecraft.
- *Surveyor 1* was its first success. It transmitted thousands of photographs from the surface.
- *Surveyor 2* failed but *Surveyor 3* made another successful landing. In 1969 the crewed Lunar Module *Intrepid* (*Apollo 12*) landed close to *Surveyor 3* and parts of the spacecraft were returned to Earth for analysis.
- *Surveyor 5, 6,* and *7* all landed successfully and returned data that was vital to the success of the later crewed Apollo missions.

Name	Country	Launch date	Mission achievements
Ranger 7	USA	July 28, 1964	close-up pictures before crash landing
Ranger 8	USA	February 17, 1965	close-up pictures before crash landing
Ranger 9	USA	March 21, 1965	close-up pictures before crash landing
Luna 9	USSR	January 31, 1966	first soft landing
Luna 10	USSR	March 31, 1966	first orbiter
Surveyor 1	USA	May 30, 1966	soft landing
Lunar Orbiter 1	USA	August 10, 1966	orbiter
Luna 11	USSR	August 24, 1966	orbiter
Luna 12	USSR	October 22, 1966	orbiter
Lunar Orbiter 2	USA	November 6, 1966	orbiter
Luna 13	USSR	December 21, 1966	lander
Lunar Orbiter 3	USA	February 5, 1967	orbiter
Surveyor 3	USA	April 17, 1967	lander, soil sampling
Lunar Orbiter 4	USA	May 4, 1967	orbiter
Lunar Orbiter 5	USA	August 1, 1967	orbiter
Surveyor 5	USA	September 8, 1967	lander
Surveyor 6	USA	November 7, 1967	lander
Surveyor 7	USA	January 7, 1968	lander
Luna 14	USSR	April 7, 1968	orbiter

Six U.S. spacecraft and 13 Soviet spacecraft failed during this period.

Surveyor

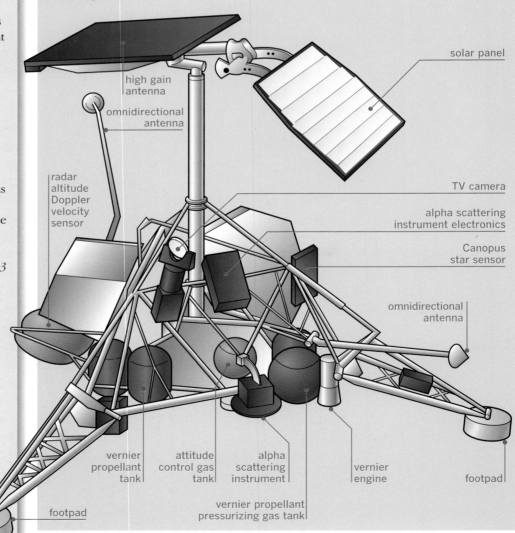

high gain antenna
omnidirectional antenna
solar panel
radar altitude Doppler velocity sensor
TV camera
alpha scattering instrument electronics
Canopus star sensor
omnidirectional antenna
vernier propellant tank
attitude control gas tank
alpha scattering instrument
vernier engine
footpad
footpad
vernier propellant pressurizing gas tank

Mars: early exploration

Mariner 4

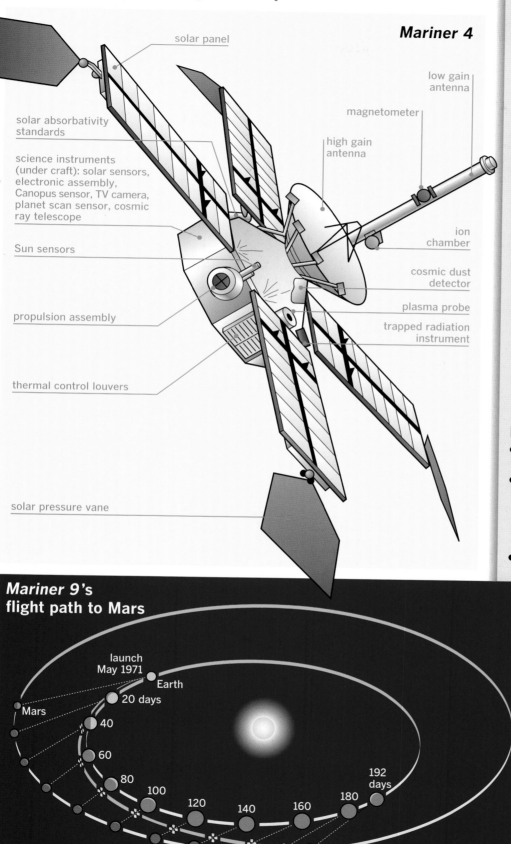

solar panel

low gain antenna

magnetometer

high gain antenna

solar absorbativity standards

science instruments (under craft): solar sensors, electronic assembly, Canopus sensor, TV camera, planet scan sensor, cosmic ray telescope

Sun sensors

propulsion assembly

thermal control louvers

solar pressure vane

ion chamber

cosmic dust detector

plasma probe

trapped radiation instrument

Mariner 9's flight path to Mars

launch May 1971

Earth

20 days

Mars

40

60

80

100

120

140

160

180

192 days

Mars encounter November 1971

Key words

flyby	spacecraft
lander	
orbit	
probe	
solar panel	

Mariner

- *Mariner 4* was a NASA spacecraft that became the first functioning spacecraft to make a close approach to Mars and also the first to transmit close-range images of the planet. The spacecraft made one flyby of Mars.
- *Mariner 6* and *Mariner 7* were identical spacecraft that both made one flyby of Mars and transmitted close-range images.
- *Mariner 9* was the first spacecraft to be put into orbit around Mars. It photographed about 80 percent of the planet's surface at much higher resolution than previous missions and measured atmospheric pressure and variations in the gravity field.

Mars

- The Soviet Union launched a series of spacecraft called *Mars*.
- *Mars 1* (actually the fourth in the series) was the first spacecraft to make a close approach to Mars, but it failed before reaching the planet and transmitted no data.
- *Mars 3* returned data from Mars orbit, but its lander failed on the surface.
- *Mars 6* returned data from orbit but its lander failed after about two minutes on the surface.

Phobos

- *Phobos 1* and *Phobos 2* were identical spacecraft launched by the Soviet Union. They were designed to orbit Mars and investigate its moon Phobos.
- *Phobos 1* failed on the way to Mars. *Phobos 2* completed part of its mission but failed just before releasing two small probes designed to land on the moon Phobos.

Key words

aerobraking	rover
atmosphere	spacecraft
lander	
orbit	
re-entry	

Mars Global Surveyor

- *Mars Global Surveyor* is a NASA spacecraft designed to orbit Mars and conduct a planet-wide mapping and surveying mission.
- Launched in November 1996, it was the first U.S. spacecraft to reach Mars for more than 20 years.
- The spacecraft was placed in a highly elliptical orbit around Mars and used aerobraking to lower and circularize its orbit prior to mapping.
- Images transmitted by *Mars Global Surveyor* have proven that large quantities of liquid water once flowed on the surface of Mars.

Mars Express

- *Mars Express* is an ESA spacecraft designed to orbit Mars and search for sub-surface water.
- *Mars Express* also released a lander called *Beagle 2* which failed before reaching the surface.

Mars Odyssey

- *Mars Odyssey* is a NASA spacecraft designed to orbit Mars and conduct a planet-wide survey of Mars' geology and atmospheric conditions.
- The spacecraft was placed in a highly elliptical orbit around Mars and used aerobraking to lower and circularize its orbit prior to mapping.
- *Mars Odyssey* is also used as a communications relay for the Mars exploration rovers *Spirit* and *Opportunity*.

Mars Reconnaissance Orbiter

- Launched in August 2005, *Mars Reconnaissance Orbiter* (MRO) is a NASA spacecraft designed to orbit and investigate Mars.
- MRO will conduct close-up photography of the planet's surface and act as a communications relay for future missions to Mars.

Mars: recent exploration

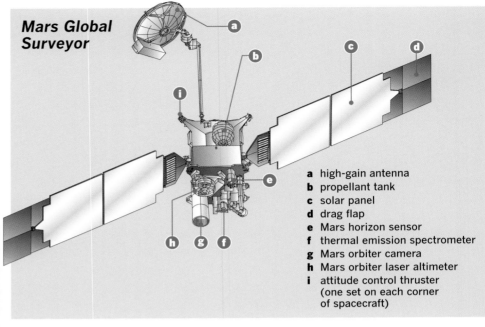

Mars Global Surveyor

a high-gain antenna
b propellant tank
c solar panel
d drag flap
e Mars horizon sensor
f thermal emission spectrometer
g Mars orbiter camera
h Mars orbiter laser altimeter
i attitude control thruster
   (one set on each corner
   of spacecraft)

Mars Express

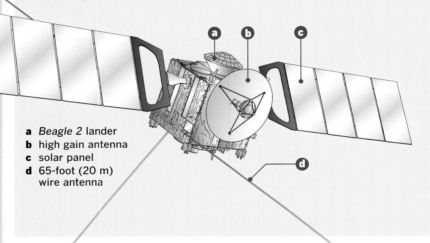

a *Beagle 2* lander
b high gain antenna
c solar panel
d 65-foot (20 m)
   wire antenna

Mars Odyssey

a gamma ray spectrometer
b solar array
c high-gain antenna
d Mars radiation environment experiment
   (located inside)
e star cameras
f high energy neutron detector
g UHF antenna
h thermal emission imaging system
i neutron spectrometer

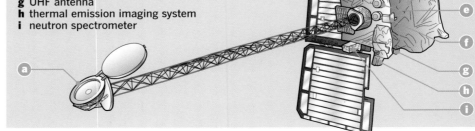

Mars: first landings

Mars Pathfinder

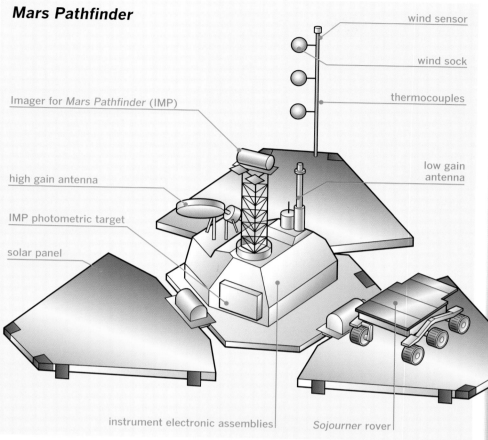

- wind sensor
- Imager for *Mars Pathfinder* (IMP)
- wind sock
- thermocouples
- high gain antenna
- low gain antenna
- IMP photometric target
- solar panel
- instrument electronic assemblies
- *Sojourner* rover

Key words

lander	rover
orbit	spacecraft
orbiter	
pole	
rocket	

Viking

- *Viking 1* and *2* (launched 1975) were near-identical NASA spacecraft consisting of a Mars orbiter and a Mars lander.
- After about a month in orbit photographing the surface to identify suitable landing sites, the landers made the descent on July 20, 1976, passing through Mars' atmosphere to the surface using parachutes and rocket engines.
- The landers transmitted stunning images of the surface, measured the local environmental conditions, and tested soil samples for signs of life.

Mars Pathfinder

- *Mars Pathfinder* (launched 1996) was a NASA spacecraft designed to deliver a lander and a rover (*Sojourner*) to the surface of Mars. The lander was later named the *Carl Sagan Memorial Station* for U.S. scientist Carl Sagan.
- The lander used a new method of reaching the surface, first descending through the atmosphere with parachutes and then inflating airbags to cushion surface impact.
- *Sojourner* became the first rover to land on the surface of another planet.
- *Sojourner* and the lander transmitted thousands of photographs of Mars' surface and conducted chemical analyses of rocks and soil.
- Both the lander and the rover far outlived their design lifetimes.

Mars Polar Lander

- *Mars Polar Lander* was a NASA spacecraft designed to land at Mars' south pole to dig for water ice.
- Contact with the spacecraft was lost as it entered Mars' atmosphere in December 1999.

Viking landing sequence

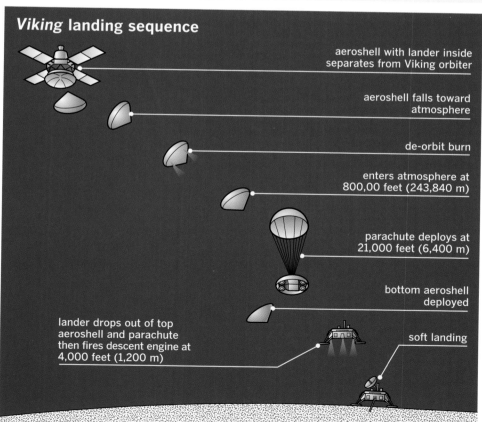

- aeroshell with lander inside separates from Viking orbiter
- aeroshell falls toward atmosphere
- de-orbit burn
- enters atmosphere at 800,00 feet (243,840 m)
- parachute deploys at 21,000 feet (6,400 m)
- bottom aeroshell deployed
- lander drops out of top aeroshell and parachute then fires descent engine at 4,000 feet (1,200 m)
- soft landing

© Diagram Visual Information Ltd.

MER

- MER is an acronym of "Mars Exploration Rover," a NASA program to land a large rover on the surface of Mars.

- Two identical MERs named *MER-A Spirit* and *MER-B Opportunity* successfully landed on Mars in January 2004 using the parachute and airbag system pioneered by the *Mars Pathfinder* lander and rover.

- Both MERs were designed to operate for 90 days on the surface, to travel across the terrain to areas of scientific interest, and to use a range of cameras and other tools to investigate geological features.

Spirit

- *MER-A Spirit* landed in the Gusev Crater, an area that orbital observations suggest may once have contained a large lake.

- *Spirit* was still operational and returning data in April 2006, having continued to function for more than 700 days beyond its design lifetime of 90 days.

Opportunity

- *MER-B Opportunity* landed in the Meridiani Planum area on the opposite side of Mars to *Spirit*'s landing site.

- *Opportunity* was still operational and returning data in April 2006, having continued to function for more than 700 days beyond its design lifetime of 90 days.

Mars: recent landings

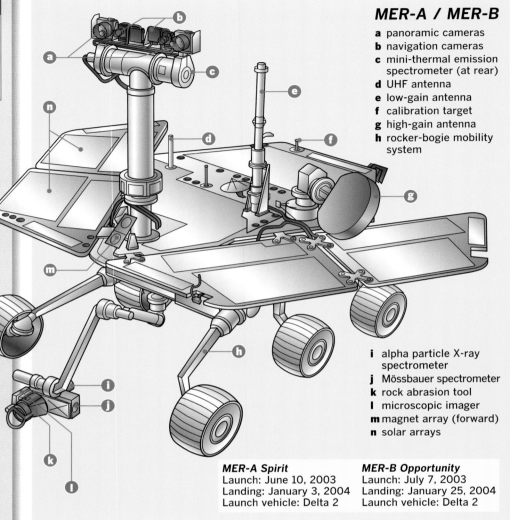

MER-A / MER-B

- **a** panoramic cameras
- **b** navigation cameras
- **c** mini-thermal emission spectrometer (at rear)
- **d** UHF antenna
- **e** low-gain antenna
- **f** calibration target
- **g** high-gain antenna
- **h** rocker-bogie mobility system

- **i** alpha particle X-ray spectrometer
- **j** Mössbauer spectrometer
- **k** rock abrasion tool
- **l** microscopic imager
- **m** magnet array (forward)
- **n** solar arrays

MER-A Spirit
Launch: June 10, 2003
Landing: January 3, 2004
Launch vehicle: Delta 2

MER-B Opportunity
Launch: July 7, 2003
Landing: January 25, 2004
Launch vehicle: Delta 2

MER landing sequence

a peak heating:	landing (L)–4 minutes	
b parachute deployment:	L–113 seconds, altitude (alt) 5.3 miles (8.6 km), speed (s) 293 miles per hour (472 kmph)	
c heatshield separation:	L–93 seconds	
d lander separation:	L–83 seconds	
e radar ground acquisition:	L–35 seconds, alt 1.5 miles (2.4 km)	
f start airbag inflation:	L–8 seconds, alt 930 feet (284 m)	
g retro rocket firing:	L–6 seconds, alt 440 feet (134 m), s 51 miles per hour (82 kmph)	
h bridle cut:	L–3 seconds, alt 33 feet (10 m)	
i bounces, rolls up to 1 km:	landing	
j roll stop:	L+10 minutes	
k airbags retracted:	L+66 minutes	
l petals opened:	L+96 minutes	

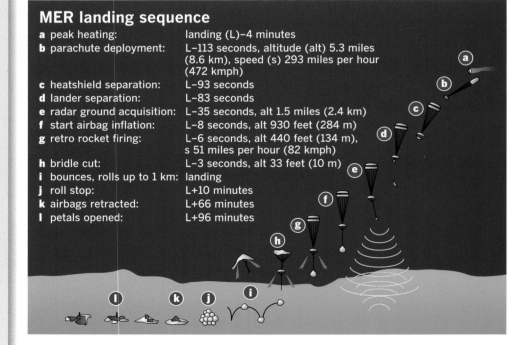

Jupiter: early exploration

Pioneer 10 and 11

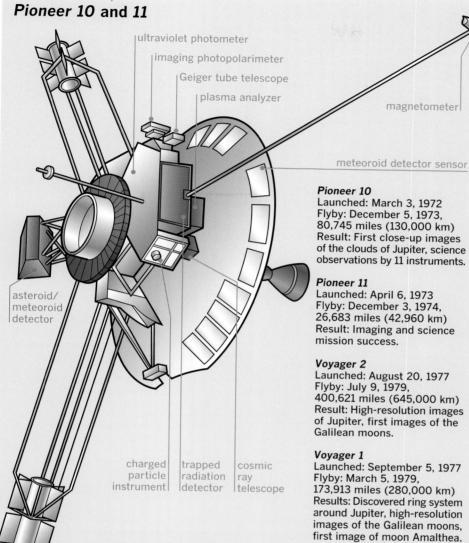

ultraviolet photometer

imaging photopolarimeter

Geiger tube telescope

plasma analyzer

magnetometer

meteoroid detector sensor

asteroid/ meteoroid detector

charged particle instrument

trapped radiation detector

cosmic ray telescope

Pioneer 10
Launched: March 3, 1972
Flyby: December 5, 1973,
80,745 miles (130,000 km)
Result: First close-up images
of the clouds of Jupiter, science
observations by 11 instruments.

Pioneer 11
Launched: April 6, 1973
Flyby: December 3, 1974,
26,683 miles (42,960 km)
Result: Imaging and science
mission success.

Voyager 2
Launched: August 20, 1977
Flyby: July 9, 1979,
400,621 miles (645,000 km)
Result: High-resolution images
of Jupiter, first images of the
Galilean moons.

Voyager 1
Launched: September 5, 1977
Flyby: March 5, 1979,
173,913 miles (280,000 km)
Results: Discovered ring system
around Jupiter, high-resolution
images of the Galilean moons,
first image of moon Amalthea.

Key words

asteroid
asteroid belt
cosmic ray
flyby
outer solar
 system

solar system
spacecraft

Pioneer

- *Pioneer 10* (launched 1972) and
  Pioneer 11 (1973) are two near-
  identical NASA spacecraft designed to
  explore the outer solar system.
- *Pioneer 10* was the first spacecraft to
  pass through the asteroid belt and the
  first spacecraft to make a close
  approach to Jupiter.
- *Pioneer 11* was the second spacecraft
  to make a close approach to Jupiter
  and the first spacecraft to make a
  close approach to Saturn.
- *Pioneer 10* and *Pioneer 11* are
  currently traveling toward the edge of
  the solar system. Communications
  with *Pioneer 11* ceased in September
  1995. Communications with *Pioneer
  10* ceased in January 2003.

Voyager

- *Voyager 1* (launched 1977) and
  Voyager 2 are two near-identical NASA
  spacecraft designed to explore the
  outer solar system.
- *Voyager 1* was the third spacecraft to
  make a close approach to Jupiter and
  Voyager 2 was the fourth.
- *Voyager 1* and *2* are still
  operational and are
  now traveling toward
  the edge of the solar
  system.

Flight paths of Pioneer 10 and 11

Callisto

Ganymede

Pioneer 10

Pioneer 11

Europa

Io

Amalthea

Key words

atmosphere	probe
comet	spacecraft
de-orbit	
flyby	
orbit	

Galileo

- *Galileo* was a NASA spacecraft designed to investigate Jupiter.
- It was the first spacecraft to enter orbit around Jupiter. It released an atmospheric probe, which became the first spacecraft to enter Jupiter's atmosphere.
- *Galileo* captured images of comet Shoemaker-Levy 9 impacting Jupiter while it was en route to the planet.
- The spacecraft's mission was extended beyond its original end date of December 1997 until September 2003. *Galileo* orbited Jupiter 34 times during its entire mission.
- *Galileo* was able to make flybys of Jupiter's moons Ganymede, Callisto, Europa, and Io that were 100 to 1,000 times closer than flybys made by the Voyager or Pioneer spacecraft.
- *Galileo* was deliberately de-orbited and destroyed in Jupiter's atmosphere to prevent the possibility of it impacting and contaminating Jupiter's moon Europa.

Galileo probe

- The Galileo probe was designed to enter Jupiter's atmosphere, brake using aerodynamic friction and then descend into the clouds using parachutes.
- The probe descended about 125 miles (200 km) into Jupiter's atmosphere and transmitted data for 58 minutes before high pressure and temperature caused it to fail.

Jupiter: recent exploration

Galileo
Launched: October 18, 1989
Jupiter orbit insertion: December 7, 1995
Jupiter atmosphere entry: September 21, 2003
Launch vehicle: Space Shuttle

Galileo probe
Release from *Galileo*: July 12, 1995
Jupiter atmosphere entry: December 7, 1995

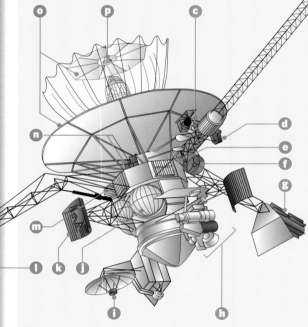

a plasma-wave antenna
b magnetometer sensors
c energetic particles detector
d plasma science
e heavy ion counter (back)
f dust detector
g radioisotope thermoelectric generators
h scan platform: includes ultraviolet spectrometer, solid-state imaging camera, near-infrared mapping spectrometer, photopolarimeter radiometer
i probe relay antenna
j retropropulsion module
k thrusters
l radioisotope thermoelectric generators
m star scanner
n extreme ultraviolet spectrometer
o Sun shields
p low-gain antenna

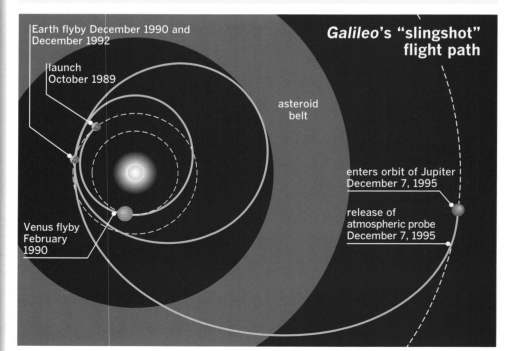

Galileo's "slingshot" flight path

Earth flyby December 1990 and December 1992

launch October 1989

asteroid belt

Venus flyby February 1990

enters orbit of Jupiter December 7, 1995

release of atmospheric probe December 7, 1995

Saturn: early exploration

Voyager spacecraft

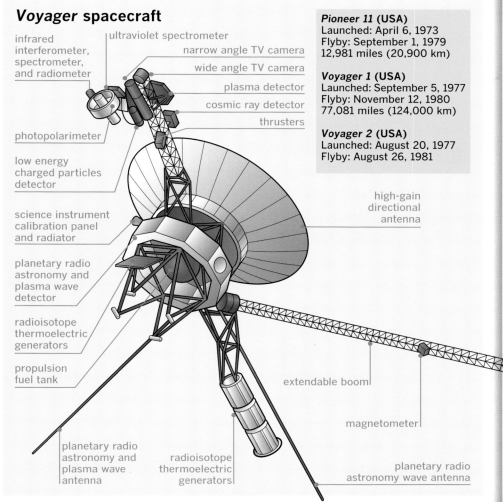

- infrared interferometer, spectrometer, and radiometer
- ultraviolet spectrometer
- narrow angle TV camera
- wide angle TV camera
- plasma detector
- cosmic ray detector
- thrusters
- photopolarimeter
- low energy charged particles detector
- science instrument calibration panel and radiator
- planetary radio astronomy and plasma wave detector
- radioisotope thermoelectric generators
- propulsion fuel tank
- high-gain directional antenna
- extendable boom
- magnetometer
- planetary radio astronomy and plasma wave antenna
- radioisotope thermoelectric generators
- planetary radio astronomy wave antenna

Pioneer 11 (USA)
Launched: April 6, 1973
Flyby: September 1, 1979
12,981 miles (20,900 km)

Voyager 1 (USA)
Launched: September 5, 1977
Flyby: November 12, 1980
77,081 miles (124,000 km)

Voyager 2 (USA)
Launched: August 20, 1977
Flyby: August 26, 1981

Key words

flyby
outer solar system
solar system
spacecraft

Pioneer 11

- *Pioneer 11* was a NASA spacecraft designed to explore the outer solar system.
- It was the first spacecraft to make a close approach to Saturn, and it discovered more rings and a new moon.

Voyager

- *Voyager 1* and *Voyager 2* are two near-identical NASA spacecraft designed to explore the outer solar system.
- They were the second and third spacecraft to make close approaches to Saturn.
- *Voyager 1* discovered three new moons, imaged fine details of the ring system, and measured the atmosphere of Titan, the largest Saturnian moon.
- *Voyager 2* discovered many more ringlets in the ring system.

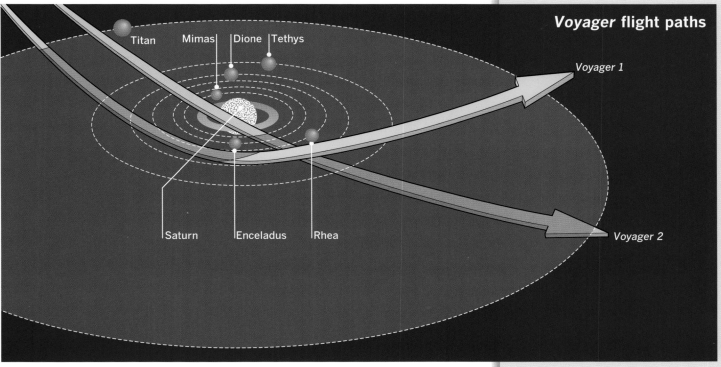

Voyager flight paths

Titan | Mimas | Dione | Tethys

Voyager 1

Voyager 2

Saturn | Enceladus | Rhea

Saturn: recent exploration

Key words

atmosphere
flyby
probe
spacecraft

Cassini

- *Cassini* is a NASA spacecraft designed to investigate Saturn and its moons.
- It was launched in October 1997 and entered orbit around Saturn in July 2004.
- *Cassini* carried the ESA probe *Huygens*, which was released and descended through the atmosphere of Saturn's moon Titan to land on its surface on January 14, 2005. The probe took photographs of the moon's surface as it descended.
- *Cassini* was the first spacecraft to enter orbit around Saturn. It is intended to complete 74 orbits of the planet before the end of its mission in 2008. It will make dozens of flybys of Titan and Saturn's other moons.

Cassini

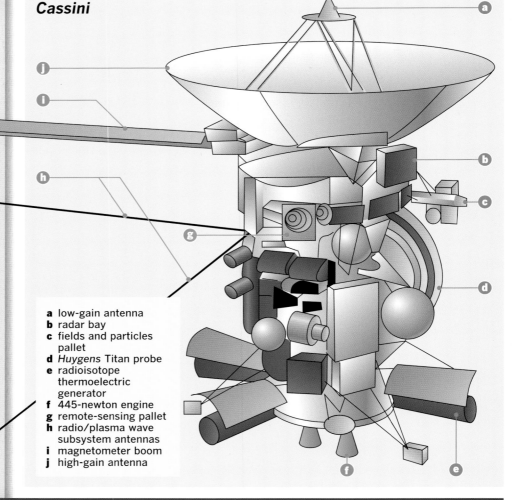

a low-gain antenna
b radar bay
c fields and particles pallet
d *Huygens* Titan probe
e radioisotope thermoelectric generator
f 445-newton engine
g remote-sensing pallet
h radio/plasma wave subsystem antennas
i magnetometer boom
j high-gain antenna

Huygens probe's descent to Titan

a entry 790 miles (1,270 km) above surface
b pilot-chute deployment
c back-cover release main parachute deployment
d front shield separation
e instrument configuration for descent
f main parachute jettison and stabilizer parachute deployment
g stabilizer parachute inflated
h surface impact
i surface mission phase

Exploring Uranus and Neptune

Key words

flyby
outer solar
  system
solar system
spacecraft

Voyager 2

- *Voyager 2* (launched 1977) is a NASA spacecraft designed to explore the outer solar system. It is the only spacecraft to have made close approaches to Uranus and Neptune.
- *Voyager 2* reached Uranus and then Neptune after making close approaches to Jupiter and Saturn, making it the only spacecraft to have visited four planets.

Uranus

- *Voyager 2* made its closest approach to Uranus on January 24, 1986 at a distance of 44,100 miles (71,000 km).
- The spacecraft photographed all five of the then-known moons and discovered ten new ones, all less than 93 miles (150 km) in diameter.
- The nine then-known rings were also photographed and two faint new rings were discovered.

Neptune

- *Voyager 2* made its closest approach to Neptune on August 25, 1989 at a distance of 3,000 miles (4,950 km).
- The spacecraft observed active weather systems in Neptune's atmosphere and discovered a giant storm known as the "great dark spot."
- Six new moons were also discovered and details of the ring system were observed.
- *Voyager 2* also made a close approach to Neptune's moon Triton and discovered that it is one of the coldest known worlds in the solar system with a temperature of −344°F (−255°C).

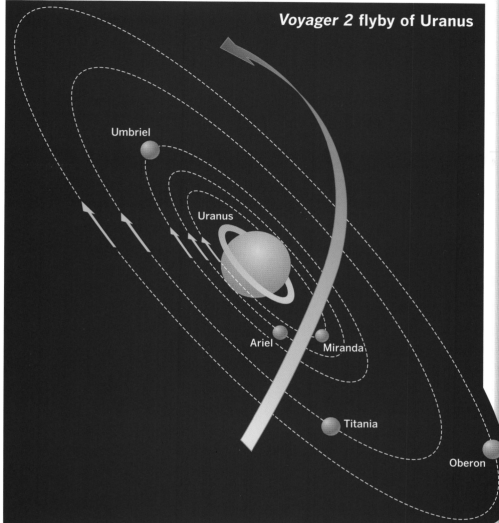

Voyager 2 flyby of Uranus

Umbriel

Uranus

Ariel

Miranda

Titania

Oberon

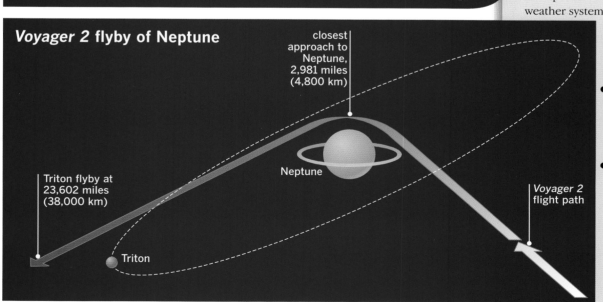

Voyager 2 flyby of Neptune

closest approach to Neptune, 2,981 miles (4,800 km)

Neptune

Triton flyby at 23,602 miles (38,000 km)

Voyager 2 flight path

Triton

Key words

asteroid
asteroid belt
comet
flyby
Near Earth
  Asteroid (NEA)

orbit
solar panel
spacecraft

Galileo

- NASA's *Galileo* spacecraft became the first to make a flyby of an asteroid when it passed close to asteroid 951 Gaspara en route to Jupiter in October 1991.
- *Galileo* also encountered asteroid 243 Ida and discovered that it has a moon.

NEAR

- *NEAR* is an acronym of *Near Earth Asteroid Rendezvous*.
- *NEAR* was a NASA spacecraft designed to orbit and study the asteroid 433 Eros.
- Eros and Mathilde are both Near Earth Asteroids (NEAs). Eros is the largest known NEA and was the first to be discovered.
- After a successful year-long survey of Eros, *NEAR* was guided to touchdown on its surface (February 2001), becoming the first spacecraft to land on an asteroid.

Hayabusa

- *Hayabusa* is a Japanese spacecraft designed to investigate the asteroid 25143 Itokawa. *Hayabusa* was originally called *Muses C*.
- *Hayabusa* reached Itokawa in November 2005, briefly landed on the surface, and collected samples. It is scheduled to return to Earth to deliver a re-entry capsule containing the samples in 2007.

Rosetta

- *Rosetta* is an ESA spacecraft designed to investigate the comet Churyumov-Gerasimenko that will also make close approaches to two asteroids.
- *Rosetta* will encounter asteroid 2867 Steins in September 2008 and asteroid 21 Lutetia in July 2010.

Exploring asteroids

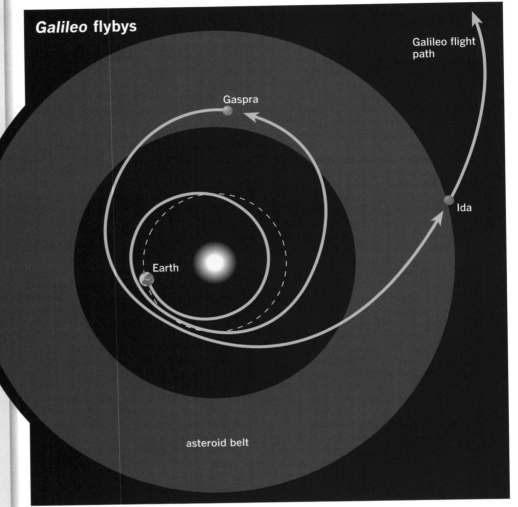

Galileo flybys

Galileo flight path

Gaspra

Ida

Earth

asteroid belt

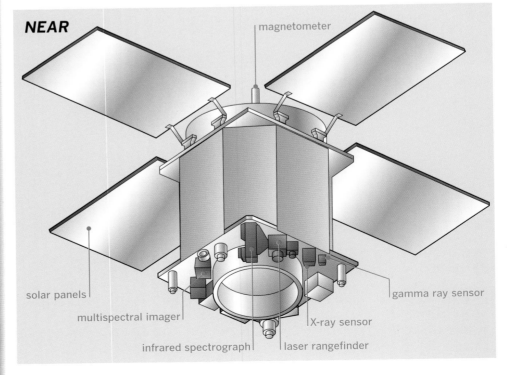

NEAR

magnetometer

solar panels

multispectral imager

infrared spectrograph

laser rangefinder

X-ray sensor

gamma ray sensor

Exploring comets

Giotto

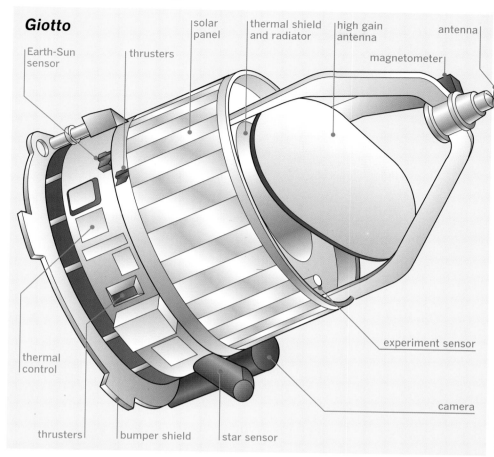

- Earth-Sun sensor
- thrusters
- solar panel
- thermal shield and radiator
- high gain antenna
- antenna
- magnetometer
- thermal control
- experiment sensor
- camera
- thrusters
- bumper shield
- star sensor

Rosetta flight path

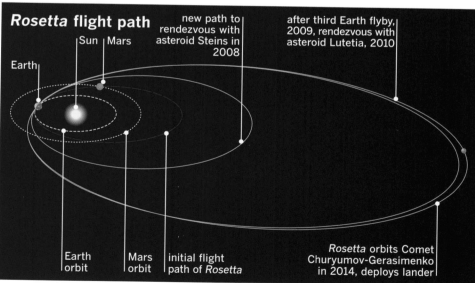

- Sun
- Mars
- Earth
- new path to rendezvous with asteroid Steins in 2008
- after third Earth flyby, 2009, rendezvous with asteroid Lutetia, 2010
- Earth orbit
- Mars orbit
- initial flight path of *Rosetta*
- *Rosetta* orbits Comet Churyumov-Gerasimenko in 2014, deploys lander

Halley's comet

- *Giotto* was just one of several spacecraft that were designed to investigate Halley's comet during its return to the inner solar system in 1986.
- *Suisei* and *Sakigake* were Japanese spacecraft that also studied the comet.

- *Vega 1* and *2* were twin Russian spacecraft that approached and studied the comet after delivering landers to the surface of Venus.
- *International Cometary Explorer* also made long-range observations of it.

Key words

comet	solar panel
inner solar system	solar system
	solar wind
lander	spacecraft
magnetosphere	

International Cometary Explorer

- *International Cometary Explorer* was a U.S. spacecraft that became the first probe to encounter a comet when it flew through the tail of Comet Giacobini-Zinner in September 1985.

Giotto

- *Giotto* was an ESA spacecraft designed to approach and study Halley's comet in 1986.
- *Giotto* took photographs of the comet's nucleus and transmitted data as it flew through the tail of the comet.
- *Giotto* later encountered Comet Grigg-Skjellerup and transmitted data.

Deep Impact

- *Deep Impact* is a NASA spacecraft designed to approach and study Comet Tempel 1.
- It released a probe that deliberately impacted the comet in July 2005.
- Cameras and other instruments aboard *Deep Impact* recorded the collision and studied resulting ejecta.

Stardust

- *Stardust* is a U.S. spacecraft designed to encounter Comet Wild 2, collect samples of dust from its coma, and return them to Earth.
- *Stardust* successfully encountered Wild 2 in January 2004 and was due to deliver its sample return capsule into Earth's atmosphere in January 2006.

Rosetta

- *Rosetta* is an ESA spacecraft currently en route to investigate Comet Churyumov-Gerasimenko. It was launched in March 2004 and will reach the comet in May 2014.
- *Rosetta* will release a small lander (*Philae*) that is designed to become the first spacecraft to make a landing on a comet nucleus.

Key words

atmosphere	orbit
attitude	re-entry
cosmonaut	retrofire
de-orbit	spacecraft
ICBM	

Vostok program

- Vostok was a Soviet space program to put a human into Earth orbit.
- It was the first program to achieve this aim successfully, in April 1961.
- There were six crewed flights in the Vostok program. All were successful.
- *Vostok* means "East" in Russian.
- The Vostok spacecraft and re-entry capsule were designed to carry a human or to act as a camera platform for reconnaissance missions.
- The Vostok rocket was an adaptation of the Soviet R7 intercontinental ballistic missile (ICBM).

Vostok 1

- *Vostok 1* was the first spacecraft to carry a human (cosmonaut Yuri Gagarin) outside of Earth's atmosphere, and the first to carry a human into Earth orbit.
- *Vostok 1* made one complete orbit of Earth in 108 minutes.
- Gagarin had no control of *Vostok 1*'s orbit or attitude, although provision was made for him to take control in an emergency.
- At the end of its orbit, *Vostok 1* fired rockets to de-orbit and re-entered Earth's atmosphere.
- Gagarin ejected from the re-entry capsule as planned at an altitude of 4.5 miles (7 km) and descended to a landing by parachute. The re-entry capsule landed separately after a parachute descent.
- Both Gagarin and the re-entry capsule touched down on land in southern Russia.

Vostok

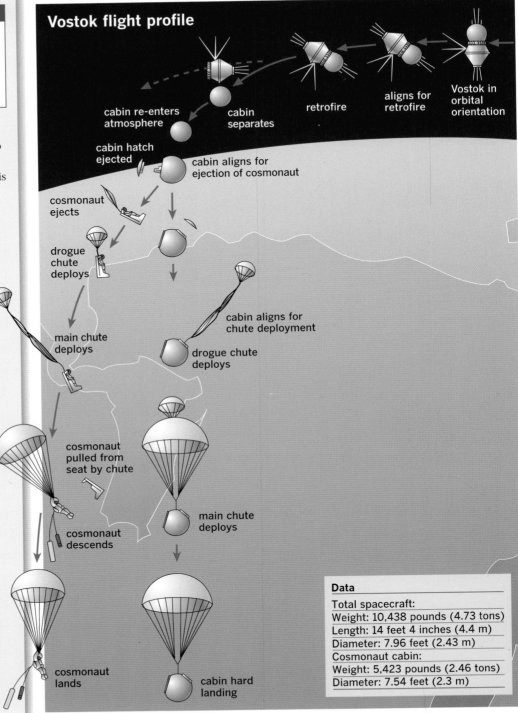

Vostok flight profile

cabin re-enters atmosphere

cabin separates

retrofire

aligns for retrofire

Vostok in orbital orientation

cabin hatch ejected

cabin aligns for ejection of cosmonaut

cosmonaut ejects

drogue chute deploys

main chute deploys

cabin aligns for chute deployment

drogue chute deploys

cosmonaut pulled from seat by chute

main chute deploys

cosmonaut descends

cosmonaut lands

cabin hard landing

Data

Total spacecraft:
Weight: 10,438 pounds (4.73 tons)
Length: 14 feet 4 inches (4.4 m)
Diameter: 7.96 feet (2.43 m)
Cosmonaut cabin:
Weight: 5,423 pounds (2.46 tons)
Diameter: 7.54 feet (2.3 m)

Vostok flights

- *Vostok 1* April 12, 1961: Yuri Gagarin becomes first human in space; flight of 1 hour 48 minutes
- *Vostok 2* August 6, 1961: Gherman Titov makes first day-long flight; flight of 1 day 1 hour 11 minutes
- *Vostok 3* August 11, 1962: Andrian Nikolyev makes flight lasting 3 days 22 hours 9 minutes
- *Vostok 4* August 12, 1962: Pavel Popovich passes close to *Vostok 3* during flight of 2 days 22 hours 44 minutes
- *Vostok 5* June 14, 1963: Valeri Bykovsky flies longest solo mission of 4 days 22 hours 56 minutes
- *Vostok 6* June 16, 1963: Valentina Tereshkova becomes first woman in space; flight of 2 days 22 hours 40 minutes

Mercury

Mercury capsule

The escape tower ejects before orbit.

Data

Length (including escape tower): 26 feet (7.9 m)
Width (across heat shield): 12 feet 2.5 inches (1.89 m)
Weight (in orbit): 2,987 pounds (1,355 kg)
Weight (at splashdown): 2,493 pounds (1,130 kg)

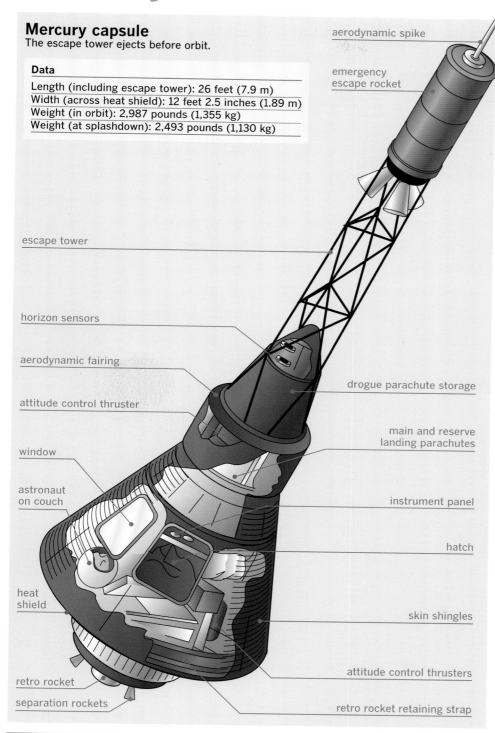

aerodynamic spike

emergency escape rocket

escape tower

horizon sensors

aerodynamic fairing

attitude control thruster

window

astronaut on couch

heat shield

retro rocket

separation rockets

drogue parachute storage

main and reserve landing parachutes

instrument panel

hatch

skin shingles

attitude control thrusters

retro rocket retaining strap

Key words

attitude	retro rocket
escape tower	spacecraft
heat shield	splashdown
orbit	suborbital
re-entry	

Mercury program

- Mercury was the first NASA program to place a human into Earth orbit.
- Mercury achieved its aim in 1961, though the Soviet Vostok program had achieved it first.
- There were six crewed flights in the Mercury program. All were successful.
- The flights were designated Mercury-Redstone (MR) or Mercury-Atlas (MA) depending on the launch vehicle used. Each spacecraft was also named.
- There were a series of uncrewed test flights of the Mercury spacecraft before the first crewed flight was attempted. Some of these flights carried chimpanzees as test subjects.

MR 3 Freedom 7

- *MR 3 Freedom 7* was the first crewed flight in the Mercury program and the first U.S. flight to carry a human (Alan Shepard) outside Earth's atmosphere.
- *MR 3 Freedom 7* did not, and was not intended to, reach Earth orbit. It was a suborbital flight of about 15 minutes in duration.
- Shepard remained in the re-entry capsule as it descended by parachute, and landed in the Atlantic Ocean.

MA 6 Friendship 7

- *MA 6 Friendship 7* was the third crewed flight in the Mercury program and the first U.S. flight to carry a human (John Glenn) into Earth orbit.
- Glenn made a successful three-orbit flight before splashing down in the Atlantic Ocean.
- More than 35 years later in October 1998 John Glenn, then aged 77, made his second space flight. Flying aboard the Space Shuttle orbiter *Discovery* (STS 95) he became the oldest person ever to travel in space.

Mercury flights

- *MR 3 (Freedom 7)* May 5, 1961
  Alan Shepard makes successful suborbital flight of 15 minutes 28 seconds
- *MR 4 (Liberty Bell 7)* July 21, 1961
  Gus Grissom makes successful suborbital flight of 15 minutes 37 seconds: capsule sinks after splashdown; Grissom survives
- *MA 6 (Friendship 7)* February 20, 1962
  John Glenn makes successful three-orbit flight of 4 hours 55 minutes

- *MA 7 (Aurora 7)* May 24, 1962
  Scott Carpenter makes successful three-orbit flight of 4 hours 56 minutes
- *MA 8 (Sigma 7)* October 3, 1962
  Wally Schirra makes successful six-orbit flight of 9 hours 13 minutes
- *MA 9 (Faith 7)* May 15, 1963
  Gordon Cooper makes successful 22-orbit flight of 34 hours 19 minutes

Key words

astronaut	orbit
attitude	propellant
docking	re-entry
ejection seat	rendezvous
extravehicular	retro rocket
activity (EVA)	spacecraft

Gemini program

- Gemini was a NASA program begun in 1965 to develop and launch a spacecraft capable of putting two astronauts into Earth orbit.
- Gemini was also intended to develop the technology and techniques, such as orbital rendezvous and docking, that would be needed for a crewed mission to the Moon.
- The Gemini program succeeded in its aims but the Soviet Voskhod program was the first to place a spacecraft carrying two crew into Earth orbit.
- There were ten crewed flights in the Gemini program. All were successful.
- Gemini 1 and 2 were uncrewed test flights.

Gemini flights

- Gemini 3 was the first U.S. spacecraft to carry two crew into Earth orbit.
- Gemini 4 was the first U.S. space mission to include a spacewalk (*extra vehicular activity, EVA*). Astronaut Ed White carried out a 22-minute EVA in Earth orbit.
- Gemini 6 and 7 were the first U.S. spacecraft to be in orbit at the same time and the first to perform a rendezvous in orbit.
- Gemini 8 was the first U.S. spacecraft to perform a rendezvous and docking in orbit (with an uncrewed Agena target rocket). An emergency re-entry and landing had to be made when both vehicles began to spin out of control.
- EVAs were also made from Gemini 9, 10, 11, and 12.
- Rendezvous and docking was also performed by Gemini 9 (rendezvous only), 10, 11, and 12.

Gemini

Gemini

Launch	Mission	Duration	Crew
March 23, 1965	Gemini 3	4 hrs 52 mins 51 s	Gus Grissom and John Young
June 3, 1965	Gemini 4	4 day 1 hr 56 mins	Ed White and Jim McDivitt
August 21, 1965	Gemini 5	7 day 22 hrs 55 mins	Gordon Cooper and Pete Conrad
December 4, 1965	Gemini 6	13 day 18 hrs 35 mins	Frank Borman and James Lovell
December 15, 1965	Gemini 7	1 day 1 hr 51 mins	Wally Schirra and Tom Stafford
March 16, 1966	Gemini 8	10 hrs 41 mins	Neil Armstrong and David Scott
June 3, 1966	Gemini 9	3 day 0 hrs 20 mins	Gene Cernan and Tom Stafford
July 18, 1966	Gemini 10	2 day 22 hrs 46 mins	Michael Collins and John Young
September 12, 1966	Gemini 11	2 day 23 hrs 17 mins	Pete Conrad and Richard Gordon
November 11, 1966	Gemini 12	3 day 22 hrs 31 mins	Buzz Aldrin and Jim Lovell

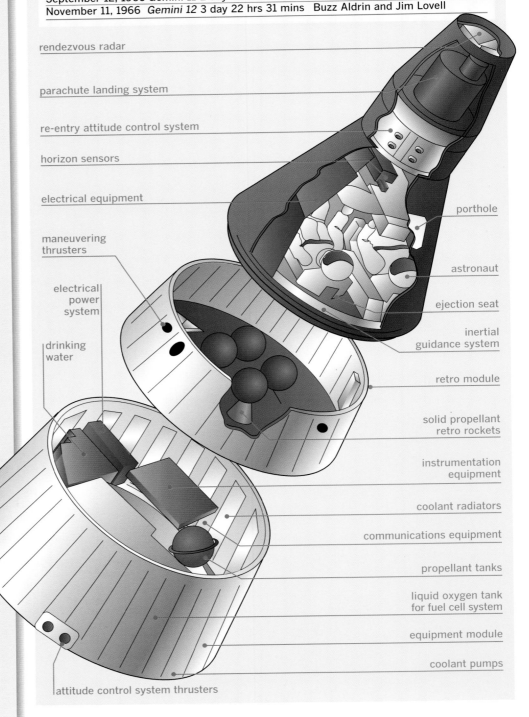

rendezvous radar

parachute landing system

re-entry attitude control system

horizon sensors

electrical equipment

maneuvering thrusters

electrical power system

drinking water

attitude control system thrusters

porthole

astronaut

ejection seat

inertial guidance system

retro module

solid propellant retro rockets

instrumentation equipment

coolant radiators

communications equipment

propellant tanks

liquid oxygen tank for fuel cell system

equipment module

coolant pumps

Voskhod

Voskhod 2

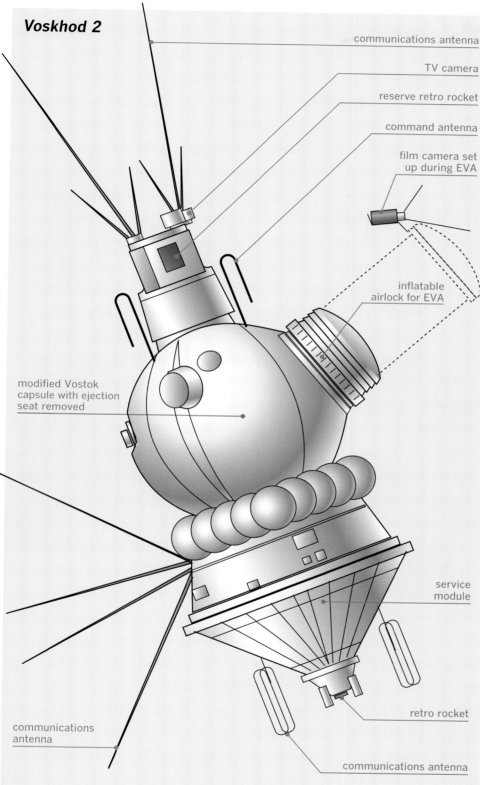

communications antenna

TV camera

reserve retro rocket

command antenna

film camera set up during EVA

inflatable airlock for EVA

modified Vostok capsule with ejection seat removed

service module

retro rocket

communications antenna

communications antenna

Launch	Mission	Duration	Crew
October 12, 1964	Voskhod 1	1 day 17 minutes 3 seconds	Vladimir Komarov, Konstantin Feoktistov, and Boris Yegorov
March 18, 1965	Voskhod 2	1 day 2 hours 2 minutes 17 seconds	Pavel Belyayev and Aleksei Leonov

Key words

airlock	orbit
cosmonauts	retro rocket
ejection seat	spacecraft
extravehicular activity (EVA)	spacesuit

Voskhod

- *Voskhod* was a Soviet program begun in 1964 to develop and launch a spacecraft capable of putting three crew into Earth orbit and to achieve the first extravehicular activity (EVA) in Earth orbit.
- The Voskhod spacecraft was a hasty adaptation of the Vostok spacecraft. Room for two more crew was created at the expense of the Vostok ejection seat and equipment for crew escape on the launch pad. The cosmonauts did not wear spacesuits in the capsule.
- There were three uncrewed test flights of the Voskhod spacecraft designated *Cosmos 47*, *Cosmos 57*, and *Cosmos 110*. *Cosmos 110* carried two dogs into Earth orbit.
- *Voskhod* means "sunrise" in Russian.

Voskhod 1

- *Voskhod 1* was the first spacecraft to carry more than one human into space. It had a crew of three.
- The spacecraft orbited Earth 16 times and collected data on the functioning of a multidisciplinary crew.

Voskhod 2

- *Voskhod 2* was the second spacecraft to carry more than one human into space. It had a crew of two.
- During the mission, cosmonaut Aleksei Leonov became the first to carry out an EVA on March 18, 1965.
- *Voskhod 2* was equipped with an inflatable airlock that allowed Leonov, dressed in a spacesuit, to exit the spacecraft without having to depressurize the entire cabin.
- Leonov's EVA lasted for about 20 minutes.
- *Voskhod 2* landed off target in a forest and the crew endured freezing conditions for 24 hours until recovery teams arrived.

Key words

attitude
de-orbit
re-entry
spacecraft
space station

Soyuz program

● Soyuz was originally a Soviet program in the late 1960s to develop and launch a spacecraft capable of taking a crew to the Moon and back.

● When the plans for a Soviet Moon landing were abandoned Soyuz became the spacecraft used to crew Soviet space stations.

● Soyuz spacecraft remain Russia's only crewed spacecraft and they are also used as uncrewed supply craft for the *International Space Station*.

● There have been several variants of the Soyuz spacecraft since the 1960s, and more than 100 Soyuz missions to date.

● *Soyuz* means "union" in Russian.

Soyuz 1

● *Soyuz 1* (launched April 23, 1967) was the first crewed launch of the Soyuz spacecraft.

● It carried one cosmonaut, Vladimir Komarov, and completed 18 orbits before successfully de-orbiting and re-entering Earth's atmosphere.

● Komarov was killed when the re-entry capsule's parachute failed to open.

Soyuz models

● The original Soyuz model, carrying a crew of three, was used from *Soyuz 1* through *11*.

● *Soyuz 12* through *40* used the ferry model, which carried a crew of two.

● The Soyuz T model was in use between 1976 and 1986 and carried a crew of three.

● The Soyuz TM model was in use between 1986 and 2003, carried a crew of three, and was used to crew and supply the *Mir* space station.

● The Soyuz TMA model is in use today. It carries three persons and is used to crew, supply, and return astronauts to Earth from the *International Space Station*.

Soyuz

Soyuz ferry

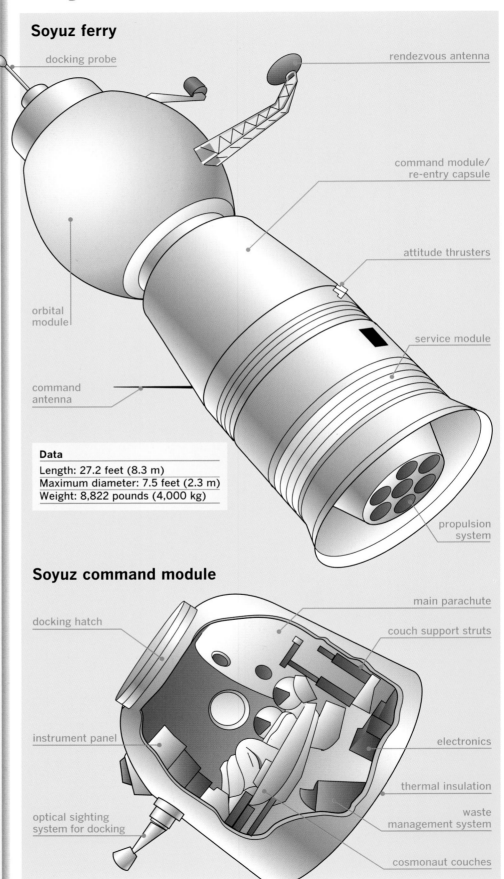

docking probe

rendezvous antenna

command module/ re-entry capsule

attitude thrusters

orbital module

service module

command antenna

propulsion system

Data
Length: 27.2 feet (8.3 m)
Maximum diameter: 7.5 feet (2.3 m)
Weight: 8,822 pounds (4,000 kg)

Soyuz command module

main parachute

couch support struts

docking hatch

instrument panel

electronics

thermal insulation

waste management system

optical sighting system for docking

cosmonaut couches

Apollo: overview

Apollo 7, 9
Earth orbit

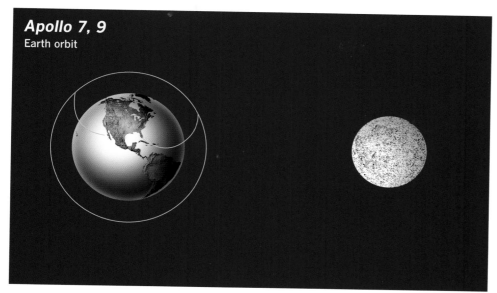

Apollo 8, 10
Lunar orbit

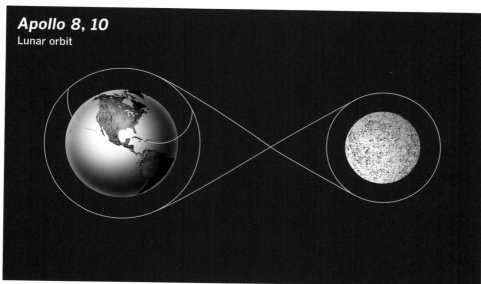

Apollo 11, 12, 14, 15, 16, 17
Lunar landing (*Apollo 13* lunar landing was aborted)

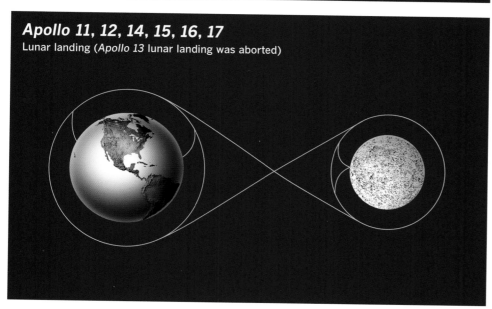

Key words

*low Earth orbit
  (LEO)*
orbit
rocket

Apollo program

- Apollo was the 1960s U.S. program to land a human crew on the Moon and return them safely to Earth.
- *Apollo 1* was one of a series of tests of the Command Module's system on the launchpad (no launch was intended). It ended in disaster in January 1967, when a fire killed all three crew. It was designated *Apollo 1* after the disaster.
- *Apollo 4, 5,* and *6* were uncrewed tests of the Saturn V rocket and spacecraft parts. There was no *Apollo 2* or *3*.
- *Apollo 7* (launched October 11, 1968) was the first crewed Apollo mission and the first three-person U.S. space mission. An Apollo Command and Service Module (CSM) was launched by a Saturn IB rocket and spent 11 days in Earth orbit.
- *Apollo 8* (launched December 21, 1968) was the first crewed spacecraft to leave low Earth orbit and the first to orbit the Moon. It was also the first crewed Apollo mission launched by Saturn V. An Apollo CSM spent 20 hours orbiting the Moon before returning to Earth.
- *Apollo 9* (launched March 3, 1969) was the first crewed Apollo mission to include a Lunar Module (LM). The crew spent ten days testing the LM and CSM docking equipment.
- *Apollo 10* (launched May 18, 1969) was the first crewed Apollo mission to take an LM to the Moon. The LM was maneuvered to within about eight miles of the Moon's surface. No landing was planned.
- *Apollo 11* was the first crewed mission to land on the Moon on July 20, 1969.
- *Apollo 12, 14, 15, 16,* and *17* also landed crews on the Moon (November 1969–December 1972).
- *Apollo 13* was planned to land on the Moon but an explosion in the Service Module (SM) en route meant that the landing had to be canceled. The crew managed to return to Earth safely.

© Diagram Visual Information Ltd.

Key words

midcourse	stage
correction	
orbit	
rocket	
spacecraft	

Earth to Moon

● All crewed Apollo flights were launched from Kennedy Space Center, Florida.

● The launch vehicle was the three-stage Saturn V rocket.

● The first stage of the Saturn V burned for two minutes 41 seconds and took the vehicle to an altitude of 42 miles (68 km). After the first stage shut down it was jettisoned and fell back to impact the Atlantic Ocean.

● The second stage burned for six minutes 29 seconds and took the vehicle to an altitude of 117 miles (188 km). The second stage was also jettisoned and impacted the Atlantic Ocean.

● The third stage burned for two minutes 25 seconds and placed the vehicle into a stable Earth orbit.

● The third stage remained attached to the rest of the vehicle for one and a half Earth orbits. At the end of that period the third stage was restarted to propel the spacecraft into an orbit that would take it around the Moon (a free return orbit). This was known as translunar injection.

● About 25 minutes after the second third stage burn, the Command and Service Module (CSM) moved away from the third stage, rotated 180°, and moved back in to dock the nose of the CSM with the top of the Lunar Module (LM) encased in its payload shroud.

● After docking, the third stage was jettisoned and the docked CSM and LM continued toward the Moon.

● The passage between Earth and the Moon was known as the translunar coast.

● During the translunar coast up to four midcourse corrections were performed using the CSMs engines.

● The spacecraft rotated slowly to ensure even heating by the Sun (know as "barbecue" mode).

Apollo: getting there

Generalized Apollo Earth-to-Moon flight path

a launch
b translunar injection
c CSM docks with LM

Apollo: landing

Generalized Apollo Earth-to-Moon flight path

a LOI 1 and LOI 2
b LM separates from CSM
c LM descent engine fires
d LM orientates to descend vertically
e LM touches down on the lunar surface

Key words

de-orbit
orbit
spacecraft

Lunar orbit

- The Service Propulsion System (SPS) was fired to slow the spacecraft into a lunar orbit at a distance of about 92 miles (148 km) above the Moon's surface. This was known as Lunar Orbit Insertion 1 (LOI 1).
- LOI 1 placed the spacecraft into a 69 by 196 mile (111 x 315 km) elliptical lunar orbit.
- After two lunar orbits, the SPS was started again (LOI 2) to place the spacecraft into a more circular 62 by 74 mile (100 x 119 km) lunar orbit.
- Both LOI burns took place when the spacecraft was on the far side of the Moon and out of radio contact.

Lunar landing

- The two landing crew transferred to the Lunar Module (LM) from the Command and Service Module (CSM) and the LM was undocked from the CSM.
- The descent engine of the LM was fired to de-orbit the LM.
- The LM descent engine was fired several times more to lower it toward the Moon's surface continuously.
- At about 7,000 feet (2,100 m) above the lunar surface the LM was orientated so that the descent engine was pointing toward the lunar surface. From an altitude of about 150 feet (45 m) the LM descended almost vertically using the descent engine continuously to slow its approach.
- The descent engine was shut down when probes extending below the LM's landing pads touched the lunar surface and the LM settled to a halt.
- Following equipment status checks, the landing crew were able to leave the LM and conduct their mission on the Moon's surface.

Key words

astronaut	orbit
atmosphere	reaction control
docking	rendezvous
midcourse	splashdown
correction	

Surface to orbit

- Once the astronauts had completed their mission on the surface, they returned to the Lunar Module (LM).
- The ascent stage of the LM was undocked from the descent stage and the ascent stage engine was fired.
- The ascent stage engine burned for seven minutes 14 seconds and propelled the LM into a 10 by 52 miles (16 x 84 km) lunar orbit.
- The LM's reaction control thrusters were then used to rendezvous with the Command and Service Module (CSM).
- After docking with the CSM, the lunar landing crew transferred to the CSM and the LM was jettisoned.

Moon to Earth

- Following a period in lunar orbit, the Service Propulsion System (SPS) on the CSM was fired to propel the spacecraft out of lunar orbit and into an Earth intercept trajectory known as the trans-Earth injection burn.
- During the trans-Earth coast a series of midcourse corrections were implemented.

Earth landing

- The CSM arrived at Earth on a trajectory that would take it direct into Earth's atmosphere.
- Before encountering the atmosphere, the Command Module (CM) separated from the Service Module (SM) and the CM was orientated so that its base struck the atmosphere first.
- Entering Earth's atmosphere at a speed of 24,700 miles per hour (40,000 kmph) the CM rapidly slowed until it was freefalling through the air.
- Drogue parachutes followed by main parachutes were deployed to slow the descent until the CM splashed down in the Pacific Ocean.
- The crew were recovered and taken aboard a U.S. Navy vessel in the area.

Apollo: getting back

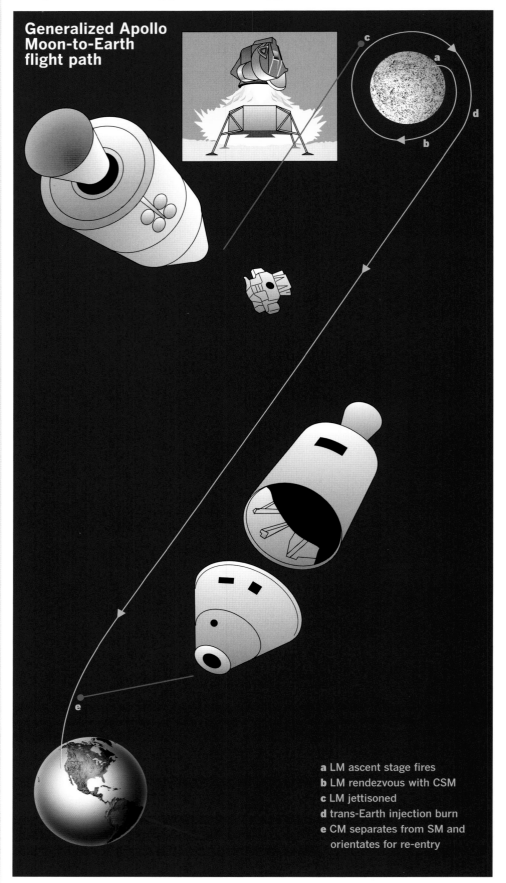

Generalized Apollo Moon-to-Earth flight path

a LM ascent stage fires
b LM rendezvous with CSM
c LM jettisoned
d trans-Earth injection burn
e CM separates from SM and orientates for re-entry

Apollo: Command Module

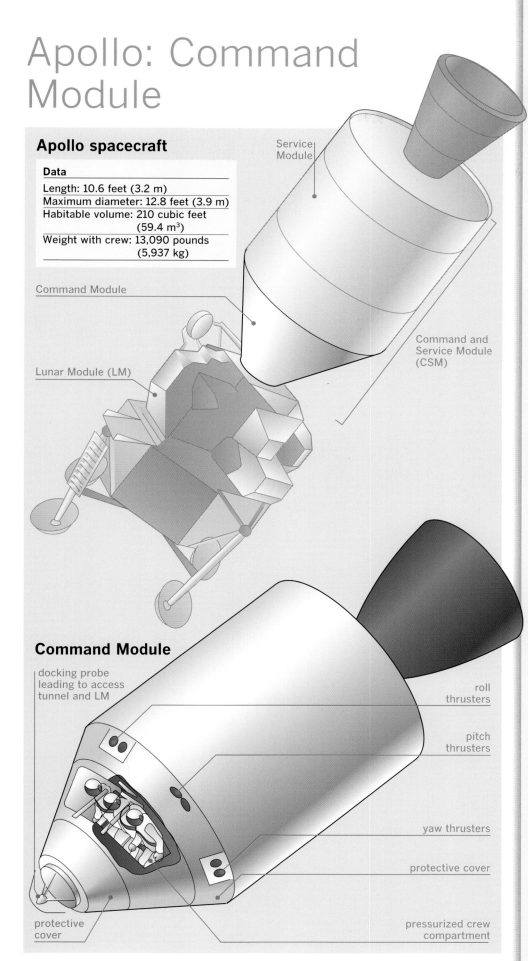

Apollo spacecraft

Data
Length: 10.6 feet (3.2 m)
Maximum diameter: 12.8 feet (3.9 m)
Habitable volume: 210 cubic feet
(59.4 m³)
Weight with crew: 13,090 pounds
(5,937 kg)

Command Module

Lunar Module (LM)

Service Module

Command and Service Module (CSM)

Command Module

docking probe leading to access tunnel and LM

roll thrusters

pitch thrusters

yaw thrusters

protective cover

protective cover

pressurized crew compartment

Key words

aerodynamic heating
astronaut
docking
heat shield
launch escape system

reaction control
re-entry
rocket
spacecraft
splashdown

Command Module

- The Apollo Command Module (CM) was the control center of the Apollo spacecraft.
- It contained the couches in which the astronauts sat during launch and all the controls and displays needed to pilot and operate the craft.
- The CM was also the only part of the Apollo spacecraft designed to return to Earth's surface.
- A forward compartment (at the apex) contained two reaction control engines and the Earth landing system, including the parachutes.
- At launch, the Launch Escape System (LES) was attached to the apex of the CM. In the event of an emergency on the launch pad, the LES would fire a rocket that would lift the CM away from the stacked spacecraft on top of the Saturn V rocket and allow it to parachute to safety.
- The crew compartment was a pressurized vessel in the middle of the CM. It contained 210 cubic feet (6 m³) of habitable space.
- The rear compartment of the CM contained ten reaction control engines, fuel tanks, helium, and water tanks.
- The entire CM was encased in a heat shield composed of a stainless steel honeycomb with an outer layer of ablative epoxy resin.
- The heat shield varied in thickness from 0.7 inches (1.8 cm) at the apex to 2.7 inches (6.9 cm) at the base.
- The CM also had a docking system and access tunnel at the apex so that the astronauts could attach to and access the Lunar Module.
- The CM and Service Module were together known as the CSM.
- The CSM remained in lunar orbit with one astronaut aboard during the lunar landing.

Key words

life support	rocket
orbit	spacecraft
propellant	
reaction control	
re-entry	

Service Module

- The Service Module (SM) contained the power systems, life support systems, and much of the fuel for the Apollo spacecraft. It was attached to the Command Module (CM) until just before re-entry . The CM and SM together were known as the CSM.

- The Service Propulsion System (SPS) was mounted on the back end of the SM. The SPS was a restartable rocket motor that provided the thrust for large changes in the spacecraft's velocity, such as those necessary to enter and leave lunar orbit.

- The SM was essentially a hollow cylinder divided into sections around a central core.

- These sections housed fuel tanks for the SPS, fuel cells for generating electricity and water, life support systems, communications equipment, and fuel for reaction control engines.

- The reaction control system on the SM consisted of four units, each with four thruster nozzles placed at equidistant intervals around the circumference of the craft. This system was completely independent of the CM reaction control system.

Apollo: Service Module

Apollo spacecraft

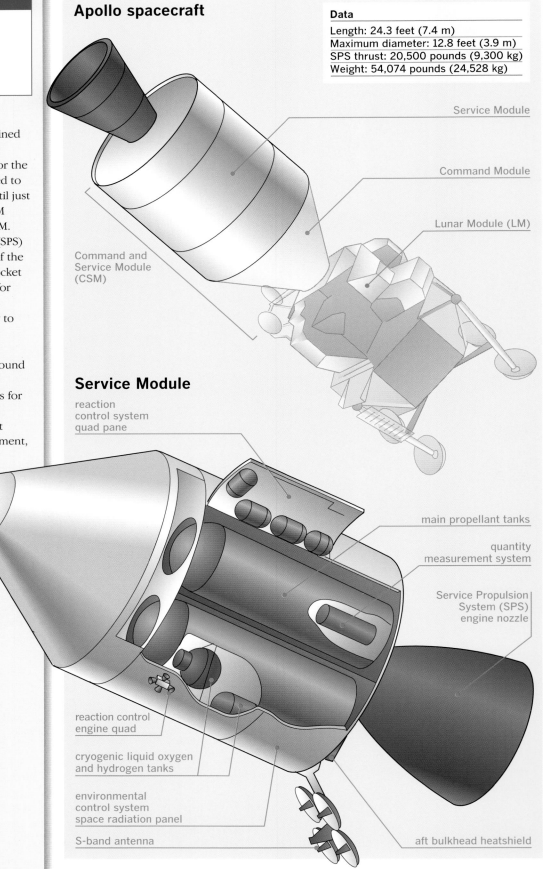

Data
Length: 24.3 feet (7.4 m)
Maximum diameter: 12.8 feet (3.9 m)
SPS thrust: 20,500 pounds (9,300 kg)
Weight: 54,074 pounds (24,528 kg)

Service Module

Command Module

Lunar Module (LM)

Command and
Service Module
(CSM)

Service Module

reaction
control system
quad pane

main propellant tanks

quantity
measurement system

Service Propulsion
System (SPS)
engine nozzle

reaction control
engine quad

cryogenic liquid oxygen
and hydrogen tanks

environmental
control system
space radiation panel

S-band antenna

aft bulkhead heatshield

Apollo: Lunar Module

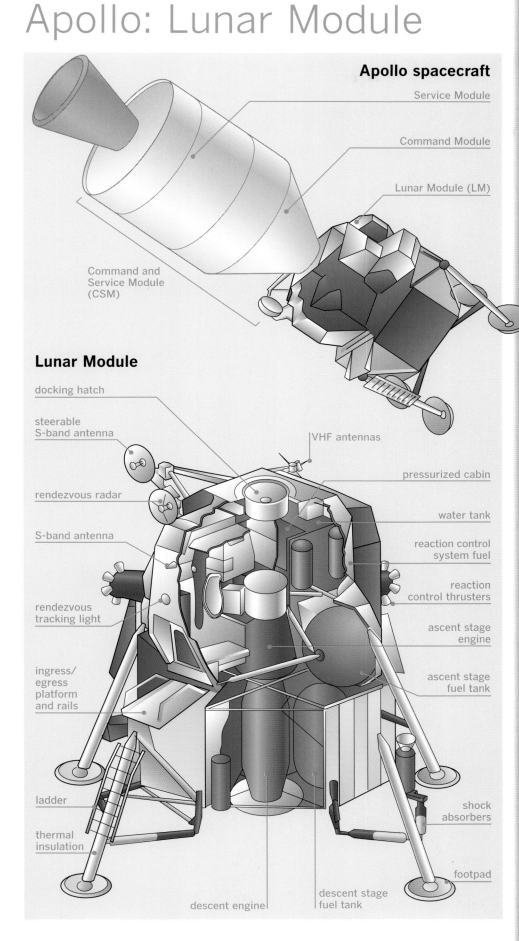

Apollo spacecraft

Service Module

Command Module

Lunar Module (LM)

Command and
Service Module
(CSM)

Lunar Module

docking hatch

steerable
S-band antenna

rendezvous radar

S-band antenna

rendezvous
tracking light

ingress/
egress
platform
and rails

ladder

thermal
insulation

VHF antennas

pressurized cabin

water tank

reaction control
system fuel

reaction
control thrusters

ascent stage
engine

ascent stage
fuel tank

shock
absorbers

footpad

descent engine

descent stage
fuel tank

Key words

attitude	reaction control
de-orbit	spacecraft
docking	
life support	
orbit	

Lunar Module

- The Lunar Module (LM or LEM) was the part of the Apollo spacecraft that landed on the Moon's surface.
- It consisted of two parts: the descent stage and the ascent stage.
- Soon after launch, the CSM docked with the LM and extracted it from the payload shroud at the top of the third stage of the Saturn V rocket.
- On the journey to the Moon, the CSM remained docked with the combined ascent and descent stages of the LM.
- The descent stage of the LM consisted of a load-carrying platform equipped with a descent engine and four extendible landing legs. The ascent stage was attached to the descent stage as it de-orbited and touched down on the lunar surface.
- The descent stage engine could be throttled for variable thrust and gimballed for attitude command.
- The ascent stage carried two crew in a pressurized cabin along with flight controls and life support equipment. It was also equipped with an ascent engine, docking equipment, and an access tunnel to allow astronauts to transfer from the LM to the CSM.
- Once the astronauts were ready to depart from the lunar surface, they undocked the ascent stage from the descent stage base and fired the ascent stage engine.
- The ascent stage engine propelled the ascent stage into lunar orbit where it docked with the Command and Service Module (CSM). The descent stage remained on the lunar surface.
- After the astronauts had transferred to the CSM in lunar orbit the LM ascent stage was jettisoned.
- The ascent engine could not be throttled or gimballed.
- The ascent stage was also equipped with reaction control motors.

© Diagram Visual Information Ltd.

Key words

astronaut
life support

Lunar rover

- The Lunar Roving Vehicle (LRV) was a vehicle designed to allow astronauts to cover more ground and carry greater loads on the Moon's surface.
- It could carry two astronauts and their life support equipment, communications equipment, scientific equipment, and 60 pounds (27 kg) of lunar samples.
- The LRV was capable of negotiating obstacles 12 inches (30 cm) high, could cross crevasses 28 inches (70 cm) wide, and could safely climb and descend slopes of 25 degrees.
- The LRV was battery-powered and had a maximum range of 57 miles (92 km) per Apollo mission.
- In practice no LRV was allowed to travel more than about six miles (9.7 km) from the Lunar Module (LM). This was the maximum distance from which the astronauts could safely walk back to the LM in the event of a total LRV failure.
- Even with this safety limit, the LRV greatly increased the area that a lunar landing crew could explore during their limited stay on the surface.
- Only *Apollo 15, 16,* and *17* carried LRVs.
- The LRV was of lightweight aluminum construction and was attached to the outside of the LM in a folded configuration for lunar landing.

Apollo: Lunar Roving Vehicle

Lunar Roving Vehicle

LRV missions

Mission	Duration	Location	Astronauts
Apollo 15	July–August 1971	Hadley Base	David Scott and James Irwin
Apollo 16	April 1972	Descartes	John Young and Charlie Duke
Apollo 17	December 1972	Taurus Littrow	Gene Cernan and Jack Schmitt

Data

Length (assembled): 10.2 feet (3.1 m)
Width (assembled): 6 feet (1.8 m)
Weight (empty): 462 pounds (210 kg)

high gain communications antenna

low gain communications antenna

TV camera

16 mm camera

display console

hand controller

sample collection bags

lunar communications relay unit

science and crew equipment

dust guards

underseat stowage

wire mesh wheels

Apollo: Saturn V

Typical Saturn V at launch

Data (typical)

Saturn V
Height: 364 feet (111 m)
Diameter: 33 feet (10 m)
Weight (fueled): 6,300,000 pounds (2,800,000 kg)
Payload to Moon: 103,600 pounds (47,000 kg)

S-IC
Thrust: 7,500,000 pounds (33.4 MN)
Burn time: 2.5 minutes

S-II
Thrust: 1,000,000 pounds (5 MN)
Burn time: 6 minutes

S-IVB
Thrust: 225,000 pounds (1 MN)
Burn times: 2.75 minutes and 5.6 minutes

Third stage
First burn to altitude of 118 miles
(190 km); second burn insertion of
Apollo into translunar orbit

Second stage
6.5-minute burn to altitude
of 115 miles (185 km)

First stage
2.5-minute burn to altitude
of 38.5 miles (62 km)

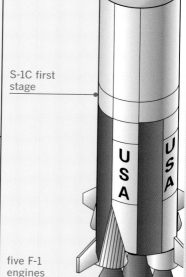

launch escape
system

Apollo Command
Module

Apollo Service
Module

Apollo Lunar
Module

Lunar Roving
Vehicle

flight control
instrument unit

S-IVB restartable
third stage

S-IVB J-2
engine

S-II second
stage

four J-2 engines

S-1C first
stage

five F-1
engines

Key words

attitude	oxidizer
launch escape	payload
system	rocket
liquid propellant	spacecraft
orbit	stage

Moon rocket

- The Saturn V is the largest operational rocket that has been built to date.
- It was designed to carry the Apollo spacecraft from the surface of Earth to lunar orbit.
- A total of 13 Saturn V rockets were launched between 1967 and 1973 and all were successful. Ten of those launches carried crewed spacecraft.

Stages

- The Saturn V was a three-stage liquid propellant expendable rocket.
- The first stage (S-IC) was equipped with five F-1 rocket engines. The center engine was fixed while the four outer engines could be gimballed for attitude control.
- S-IC burned a kerosene fuel known as Rocket Propellant 1 (RP-1) with liquid oxygen as an oxidizer. It was built by the Boeing company.
- The second stage (S-II) was equipped with five J-2 rocket engines. The center engine was fixed while the four outer engines could be gimballed for attitude control.
- S-II burned liquid hydrogen and liquid oxygen. It was built by North American Aviation.
- The third stage (S-IVB) was equipped with one J-2 rocket engine that could be gimballed for attitude control.
- The J-2 engine on the third stage was restartable. The first burn of the third stage's J-2 engine took the Apollo spacecraft to Earth orbit. The engine was restarted one and a half orbits later to propel the spacecraft toward the Moon.
- S-IVB burned liquid hydrogen and liquid oxygen. It was built by the Douglas Aircraft Company.
- Stages 1 and 2 could survive the shutdown of an engine and still achieve their altitude goals by burning the other engines for longer.

Apollo: launch site

© Diagram Visual Information Ltd.

Key words

ordnance
rocket

Launch Control Center

● All launches were controlled from one of four firing rooms, each with 470 sets of monitoring equipment.
● It included a specially-built four-story "electronic brain" called LC-39.

Mobile Launch Platform

● A Mobile Launch Platform is a 46-foot (136 m) tall structure able to hold an upright Saturn V.
● Its base is two stories high with an exhaust hole and four arms that kept the Saturn V on the pad until its engines had built up 95 percent of thrust.

Transporters

● These transporters were used to carry a Saturn V and its Mobile Launch Platform the 3.4 miles (5.5 km) from the VAB to the launch pad.
● Each tracked vehicle weighs 2,720 tons and has a top deck about the size of a baseball infield.
● Each of the four double tracks of the transporter is 10 feet (3 m) high and 40 feet (12 m) long.
● Two were built and are still in use today.

Kennedy Space Center

● All Apollo missions were assembled at and launched from the Kennedy Space Center (KSC), Florida.
● Kennedy Space Center is still in use today and is the launch site for the Space Shuttle.

Vertical Assembly Building

● The Vertical Assembly Building covers an area of eight acres (32,500 m²) and is 542 feet (160 m) tall.
● It was used to assemble the 363-foot (111 m) tall Saturn V rockets on top of the tracked transporter.
● It is now known as the Vehicle Assembly Building (VAB) and is used to assemble Space Shuttle systems for launch. It remains the largest enclosed space in the world.

Kennedy Space Center launch complex

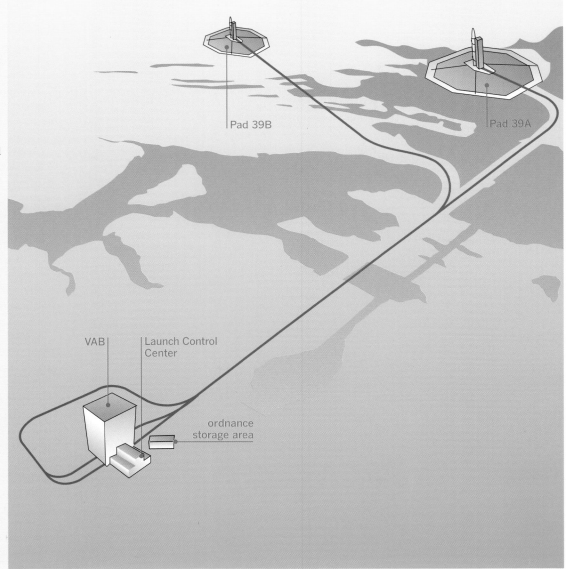

Pad 39B

Pad 39A

VAB

Launch Control Center

ordnance storage area

Apollo: landing sites

Lunar features

1. Kepler
2. Plato
3. Lagrange
4. Theophilus
5. Tycho
6. Clavius
7. Ptolemy
8. Copernicus
9. Sea of Clouds
10. Sea of Crises
11. Sea of Cold
12. Sea of Serenity
13. Sea of Tranquility
14. Sea of Storms
15. Sea of Nectar
16. Sea of Fertility
17. Central Bay

Landing sites

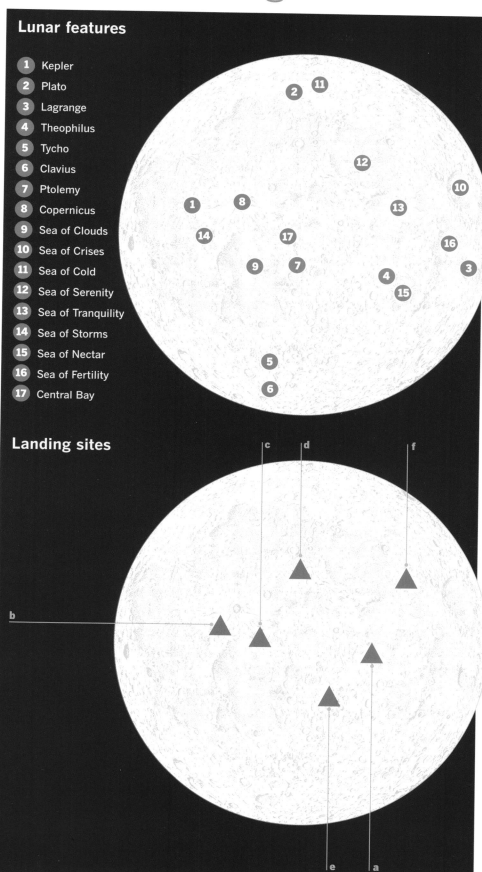

Key words

crater
mare
Moonwalk

Apollo landings

a *Apollo 11*
Launched: July 16, 1969
Lunar module: *Eagle*: stayed on surface
at Tranquility Base (0.41° N, 23.36° E) for
21 hrs 30 mins
Moonwalk time: 2 hrs 21 mins
Moonrock cargo: 48.5 pounds (21.99 kg)

b *Apollo 12*
Launched: November 14, 1969
Lunar module: *Intrepid*: stayed on
surface in Sea of Storms (3.11° S,
23.23° W) for 1 day 7 hrs 31 mins
Moonwalks: two lasting 7 hrs 45 mins
Moonrock cargo: 74.7 pounds (33.88 kg)

c *Apollo 14*
Launched: January 31, 1971
Lunar module: *Antares*: stayed on
surface at Fra Mauro (3.40° S 17.28° W)
for 1 day 9 hrs 31 mins
Moonwalks: two lasting 9 hrs 22 mins
Moonrock cargo: 98 pounds (44.45 kg)

d *Apollo 15*
Launched: July 26, 1971
Lunar module: *Falcon*: stayed on surface
at Hadley Base (26.5° N, 3.40° E) for
2 days 18 hrs 55 mins
Moonwalks: three lasting 18 hrs 25 mins
Moonrock cargo: 173 pounds (78.47 kg)

e *Apollo 16*
Launched: April 16, 1972
Lunar module: *Orion*: stayed on surface
at Descartes (8.59° S, 15.30° E) for
2 days 23 hrs 14 mins
Moonwalks: three lasting 20 hrs 14 mins
Moonrock cargo: 213 pounds (96.61 kg)

f *Apollo 17*
Launched: December 7, 1972
Lunar module: *America*: stayed on
surface at Taurus Littrow (20.10° N,
30.45° E) for 3 days 2 hrs 59 mins
Moonwalks: three lasting 22 hrs 5 mins
Moonrock cargo: 243 pounds (110.2 kg)

Apollo: science

Apollo Lunar Surface Experiment Package (ALSEP)

	Principal experiments	Other experiments

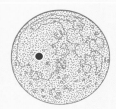

Apollo 11
Lunar passive seismology
Lunar dust detector

Lunar geology investigation
Lunar ranging retro-reflector
Solar wind composition
Helmet mounted cosmic ray detector
Lunar surface close-up camera

Apollo 12
Lunar passive seismology
Lunar tri-axis magnetometer
Solar wind spectrometer
Suprathermal ion detector
Cold cathode gauge
Lunar dust detector

Lunar geology investigation
Solar wind composition
Lunar surface close-up camera

Apollo 14
Lunar passive seismology
Lunar active seismology
Suprathermal ion detector
Lunar environment charged particle detector
Cold cathode gauge
Lunar dust detector

Lunar geology investigation
Laser ranging retro-reflector
Solar wind composition
Lunar surface close-up camera (failed)
Portable magnetometer
Soil mechanics

Apollo 15
Lunar passive seismology
Lunar tri-axis magnetometer
Solar wind spectrometer
Suprathermal ion detector
Cold cathode gauge
Lunar dust detector

Lunar geology investigation
Laser ranging retro-reflector
Solar wind composition
Soil mechanics

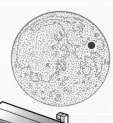

Apollo 16
Lunar passive seismology
Lunar active seismology
Lunar tri-axis magnetometer
Lunar heat flow

Lunar geology investigation
Solar wind composition
Portable magnetometer
Soil mechanics
Cosmic ray sheet detector
Far ultraviolet camera/spectrometer

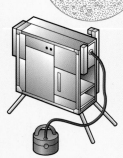

Apollo 17
Lunar heat flow
Lunar ejecta and meteorites
Lunar seismic profiling
Lunar atmospheric composition
Lunar surface gravimeter

Lunar geology investigation
Lunar gravity traverse
Soil mechanics
Surface electrical properties

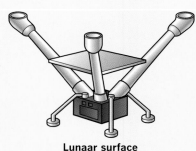

**Superthermalion
detector experiment**

**Solar wind
spectrometer**

**Lunaar surface
magnetometer**

**Passive lunar surface
seismic experiment**

Salyut 1–5

Salyut 1
- Launched: April 19, 1971
- Re-entered: October 11, 1971
- First crew (*Soyuz 10*) failed to dock
- Second crew (*Soyuz 11*) docked and made a 23-day flight: all three cosmonauts were killed when their Soyuz capsule depressurized during re-entry

Salyut 2
- Failed in orbit

Salyut 3
- Launched: June 25, 1974
- Re-entered: January 24, 1975
- A military space station
- One two-man crew (*Soyuz 14*) docked successfully
- A second crew (*Soyuz 15*) failed to dock
- *Salyut 3* successfully ejected military film pods for return to Earth

Salyut 4
- Launched: December 26, 1974
- Re-entered: February 3, 1977
- Received two two-man crews (*Soyuz 17* and *18*)
- Uncrewed test vehicle (*Soyuz 20*), later known as the Progress tanker: successfully docked

Salyut 5
- Launched: June 22, 1976
- Re-entered: August 8, 1977
- A military space station
- Received two two-man crews (*Soyuz 21* and *25*)
- A third crew (*Soyuz 23*) failed to dock
- *Salyut 5* successfully ejected military film pods for return to Earth

Key words

atmosphere	orbit
attitude	propellant
cosmonaut	re-entry
de-orbit	solar panel
extravehicular	space station
activity (EVA)	

Salyut program
- Salyut was a Soviet program to develop and launch a series of space stations into Earth orbit.
- *Salyut 1*, the world's first space station, was launched on April 19, 1971.
- *Salyut 1* was followed by a series of Salyut space stations in which cosmonauts set new space endurance records and gained a great deal of experience of long-term exposure to living in space.
- The Salyut series was the foundation of the *Mir* space station.
- Cosmonaut crews and supplies were ferried to and from the Salyut stations in Soyuz ferry craft.
- When their operational lives were over and the last crew had left, the Salyut space stations were deliberately de-orbited to burn up on re-entry into Earth's atmosphere.

Salyut 1

Labels: Soyuz ferry craft; one pair of solar panels; rendezvous antennas; EVA access hatch; atmospheric regeneration system; forward work section; movie camera; photographic camera; biological research equipment; food refrigeration unit; rear work section; attitude control engines; main propulsion system; propellant tanks; treadmill; Orion stellar telescope

Data (*Salyut 1*)
Weight: 40,785 pounds (15,500 kg)
Length: 47.3 feet (14.4 m)
Width (narrowest): 6.56 feet (2 m)
Width (widest): 13.6 feet (4.2 m)

Key words

airlock	solar panel
cosmonaut	spacecraft
extravehicular	space station
activity (EVA)	
re-entry	

Salyut 6 and 7

Salyut 6 and 7

- Following the success of *Salyut 1–5*, the program was extended with a new generation of Salyut space stations.
- *Salyut* 6 and 7 were designed to accommodate crews for longer durations in space.
- Unlike *Salyut 1–5*, *Salyut* 6 and 7 had two docking ports. This meant that while one port was occupied by the resident crew's Soyuz spacecraft, the other port could be used to receive Soyuz supply ferries and "guest" crews.
- Uncrewed Soyuz supply ferries docked automatically with the stations, proving technology that would later be vital for the construction and resupply of modular space stations such as *Mir* and the *International Space Station*.
- Visiting crews often included cosmonauts from Soviet bloc countries other than the USSR. Vladimir Remek of Czechoslovakia became the first non-U.S., non-Soviet citizen in space when he visited *Salyut 6* in 1978.
- Cosmonauts from Hungary, Poland, Romania, Cuba, Mongolia, Vietnam, and East Germany also visited *Salyut 6*.

Salyut 6
- Launched: September 29, 1977
- Re-entered: July 28, 1982
- Visited by 16 crews: occupied for 676 days
- New Soyuz T ferry introduced for crew rotations

Salyut 7
- Launched: April 19, 1982
- Re-entered: February 7, 1991
- Visited by nine crews
- Declared retired in March 1985, then reactivated by *Soyuz T13* crew in June 1985
- Evacuated in September 1985, then revisited by *Soyuz T15* crew stationed on the new *Mir* space station

Salyut 7

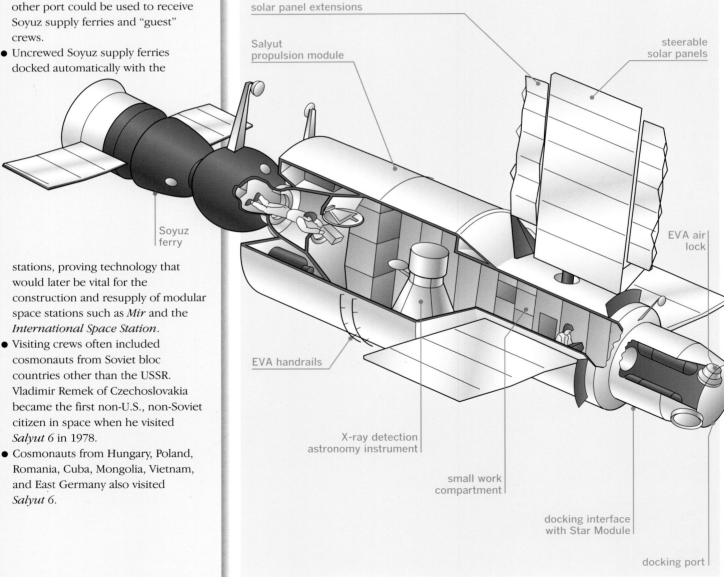

solar panel extensions

Salyut propulsion module

steerable solar panels

Soyuz ferry

EVA air lock

EVA handrails

X-ray detection astronomy instrument

small work compartment

docking interface with Star Module

docking port

Skylab

Skylab

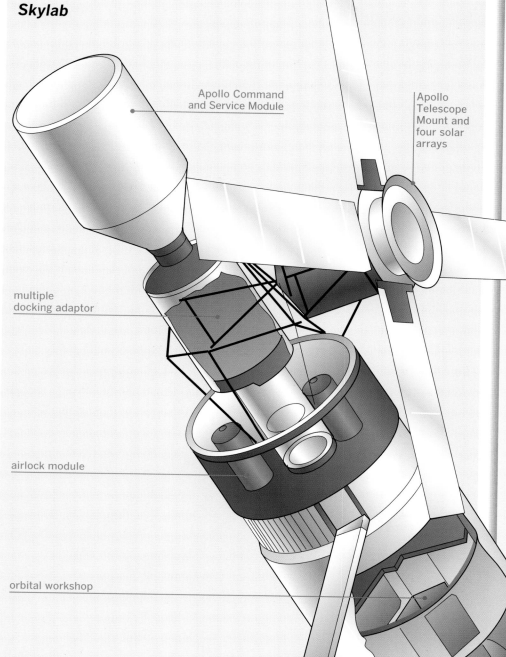

Apollo Command and Service Module

Apollo Telescope Mount and four solar arrays

multiple docking adaptor

airlock module

orbital workshop

solar array

Data

(*Skylab* and Apollo CSM combined)
Length: 118.5 feet (36.1 m)
Width (maximum): 21.6 feet (6.6 m)
Weight: 200,000 pounds (90,720 kg)

Key words

airlock	solar array
docking	space station
orbit	stage
re-entry	
rocket	

Apollo Applications Program

- The Apollo Applications Program (AAP) was a plan to put existing hardware into use for the building of a U.S. space station.
  - The AAP space station was to be launched with a Saturn V booster.
    - The space station itself would be built around a modified Saturn V third stage.
- Once in orbit the space station would be crewed and supplied by astronauts flying Apollo Command and Service Modules.
- Apollo Lunar Module hardware was to be used in the construction of a solar telescope.
- All of these objectives were achieved and the space station became known as *Skylab*.

Skylab

- *Skylab* was launched on May 14, 1973 by a Saturn V booster—the last Saturn V to fly.
- During launch, one solar panel and one micrometeorite panel were ripped away from *Skylab*'s hull.
  - The second solar array failed to deploy once the station was in orbit, leaving *Skylab* without electrical power.
    - The panel was finally deployed by the first *Skylab* crew during a dangerous spacewalk.
    - *Skylab* was crewed by three sets of three astronauts during stays lasting 28, 59, and 84 days.
    - Re-entry into Earth's atmosphere occurred on July 11, 1979.

Key words

space station

Building on Salyut

- Following the success of their Salyut series of space stations, the Soviets started a more ambitious space station program known as *Mir*.
- The *Mir* space station was assembled using several Salyut-class modules (the core module was launched in February 1986).
- Once completed (1996), it was by far the largest structure that had ever been assembled in space.
- *Mir* was crewed for most of its operational lifetime and supplied by Soyuz TM crewed ferries and uncrewed Progress supply tankers.
- *Mir* allowed the Soviet Union to become the world leader in long-duration spaceflight and hosted several international crews, providing valuable experience for the *International Space Station* project.
- With the collapse of the Soviet Union in 1991, a planned successor to *Mir* had to be canceled.

- *Mir* remained in service far beyond its intended five-year operational life.
- *Mir* means "peace" in Russian.

Mir

Mir components

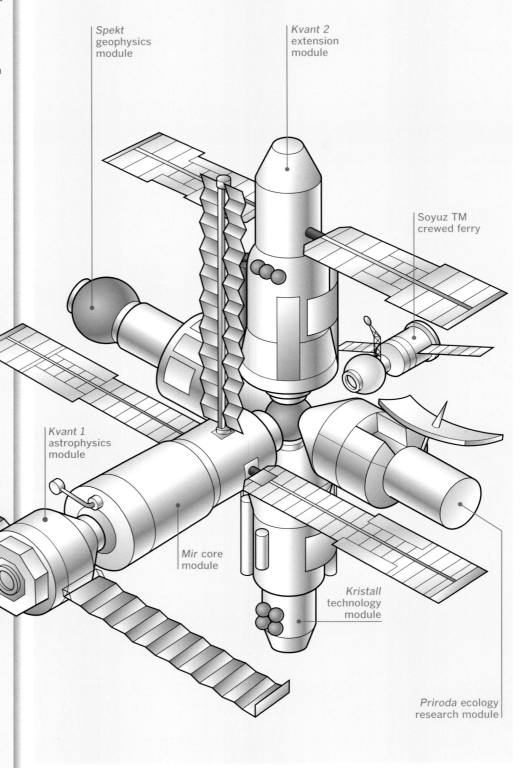

Spekt geophysics module

Kvant 2 extension module

Soyuz TM crewed ferry

Kvant 1 astrophysics module

Mir core module

Kristall technology module

Priroda ecology research module

Progress uncrewed supply tanker

Mir parts

The separate *Mir* modules

Key words

space station

Mir modules

a   *Mir* core module
     Launched: February 20, 1986
     Length: 43.04 feet (13.13 m)
     Weight: 44,973 pounds (20,400 kg)

b   *Kvant 1* astrophysics module
     Launched: March 30, 1987
     Length: 20.65 feet (6.3 m)
     Weight: 24,250 pounds (11,000 kg)

c   *Kristall* technology module
     Launched: May 31, 1990
     Length: 43.04 feet (13.13 m)
     Weight: 43,298 pounds (19,640 kg)

d   *Kvant 2* extension module
     Launched: November 26, 1989
     Length: 45 feet (13.73 m)
     Weight: 43,132 pounds (19,565 kg)

e   *Priroda* ecology research module
     Launched: April 23, 1996
     Length: 39.34 feet (12 m)
     Weight: 43,430 pounds (19,700 kg)

f   *Spekt* geophysical module
     Launched: May 23, 1995
     Length: 47.21 feet (14.4 m)
     Weight: 42,636 pounds (19,340 kg)

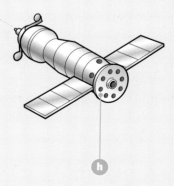

g   Soyuz ferry craft

h   Progress tanker

Key words

astronaut
cosmonaut
docking
space station

Mir 2

- Plans for a second-generation *Mir* space station to rival the U.S.-led *International Space Station* project were canceled soon after the collapse of the Soviet Union in 1991.
- In 1994 Russia and the United States agreed to a series of Space Shuttle missions to *Mir* as a prelude to further bilateral cooperation in space.
- The first Shuttle/*Mir* Mission (SMM 1) flew in June 1995. Eight more were to follow.
- By the time of SMM 1, *Mir* was reaching the end of its planned operational life and the *International Space Station (ISS)* project was facing cancellation due to spiralling costs.
- The United States needed Russia as a partner in the *ISS* project to help spread costs, while Russia needed to be involved in the *ISS* if its crewed space program was to have a future.
- Russia joined the *ISS* project and SMMs were flown to enable both nations to develop methods of working together in space.

Shuttle-*Mir*

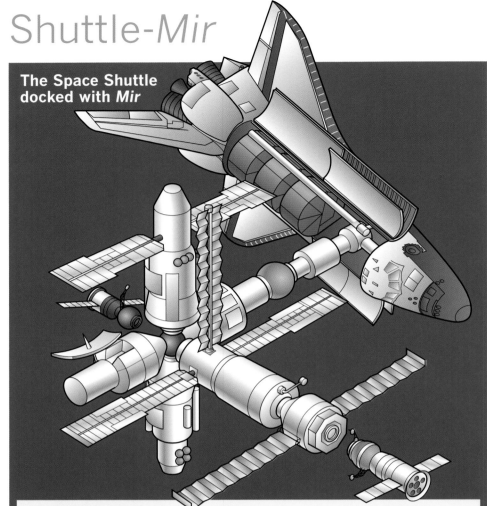

The Space Shuttle docked with *Mir*

Shuttle/*Mir* missions

June 27, 1995	*Shuttle Transportation System (STS) 71 Atlantis* on SMM 1; first joint U.S./Russian flight since 1975 Apollo/Soyuz mission; two Russian cosmonauts transfer to *Mir*; two Russian cosmonauts and U.S. astronaut, Norman Thagard, launched in *Soyuz TM21*, return to Earth aboard *Atlantis*.
November 12, 1995	*STS 74 Atlantis* on SMM 2 visits *Mir* and attaches a new docking module and transfer compartment.
March 22, 1996	*STS 76 Atlantis* on SMM 3 delivers U.S. astronaut Shannon Lucid for a 188-day stay: her stay is considered a great success with excellent crew compatibility.
September 16, 1996	*STS 79 Atlantis* on SMM 4 delivers U.S. astronaut John Blaha for 128-day stay and returns Shannon Lucid. Blaha's stay onboard is difficult as he has problems in relating to the Russian crew members.
January 12, 1997	*STS 81 Atlantis* on SMM 5 delivers Jerry Linenger for 132-day stay and returns John Blaha: Linenger plays a major part in *Mir*'s recovery from a serious fire.
May 15, 1997	*STS 84 Atlantis* on SMM 6 delivers Micheal Foale for 144-day stay and returns Jerry Linenger. Foale is considered the best of all SMM astronauts, integrating easily with the Russian crew, who face a serious crisis when an uncrewed Progress supply shuttle collides with the station.
September 26, 1997	*STS 86 Atlantis* on SMM 7 delivers U.S. astronaut David Wolf for 127-day stay and returns Micheal Foale. The first joint U.S./Russian spacewalk is made from the Shuttle.
January 23, 1998	*STS 89 Endeavor* on SMM 8 delivers Andrew Thomas for 141-day stay and returns David Wolf.
June 2, 1998	*STS 91 Discovery* on SMM 9 crewed with veteran Russian cosmonaut and head of the *Mir* program Valeri Ryumin; returns Andrew Thomas.

International Space Station

Key words

docking
orbit
rocket
solar array
space station

ISS expeditions

Expedition 1
ISS resident: November 2, 2000–
March 18, 2001
Launch vehicle: Soyuz TM 31
Return vehicle: STS 102 (Discovery)

Expedition 2
ISS resident: March 10, 2001–
August 20, 2001
Launch vehicle: STS 102 (Discovery)
Return vehicle: STS 105 (Discovery)

Expedition 3
ISS resident: August 12, 2001–
December 15, 2001
Launch vehicle: STS 105 (Discovery)
Return vehicle: STS 108 (Endeavour)

Expedition 4
ISS resident: December 7, 2001–
June 15, 2002
Launch vehicle: STS 108 (Endeavour)
Return vehicle: STS 111 (Endeavour)

Expedition 5
ISS resident: June 7, 2002–
December 2, 2002
Launch vehicle: STS 111 (Endeavour)
Return vehicle: STS 113 (Endeavour)

Expedition 6
ISS resident: November 25, 2002–
May 3, 2003
Launch vehicle: STS 113 (Endeavour)
Return vehicle: Soyuz TMA 1

Expedition 7
ISS resident: April 28, 2003–
October 27, 2003
Launch vehicle: Soyuz TMA 2
Return vehicle: Soyuz TMA 2

Expedition 8
ISS resident: October 20, 2003–
April 29, 2004
Launch vehicle: Soyuz TMA 3
Return vehicle: Soyuz TMA 3

Expedition 9
ISS resident: April 21, 2004–
October 23, 2004
Launch vehicle: Soyuz TMA 4
Return vehicle: Soyuz TMA 4

Expedition 10
ISS resident: October 15, 2004–
April 24, 2005
Launch vehicle: Soyuz TMA 5
Return vehicle: Soyuz TMA 5

Expedition 11
ISS resident: April 16, 2005–
October 10, 2005
Launch vehicle: Soyuz TMA 6
Return vehicle: Soyuz TMA 6

Expedition 12
ISS resident: October 3, 2005–
April, 2006 (scheduled)
Launch vehicle: Soyuz TMA 7
Return vehicle: Soyuz TMA 7 (scheduled)

International Space Station

- The *International Space Station* (ISS) is a U.S.-led international program to build a large space station that can sustain a three-person crew in permanent Earth orbit.

- The *ISS* is being built by the United States, Russia, Canada, Japan, Brazil, and the nations of the European Space Agency (ESA).

- The station is being assembled from components launched into orbit by Russian Proton and Soyuz rockets and by the Space Shuttle.

- The command and control module *Zarya* was the first element of the *ISS* to be placed in Earth orbit. It was Russian-built and U.S.-funded.

- The habitation and docking module *Unity* was the second *ISS* module to be placed in orbit. It is a U.S.-built component and is also known as *Node 1* because it acts as a central connector for later units.

- *Zarya* and *Unity* were docked and connected on December 7, 1998.

Completed International Space Station

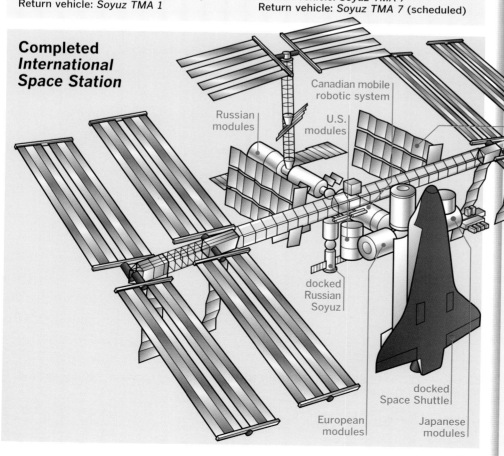

Canadian mobile robotic system

Russian modules

U.S. modules

radiators

solar arrays

docked Russian Soyuz

docked Space Shuttle

European modules

Japanese modules

- The first permanent crew (Expedition 1) to inhabit the *ISS* arrived by Soyuz spacecraft in November 2000. The *ISS* has been continually crewed by at least two astronauts or cosmonauts since that time.

- Crews usually return to Earth in the vehicle that delivers their successors. A Soyuz spacecraft is permanently docked with the station to provide a backup.

International Space Station: U.S./Russia

© Diagram Visual Information Ltd.

Key words

solar array
space station

ISS main components

- The main structural components of the *International Space Station* are being built by the United States and Russia.
- U.S. components include the eight main solar arrays and the thermal control panels. The USA is also supplying the "truss" elements that support the solar arrays and form the structural backbone of the station.
- *Node 1* (*Unity*) and *Node 2*, both connecting modules, the *Destiny* laboratory, the *Quest* airlock, and the *SPACEHAB* pressurized logistics module are also U.S.-built.
- *Zvezda*, a crew compartment, and *Zarya*, a propulsion and control module, are the two critical Russian components.

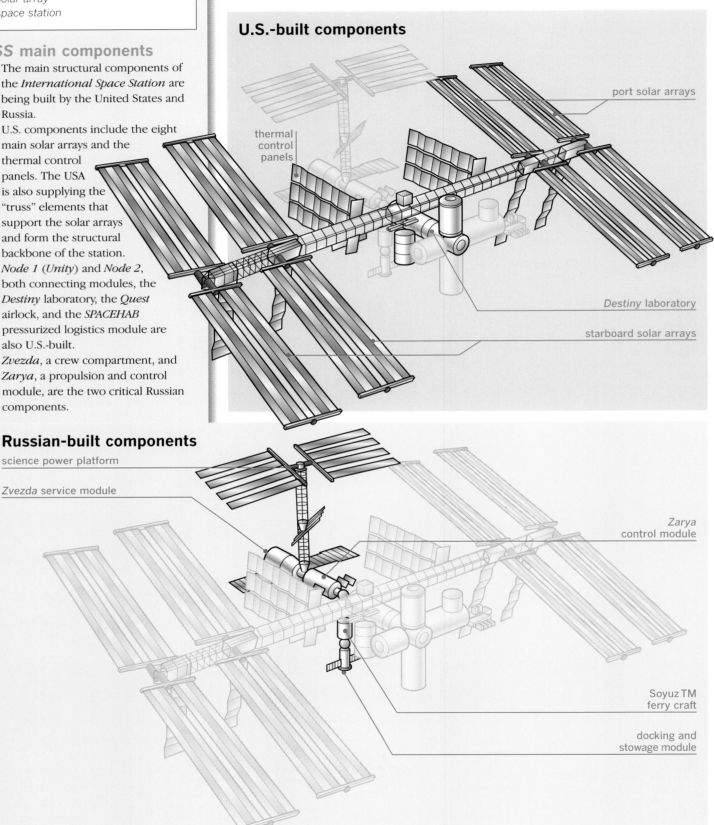

U.S.-built components

port solar arrays

thermal control panels

Destiny laboratory

starboard solar arrays

Russian-built components

science power platform

Zvezda service module

Zarya control module

Soyuz TM ferry craft

docking and stowage module

International Space Station: other countries

Key words

space station

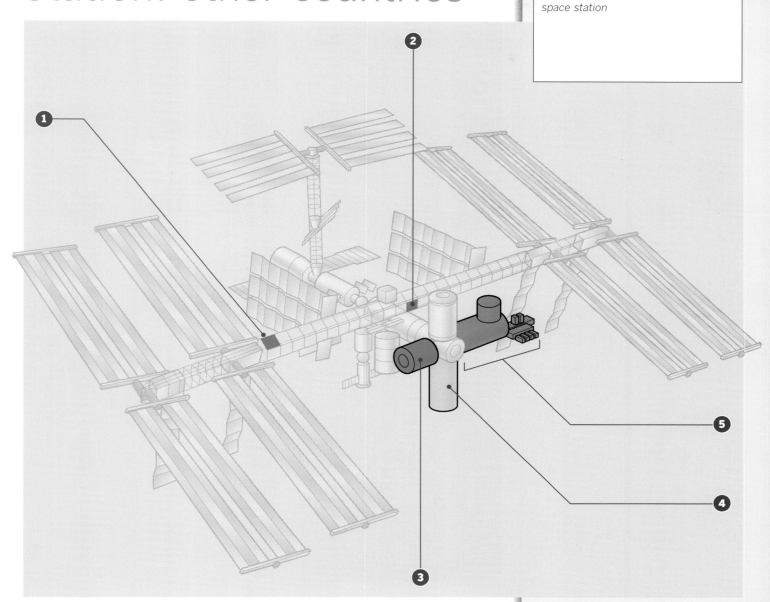

1 Brazil
Express pallet
A cradle for pressurized experiments that can be attached to any truss section or the outside of the Japanese Experiment Module.

2 Canada
Remote Manipulator System
A remotely controlled robotic arm that can move around the station on a system of rails.

3 Europe
Columbus Orbital Facility
A pressurized laboratory containing ten experiment pallets.

4 Italy
Multipurpose Logistics Module
One of three pressurized modules containing experiments and carried to and from the *ISS* by the Space Shuttle.

5 Japan
Japanese Experiment Module (JEM)
A six-element science station that includes a pressurized laboratory, pressurized logistics support, an exposed cradle for experiments, an airlock, a remote manipulator system, and communications equipment.

Shenzhou

Key words

astronaut
orbit
re-entry
retro rocket
spacecraft

Shenzhou program

- Shenzhou is the name of a series of spacecraft built and operated by China.
- Four uncrewed Shenzhou spacecraft (*Shenzhou 1, 2, 3,* and *4*) were launched between November 1999 and December 2002.
- *Shenzhou 5,* launched in October 2003, carried astronaut Yang Liwei on a 21-hour mission during which 14 orbits of Earth were completed. This was the first launch of a crewed spacecraft by any nation other than the USA or USSR/Russia.
- *Shenzhou 6,* launched in October 2005, carried two Chinese astronauts on a mission lasting four days 19 hours.
- Chinese astronauts are sometimes refered to as *taikonauts* from the Chinese word for "space."

Shenzhou spacecraft

- The Shenzhou spacecraft resemble Soyuz spacecraft, but are larger.
- A Shenzhou spacecraft consists of three major elements: an orbital module, a re-entry module, and a service module.
- The orbital module contains living space and facilities for experiments. It has its own propulsion system and can be left in orbit.
- The re-entry module is the main crew compartment and can accommodate up to three astronauts. It detaches from the rest of the spacecraft at the end of the flight and re-enters Earth's atmosphere before parachuting to a landing.
- The service module houses the power systems, life support systems, and the retro rockets used to slow the spacecraft before re-entry.
- Both the orbital module and the service module have two solar panels.

Shenzhou 5

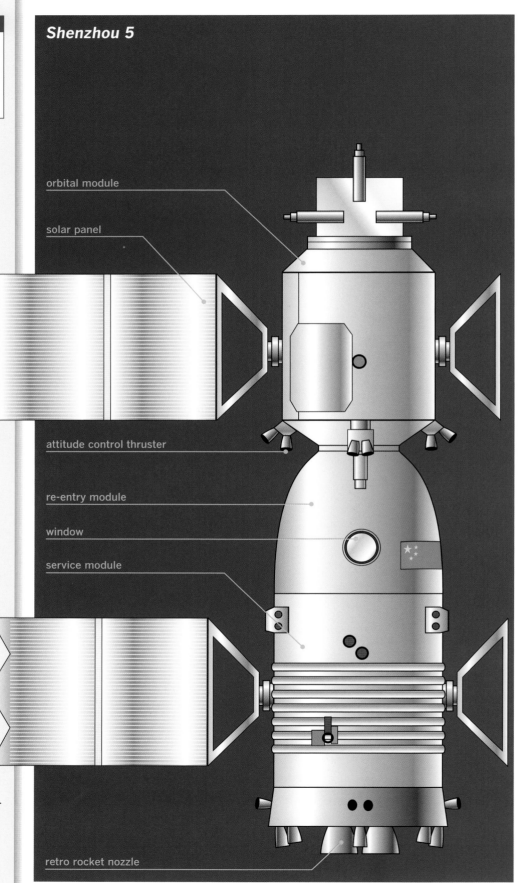

orbital module

solar panel

attitude control thruster

re-entry module

window

service module

retro rocket nozzle

Space travelers

Space experience			
Days	Astronaut	Country	Total experience (days)
800+	Sergei Krikalev	Russia	804
700+	Sergei Avdeyev	Russia	747
600+	Valeri Poliakov	Russia	678
	Anatoli Solovyov	Russia	651
	Alexander Kaleri	Russia	610
500+	Viktor Afanasyev	USSR/Russia	555
	Yuri Usachev	Russia	553
	Musa Manarov	USSR	541
400+	Alexander Viktorenko	USSR	489
	Nikolai Budarin	Russia	444
	Yuri Romanenko	USSR	430
300+	Alexander Volkov	USSR	391
	Yuri Onufrienko	Russia	389
	Vladimir Titov	Russia	387
	Gennady Padalka	Russia	386
	Vasily Tsiblyev	Russia	381
	Valeri Korzun	Russia	381
	Leonid Kizim	USSR	374
	Michael Foale	USA/UK	373
	Alexander Serebrov	USSR	372
	Vladimir Solovyov	USSR	361
	Talgat Musabayev	USSR/Kazakhstan	339
	Vladimir Lyakhov	USSR	333
	Yuri Gidzenko	Russia	329
	Yuri Malenchenko	Russia	322
	Gennadi Manakov	USSR	309
	Alexander Alexandrov	USSR	309
200+	Valeri Ryumin	USSR	297
	Gennadi Strekalov	USSR/Russia	268
	Vladimir Lyakhov	USSR	259
	Viktor Savinykh	USSR	252
	Vladimir Dezhurov	USSR/Russia	244
	Oleg Atkov	USSR	252
	Carl Walz	USA	230
	Daniel Bursch	USA	226
	Shannon Lucid	USA	223
	Valentin Lebedev	USSR	219
	Vladimir Kovalyonok	USSR	216
	Keneth Bowersox	USA	211
	Anatoli Berezovoi	USSR	211
	Susan Helms	USA	211
	Jean-Pierre Haigneré	France	209
	Edward Lu	USA	205
	Jim Voss	USA	202
	Leonid Popov	USSR	200

Most individual spaceflights

Franklin Chang-Diaz	USA	7		Story Musgrave	USA	6
Jerry Ross	USA	7		Gennady Strekalov	Russia	6
Curtis Brown	USA	6		James Wetherbee	USA	6
Michael Foale	USA/UK	6		John Young	USA	6
Sergei Krikalev	Russia	6				

Key words

astronaut
cosmonaut

Human spaceflight

- Since the first human spaceflight—by Soviet cosmonaut Yuri Gagarin aboard *Vostok 1* in 1961—more than 450 people have traveled into space.

- Some of those astronauts and cosmonauts have made multiple journeys on the same or different spacecraft. For example, Franklin Chang-Diaz is a U.S. astronaut who has flown into space on seven separate Space Shuttle missions. Michael Foale is an astronaut with dual U.S.–British citizenship who has flown on both Space Shuttle and Soyuz missions, and spent time on both *Mir* and the *International Space Station* (*ISS*).

- Unlike the U.S. space program, the USSR/Russian program has concentrated on maintaining space stations in Earth orbit since the early 1970s. The Salyut series of space stations and their sucessor *Mir* enabled many cosmonauts to spend long periods in space. Of the 46 astronauts and cosmonauts who have spent more than 200 days in space, only nine have been non-Soviet/Russian.

- One of the aims of the *ISS* program is to maintain a permanent human presence in space. It has been continuously inhabited by a crew of at least two since November 2000. *ISS* crews usually spend about six months onboard the station before being replaced by another crew.

- Studying the effects on humans of long periods spent in space will be essential to the success of future human spaceflight programs. A crewed mission to Mars, or the establishment of a permanent habitation on the Moon, will require astronauts to spend many months or even years in space.

Space Shuttle

Key words

atmosphere	space station
booster	spacecraft
orbiter	
solid propellant	

Space Transportation System

- The Space Transportation System (STS), or "Space Shuttle" as it is better known, is the world's first partly reusable spacecraft.
- It is currently the only U.S. crewed spacecraft still in operation.
- The first Space Shuttle mission (*STS 1*) was launched on April 12, 1981.
- The orbiter is launched using the thrust of its own engines supplemented by the thrust from two solid propellant boosters. Fuel for the orbiter's launch engines is contained in a large external fuel tank.
- The orbiter and the solid fuel boosters are reusable: the external tank is not.
- The orbiter is the only part of the stack that reaches orbit. After a mission, it re-enters Earth's atmosphere and glides to a controlled landing on a runway.

Shuttle Transportation System (STS)

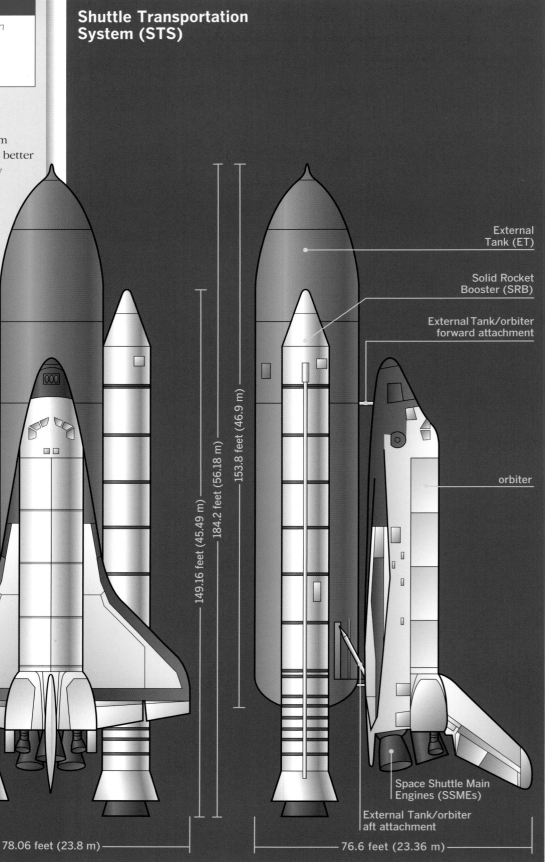

External Tank (ET)

Solid Rocket Booster (SRB)

External Tank/orbiter forward attachment

orbiter

Space Shuttle Main Engines (SSMEs)

External Tank/orbiter aft attachment

149.16 feet (45.49 m)

184.2 feet (56.18 m)

153.8 feet (46.9 m)

78.06 feet (23.8 m)

76.6 feet (23.36 m)

Orbiter

Orbiter

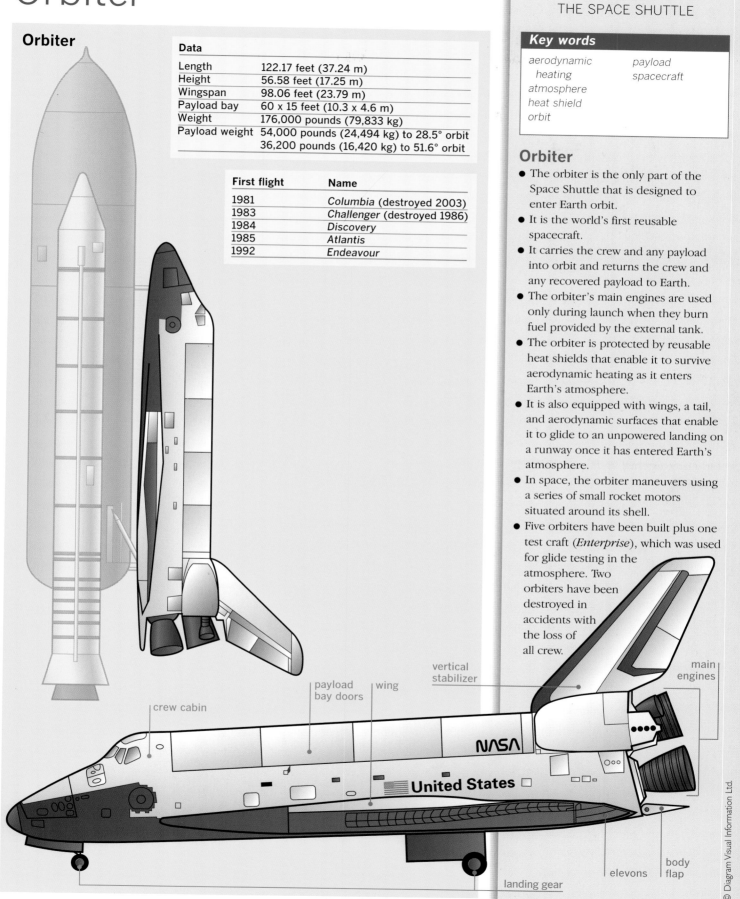

Data	
Length	122.17 feet (37.24 m)
Height	56.58 feet (17.25 m)
Wingspan	98.06 feet (23.79 m)
Payload bay	60 x 15 feet (10.3 x 4.6 m)
Weight	176,000 pounds (79,833 kg)
Payload weight	54,000 pounds (24,494 kg) to 28.5° orbit
	36,200 pounds (16,420 kg) to 51.6° orbit

First flight	Name
1981	*Columbia* (destroyed 2003)
1983	*Challenger* (destroyed 1986)
1984	*Discovery*
1985	*Atlantis*
1992	*Endeavour*

Orbiter

- The orbiter is the only part of the Space Shuttle that is designed to enter Earth orbit.
- It is the world's first reusable spacecraft.
- It carries the crew and any payload into orbit and returns the crew and any recovered payload to Earth.
- The orbiter's main engines are used only during launch when they burn fuel provided by the external tank.
- The orbiter is protected by reusable heat shields that enable it to survive aerodynamic heating as it enters Earth's atmosphere.
- It is also equipped with wings, a tail, and aerodynamic surfaces that enable it to glide to an unpowered landing on a runway once it has entered Earth's atmosphere.
- In space, the orbiter maneuvers using a series of small rocket motors situated around its shell.
- Five orbiters have been built plus one test craft (*Enterprise*), which was used for glide testing in the atmosphere. Two orbiters have been destroyed in accidents with the loss of all crew.

crew cabin

payload bay doors

wing

vertical stabilizer

main engines

NASA

United States

landing gear

elevons

body flap

Key words

booster
orbit
orbiter
oxidizer
propellant

rocket
solid propellant

Main engines

- Each orbiter is equipped with three Space Shuttle Main Engines (SSMEs).
- The SSME is the world's first re-usable rocket engine designed to reach Earth orbit.
- During launch, the SSMEs augment the thrust of the Solid Rocket Boosters (SRBs).
- The SSMEs burn liquid oxygen and liquid hydrogen stored in the External Tank.
- The SSMEs continue to burn after the SRBs have stopped and have been ejected.

Solid Rocket Boosters

- The two Solid Rocket Boosters (SRBs) provide most of the thrust required to put the Space Shuttle into orbit.
- The SRBs are packed with an aluminum powder fuel and ammonium percholate oxidizer bound into a solid mass with curing agents.
- They are ignited at launch and burn for about two minutes before being jettisoned at an altitude of about 27 miles (45 km).
- Once jettisoned, parachutes deploy from the SRBs and they land in the sea, to be retrieved and reused.
- The use of solid propellant boosters adds to the risks of crewed spaceflights since once ignited they cannot be turned off.

Launch engines

Space Shuttle Main Engines (SSMEs)

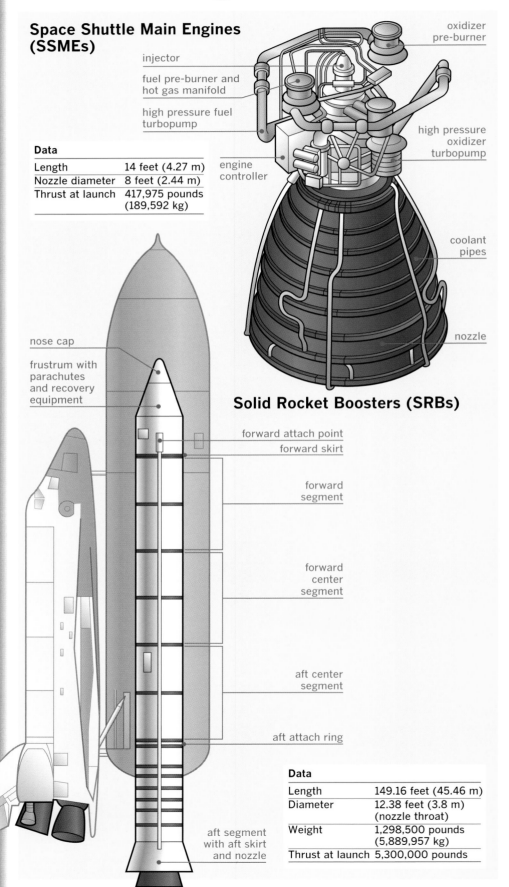

oxidizer pre-burner

injector

fuel pre-burner and hot gas manifold

high pressure fuel turbopump

high pressure oxidizer turbopump

engine controller

coolant pipes

nozzle

Data

Length	14 feet (4.27 m)
Nozzle diameter	8 feet (2.44 m)
Thrust at launch	417,975 pounds (189,592 kg)

nose cap

frustrum with parachutes and recovery equipment

Solid Rocket Boosters (SRBs)

forward attach point

forward skirt

forward segment

forward center segment

aft center segment

aft attach ring

aft segment with aft skirt and nozzle

Data

Length	149.16 feet (45.46 m)
Diameter	12.38 feet (3.8 m) (nozzle throat)
Weight	1,298,500 pounds (5,889,957 kg)
Thrust at launch	5,300,000 pounds

Fuel tank

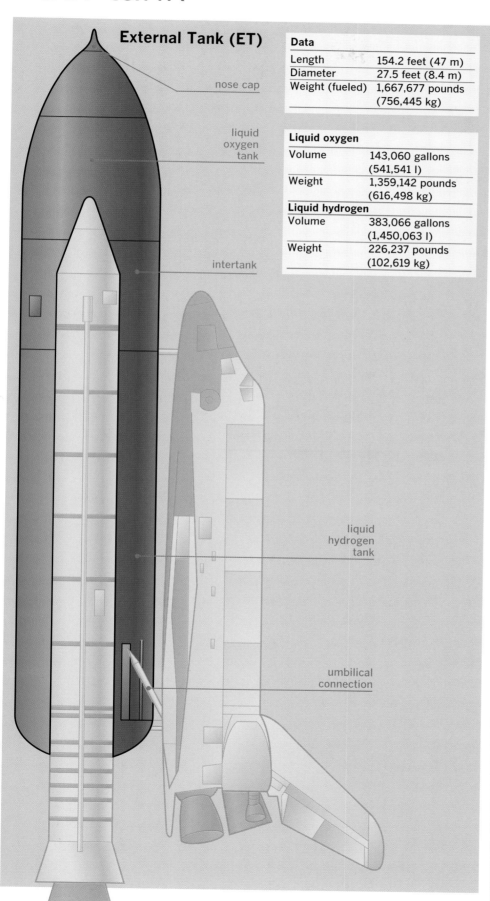

External Tank (ET)

nose cap

liquid oxygen tank

intertank

liquid hydrogen tank

umbilical connection

Data	
Length	154.2 feet (47 m)
Diameter	27.5 feet (8.4 m)
Weight (fueled)	1,667,677 pounds (756,445 kg)

Liquid oxygen	
Volume	143,060 gallons (541,541 l)
Weight	1,359,142 pounds (616,498 kg)
Liquid hydrogen	
Volume	383,066 gallons (1,450,063 l)
Weight	226,237 pounds (102,619 kg)

Key words

atmosphere	oxidizer
launch pad	propellant
liquid propellant	re-entry
orbit	
orbiter	

External Tank

- The External Tank (ET) holds the liquid propellants that are burned by the Space Shuttle Main Engines.
- It is the only part of the Space Shuttle system that is not re-used.
- Once the orbiter has achieved its initial 70-mile (112 km) altitude orbit, the ET is jettisoned and re-enters the atmosphere where most of it is burned up. Debris then splashes down in the Indian Ocean.
- The ET acts as the "backbone" of the assembled Space Shuttle system on the launch pad and during launch.
- Propellants are fed to the orbiter through a 17-inch (43 cm) diameter umbilical connection.
- There are two separate tanks inside the ET: one for liquid hydrogen, the fuel; and a smaller one for liquid oxygen, the oxidizer. These two tanks are separated by an intertank structure.
- For the first few Space Shuttle missions the ET was painted white. Later, it was left unpainted to save weight. Its orange color is the color of the insulation material on its surface.

Key words	
atmosphere	orbiter
booster	payload
de-orbit	propellant
heat shield	re-entry
Mach	
orbit	

Typical flight profile

1 Orbiter, External Tank (ET), and Solid Rocket Boosters (SRBs) are assembled and mated in the Vehicle Assembly Building (VAB) at Kennedy Space Center (KSC) and rolled out to the pad for launch.

2 Space Shuttle system is launched.

3 SRBs are jettisoned and parachute into the Atlantic. They are recovered and sent to a contractor, by which they are refilled with propellant.

4 Once the orbiter has reached orbit, the ET is jettisoned and partially destroyed during re-entry.

5 The orbiter fires its Orbital Maneuvering System (OMS) engines to raise its orbit.

6 The orbiter's payload bay doors are opened and the mission begins.

7 Orbital operations can include assembly of the *International Space Station*, satellite deployment and retrieval, and satellite servicing.

8 Payload bay doors are closed and OMS engines are fired to de-orbit the orbiter.

9 Flying at Mach 25 the orbiter re-enters Earth's atmosphere.

10 The orbiter glides through the atmosphere making large S-shaped turns to reduce its velocity.

11 The orbiter approaches the runway descending at an angle seven times steeper than an airliner and flying at over 200 miles per hour (322 kmph).

Flight path

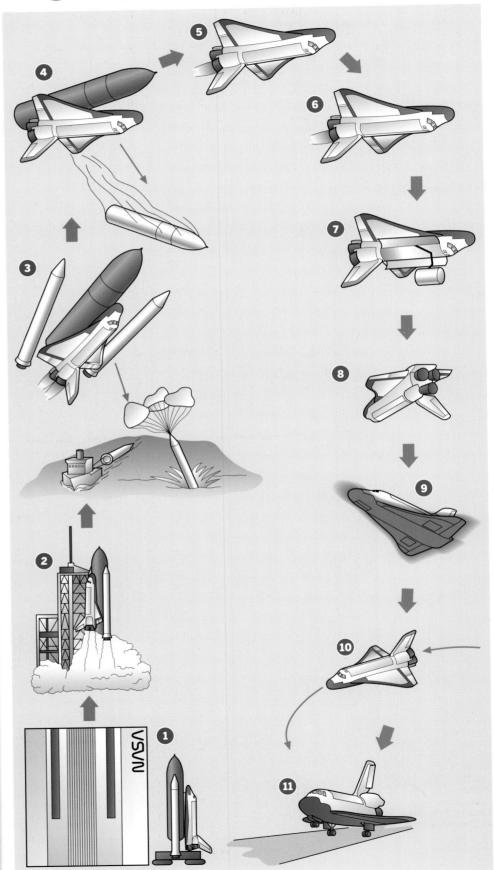

Emergencies

Launchpad abort
In the event of a fire onboard the orbiter while it is still on the launchpad, the crew can escape through the hatch, ride in baskets down slide wires to the ground, and take refuge in escape vehicles or an underground bunker.

Contingency abort
In the event of a multiple engine failure soon after SRB separation, the crew would shut down all engines and attempt to glide to landing at the nearest possible site—possibly putting down in the sea, though it is unlikely that this would be survivable. This is not an official abort procedure due to its very high risk.

Return To Launch Site (RTLS)
In the event of an engine failure soon after SRB separation, the orbiter and External Tank would continue their ascent **1**, then turn around and use the remaining engines to stop the ascent and send the vehicle back toward the launch site **2**. After shutting down the engines, the External Tank would be jettisoned **3** and the orbiter would glide in for a landing **4**.

Key words

abort	launch pad
atmosphere	orbiter
booster	re-entry
countdown	
fuel cell	

Problems and emergencies

- At any time during the countdown to launch or the launch itself a problem may occur that threatens the safety of the crew of the Space Shuttle system. If such a problem occurs, there are a number of practiced emergency procedures that will allow the crew to return safely to Earth.
- The most likely problems are shutdown of one or more of the Space Shuttle main engines. Other emergencies such as fires, structural failure, or collision are unlikely to be survivable.
- Because the Solid Rocket Boosters (SRBs) cannot be turned off once they have been ignited there is no chance of making an abort maneuver during the first two minutes of flight.
- The SRB failure that caused the destruction of the orbiter *Challenger* and the death of its crew occurred in a fraction of a second and no abort procedure was possible.
- The failure that caused the destruction of the orbiter *Columbia* and the death of its crew occurred during atmospheric re-entry, when the orbiter has very limited maneuverability.

Flight path of a Return To Launch Site abort

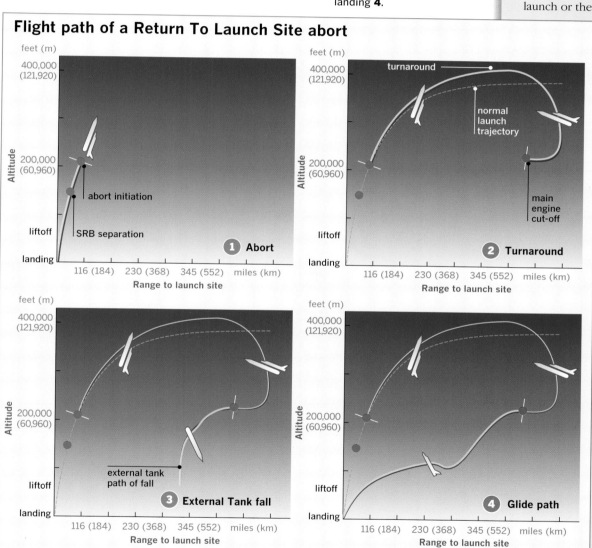

1 Abort — abort initiation, SRB separation (feet (m): 400,000 (121,920), 200,000 (60,960), liftoff, landing; Range to launch site miles (km): 116 (184), 230 (368), 345 (552))

2 Turnaround — turnaround, normal launch trajectory, main engine cut-off

3 External Tank fall — external tank path of fall

4 Glide path

Trans-Atlantic Landing (TAL)
In the event of a problem after the opportunity to perform an RTLS abort has passed, the orbiter would shut down engines, jettison the External Tank and attempt to glide to a landing at pre-selected airfields in Europe or North Africa.

Abort to Orbit (ATO)
In the event of a problem after the opportunity to perform a TAL has passed, the orbiter would continue into orbit using its remaining engines and possibly its Orbital Maneuvering System engines as well. Once in orbit, the decision can be made to make an emergency re-entry and landing or the mission may be able to continue as planned.

Abort Once Around (AOA)
If, following an ATO, the decision is made to return the orbiter to Earth, or if an emergency such as a fuel cell failure occurs in orbit, the orbiter can make a re-entry burn after just one orbit, and return for a normal approach and landing at a designated landing site.

Key words

airlock
flight deck
galley
life support
orbit

Crew accommodation

- Two crew members are needed to fly a Shuttle mission: a pilot and a commander.
- Except during test flights, these two will also be joined by at least one mission specialist.
- Up to seven crew members can fly on a single mission.
- All crew members are accommodated during launch and in orbit in the crew compartment.
- The crew compartment consists of three levels or decks: the flight deck, the mid deck, and the lower deck.

Flight deck

- The pilot, commander, and one or two other crew members are seated on the flight deck during launch, orbital maneuvers, and landing.
- The flight deck contains all flight controls and workstations for using the Remote Manipulator System.

Mid deck

- The mid deck houses the galley, sleeping bunks, crew storage lockers, the personal hygiene station, and the waste management station.
- The main crew hatch for entering and leaving the orbiter on the ground is on the mid deck.
- Access to the airlock is also from the mid deck.
- Other crew members may be seated on the mid deck during launch, orbital maneuvers, and landing. Their seats are stowable.

Lower deck

- Accessible from the mid deck, the lower deck is essentially a storage area for equipment required during the mission and contains parts of the waste disposal and life support systems.

Crew quarters

Flight deck

pilot's seat

workstations

other crew seats

interdeck access

commander's seat

Crew accommodation

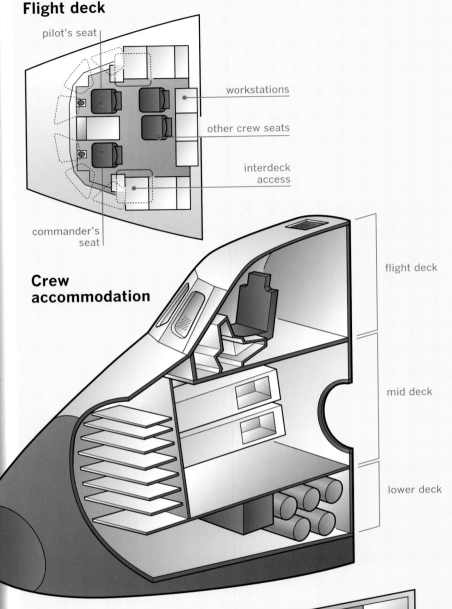

flight deck

mid deck

lower deck

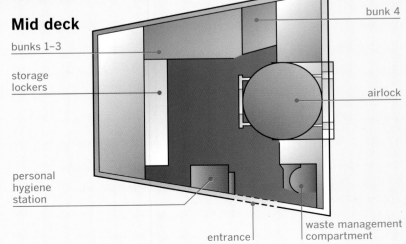

Mid deck

bunks 1–3

storage lockers

bunk 4

airlock

personal hygiene station

entrance

waste management compartment

Space walking

Donning the Extravehicular Mobility Unit (EMU)

1 one piece water-cooled undergarment

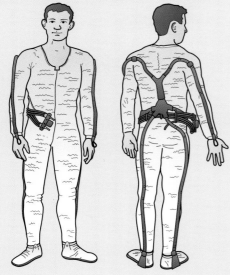

2 lower and upper torso assemblies join at waist

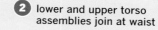

3 helmet and gloves join to upper torso

Manned Maneuvering Unit (MMU)

- Some early Shuttle EVAs made use of a chairlike device that enabled astronauts to fly independently of the Shuttle.
- The MMU is equipped with 24 nozzles that eject nitrogen gas to provide thrust in any direction.
- It was used to allow astronauts to capture stranded satellites so that they could be repaired or returned to Earth in the Shuttle's cargo bay.
- MMUs are no longer used. Astronauts now have chest-mounted devices known as Safers which also use nitrogen gas thrusters in case an astronaut becomes separated from the Shuttle.

Key words

astronaut	MMU
EMU	orbiter
extravehicular	satellite
activity (EVA)	spacesuit
life support	

Spacewalking

- Leaving a spacecraft in space to carry out operations outside the vehicle is known as spacewalking or extravehicular activity (EVA).
- Every Shuttle mission includes training for EVA. Sometimes EVAs are part of the planned mission but they may also be needed to carry out emergency repairs or even to evacuate the orbiter.
- During an EVA an astronaut remains attached to the orbiter by means of a harness and tether system.

EVA suit

- If an astronaut is required to do an EVA, either as part of the mission plan or in an emergency, an Extravehicular Mobility Unit (EMU), or spacesuit, is worn.
- The EMU provides an astronaut with all he or she needs to survive and work in space outside the orbiter.
- Suit segments are made in different sizes and can be assembled in any combination to fit a particular astronaut but, unlike spacesuits for the Apollo missions, they are not individually tailored.
- The EMU—with helmet, boots, and gloves—is worn over a one-piece garment that includes water-cooling tubes and a urine collection system.
- Permanently attached to the upper half of the EMU is the Primary Life Support System (PLSS): a backpack that includes systems to provide breathable air, maintain suit pressure, cool the astronaut, and absorb carbon dioxide and other gases.
- A communications unit is attached to the top of the PLSS.
- A backup oxygen supply is attached to the bottom of the PLSS.
- The PLSS is monitored and controlled from a chest-mounted control panel.

© Diagram Visual Information Ltd.

Maneuvering

Orbital Maneuvering System (OMS)

- Each orbiter has two OMS engines mounted in pods—one on each side of the vertical stabilizer.
- OMS engines are used during orbital insertion, de-orbiting, and for large changes of orbit.
- They may also be used in the event of a main engine failure to achieve an Abort to Orbit.
- OMS engines burn monomethyl hydrazine (fuel) and nitrogen tetroxide (oxidizer).

Reaction Control System (RCS)

- Each orbiter has 44 small rocket engines in three modules—one in the nose and one of each in the OMS engine pods.
- RCS engines are used to make small orbital changes and to change the attitude of the orbiter.
- In the event of an OMS engine failure, they may also be used to achieve a de-orbit burn.
- RCS engines use the same fuel as OMS engines and propellants can be transferred from one to the other if necessary.
- There are 38 primary RCS engines with 870 pounds (3,870 newtons) of thrust each and six secondary (vernier) engines with 25 pounds (110 newtons) of thrust each.

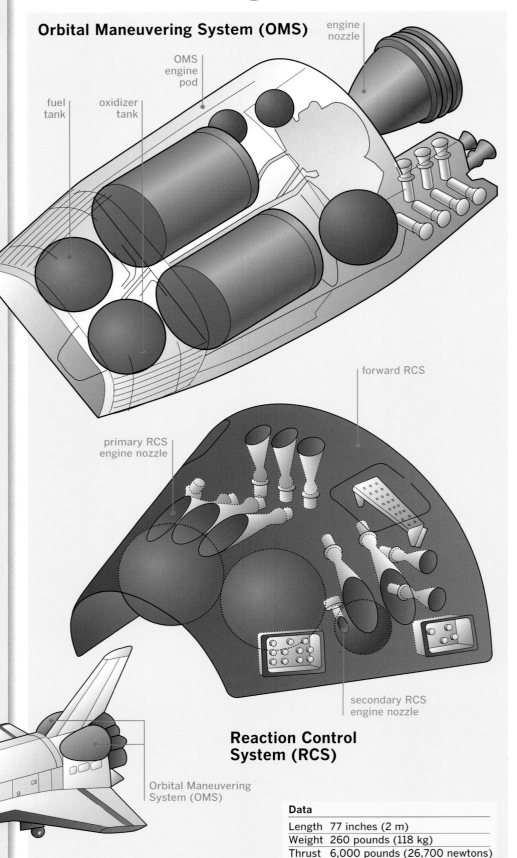

Orbital Maneuvering System (OMS)

engine nozzle

OMS engine pod

fuel tank

oxidizer tank

forward RCS

primary RCS engine nozzle

secondary RCS engine nozzle

Reaction Control System (RCS)

Reaction Control System (RCS)

Orbital Maneuvering System (OMS)

Data	
Length	77 inches (2 m)
Weight	260 pounds (118 kg)
Thrust	6,000 pounds (26,700 newtons)

Heat protection

Thermal Protection System (TPS) materials

- ■ reinforced carbon-carbon tiles up to 3,000°F (1,650°C)
- ▨ high-temperature reusable surface insulation up to 2,300°F (1,275°C)
- ▨ advanced flexible reusable surface insulation up to 1,200°F (650°C)
- □ coated Nomex felt reusable surface insulation up to 700°F (370°C)

Note: The orbiters have individual configurations of thermal protection materials.

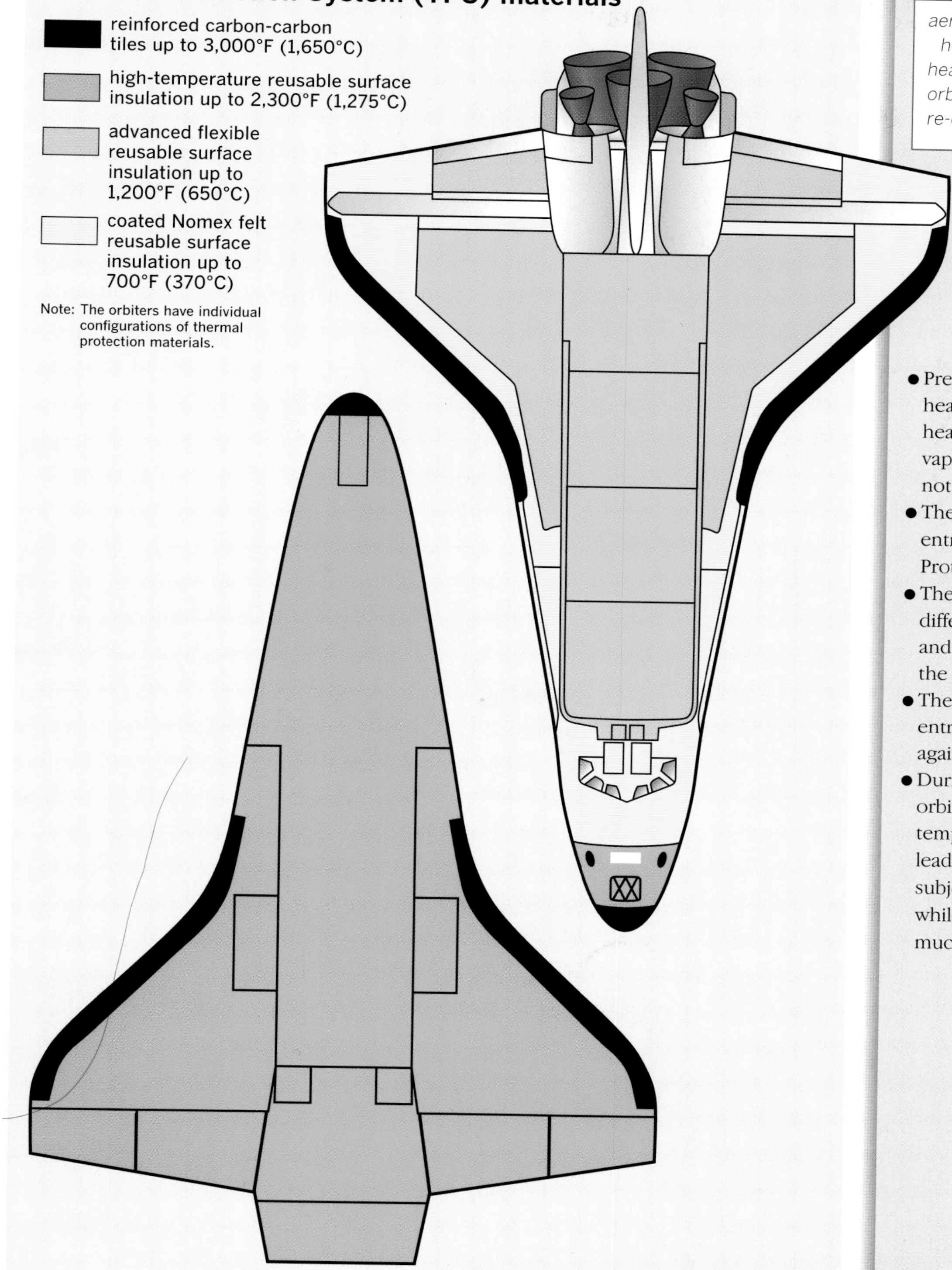

Key words

aerodynamic heating
heat shield
orbiter
re-entry

Thermal stresses

- During re-entry any spacecraft is subjected to very high temperatures as it passes through Earth's atmosphere and undergoes aerodynamic heating.
- Previous spacecraft have used ablative heat shields for re-entry. These carry heat away from the spacecraft by vaporizing but they are heavy and not reusable.
- The orbiter is protected during re-entry by a unique re-usable Thermal Protection System (TPS).
- The TPS is made up of several different kinds of heat-resistant tiles and fabrics that cover the outer skin of the orbiter.
- These materials absorb the heat of re-entry and are able to radiate it away again very quickly.
- During re-entry different parts of the orbiter experience different temperature levels. The nose cone and leading edges of the wings are subjected to the highest temperatures, while the upper fuselage experiences much lower temperatures.

© Diagram Visual Information Ltd.

Key words

orbiter

Space toilet

- The Waste Collection System (WCS), or toilet, is a vital piece of equipment. Disposal of bodily wastes is critical in a totally closed environment such as the orbiter's crew compartment.
- The WCS is designed for use by both male and female astronauts.
- Separate systems dispose of solid and liquid wastes.
- Liquid waste is conveyed from the urinal to a waste water tank by an airflow. This tank is periodically emptied into space.
- Solid waste is drawn into a chamber by an airflow where it is shredded and deposited on the walls of the chamber by a rapidly rotating assembly known as a slinger.
- When the WCS is closed and switched off, the chamber is exposed to space, causing solid wastes to dry solid on the chamber walls.
- The WCS has thigh and foot restraints to hold an astronaut in place while using the equipment.

Personal hygiene station

- All astronauts are issued with a personal hygiene kit containing essential items.
- The personal hygiene station is equipped with a mirror, a light, and a hand-washing enclosure.
- Astronauts wash using washcloths and are issued with towels.
- Waste water is drawn by an airflow into a waste water tank.
- The WCS and hygiene station are equipped with a fold-out door and curtain for privacy.

Hygiene

Waste Collection System (WCS)

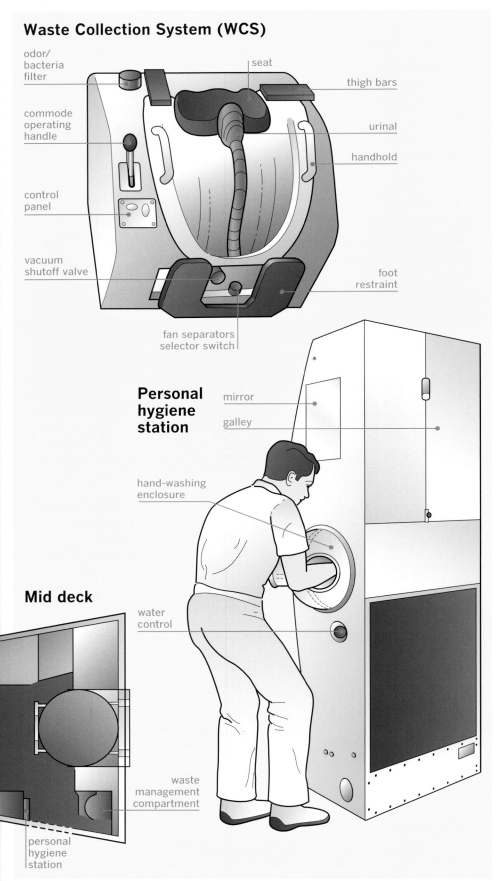

odor/bacteria filter

commode operating handle

control panel

vacuum shutoff valve

seat

thigh bars

urinal

handhold

foot restraint

fan separators selector switch

Personal hygiene station

mirror

galley

hand-washing enclosure

Mid deck

water control

waste management compartment

personal hygiene station

Robotic arm

Remote Manipulator System (RMS)

Key words

astronaut
extravehicular
 activity (EVA)
payload
satellite

end
effector

television
camera

wrist
joint

lower boom

television
camera

elbow joint

upper
boom

shoulder
joint

control panels
(inside orbiter)

Robotic arm

● The Remote Manipulator System
(RMS) uses a robotic arm that allows
shuttle astronauts to deploy and
retrieve payloads without undertaking
hazardous extravehicular activity
(EVA).

 ● The RMS arm has six joints and an
 end effector that can latch
 securely onto the attachments
 included on satellites.

 ● The RMS arm is controlled by
 mission specialists from a
 control panel at the rear
 of the flight deck. Two
 windows allow the
 operator to see the
payload bay and television cameras
can be mounted on the wrist and the
elbow of the arm.

● Capable of manipulating payloads up
to 65,000 pounds (29,500 kg), the
RMS can capture stranded satellites
and hold them in position for repair
or stow them in the cargo bay for
return to Earth. It can also be used as
a work platform by an astronaut on
an EVA.

© Diagram Visual Information Ltd.

Key words	
docking	satellite
fuel cell	
orbit	
orbiter	
payload	

Carrying capacity

- The main job of the Space Shuttle system is to carry satellites, equipment, and other cargoes into space.
- All of these things are stored in the payload bay so that they can be exposed to space or deployed in orbit.
- The payload bay is configured differently for each mission.
- The dimensions of the payload bay are roughly cylindrical: 60 feet (18 m) long and 15 feet (4.5 m) in diameter.

Power supply

- Orbiter systems and onboard experiments require electrical power.
- Electrical power is provided by the Power and Reactant Storage and Distribution system on the orbiter.
- Electricity is generated by three fuel cells located beneath the payload bay floor.

Fuel cells

- Fuel cells were developed for use on the Apollo missions.
- Shuttle fuel cells are the same size as those used on Apollo missions but produce six times more power.
- A fuel cell of the type used on the shuttle produces electricity from a continuous supply of hydrogen and oxygen. The only by product is water vapor.
- Cryogenic oxygen and hydrogen for the fuel cells are stored in high-pressure spherical tanks.
- A maximum of 12,000 watts is available from the system in orbit.

Cargo

Orbiter power supply

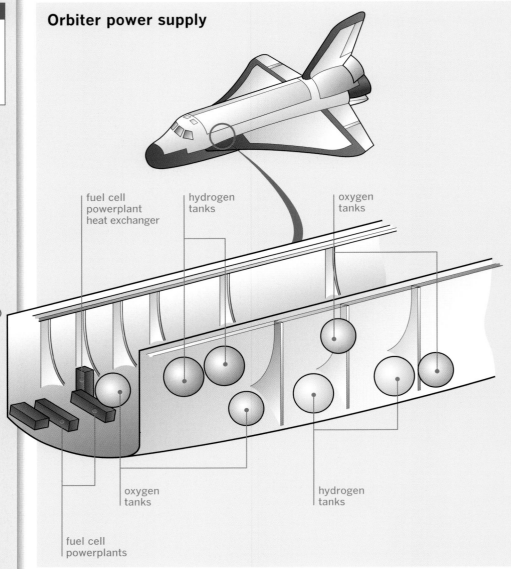

fuel cell powerplant heat exchanger

hydrogen tanks

oxygen tanks

oxygen tanks

hydrogen tanks

fuel cell powerplants

STS 89 Endeavour payload bay configuration
The Shuttle carried equipment for Shuttle/Mir mission transfers.

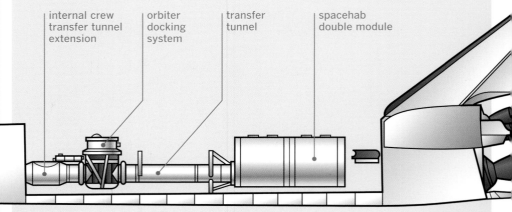

internal crew transfer tunnel extension

orbiter docking system

transfer tunnel

spacehab double module

Cockpit flight controls

Key words

abort
attitude
flight deck
orbiter

Layout of central flight control panels

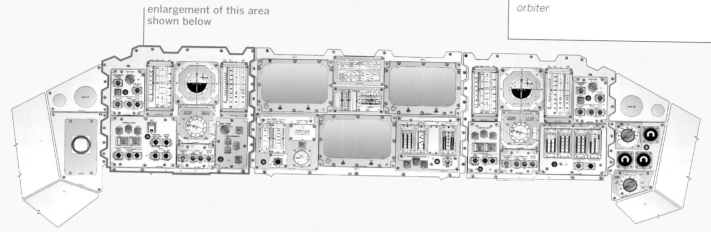

enlargement of this area
shown below

Detail of some critical flight controls and indicators

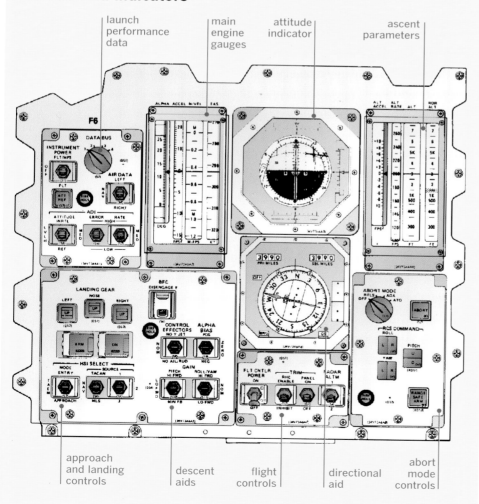

launch performance data

main engine gauges

attitude indicator

ascent parameters

approach and landing controls

descent aids

flight controls

directional aid

abort mode controls

Flight controls

- On the flight deck the pilot's and commander's seats are surrounded by the orbiter's flight controls.
- Originally designed in the 1970s, they use traditional mechanical gauges and cathode ray tube displays.
- The flight controls of all orbiters are currently being updated to the "glass cockpit" type systems used in modern military aircraft and civilian airliners such as the Boeing 777.
- The new Multifunction Electronic Display System (MEDS) was first installed on the orbiter *Atlantis*. It utilizes 11 full-color flat panel screens to display two- and three-dimensional graphical displays of key flight indicators.

Key words

astronaut
galley

Space food

- During missions astronauts on the Space Shuttle have access to a varied diet.
- The galley is equipped with an oven and hot and cold water dispensers.
- Water is added to dehydrated food using the water dispensers.
- Sealed meal packages are heated in the oven.
- Food may be freeze-dried, dehydrated, heat-treated (thermostabilized), or irradiated to preserve it: there is no refrigeration unit.
- Food in natural states, such as nuts or fruit, may also be available.
- Menus for each day, providing 3,000 calories per astronaut, are selected by crew members before the mission.
- After preparation, food is placed in individual food trays for consumption.

Food

Galley

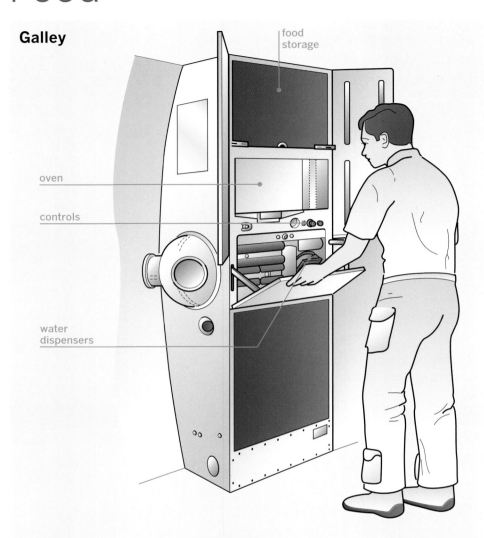

food storage

oven

controls

water dispensers

Mid deck

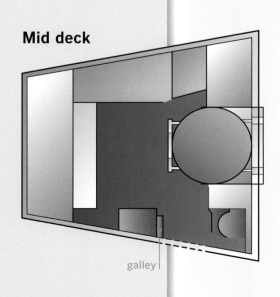

galley

Typical menu (1 day)

Breakfast
Dried peaches IM
Sausage R
Scrambled eggs R
Cornflakes R
Cocoa B
Orange drink B

Lunch
Ham T I
Cheese spread T
Bread I NF
Green beans and broccoli R
Crushed pineapple T
Bananas FD
Shortbread cookies NF
Cashew nuts NF
Lemon tea with sugar B

Dinner
Cream of mushroom soup R
Smoked turkey T I
Mixed vegetables R
Vanilla pudding T R
Strawberries R
Tropical punch B

Key
B beverage
FD freeze-dried
I irradiated
IM intermediate moisture
NF natural form
R rehydratable
T thermostabilized

Living

Work

Exercise

Eating

Recreation

Sleeping

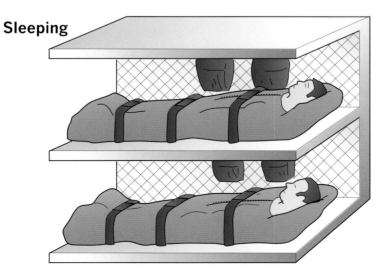

Key words
astronaut
microgravity

Mission plan

- Life onboard the Space Shuttle is carefully planned and highly structured.
- A mission flight plan will include periods for work, exercise, eating, hygiene, recreation, and sleeping.
- On almost all missions, problems will result in delays, so the flight plan has to be flexible.

Exercise

- Shuttle missions carry exercise machines such as a treadmill or pulley machine, which allow the astronauts to exercise in *microgravity* (the near-complete absence of gravity).
- To offset the degenerative effects of microgravity on the body, astronauts need to exercise vigorously for about an hour every day.

Eating

- Food preparation and consumption requires a lot of time, especially with the added difficulty of microgravity.
- Crew members usually take turns preparing meals for the whole crew.

Recreation

- Most crews play music on personal stereos during work periods.
- There is little time for sheer relaxation, although some time is considered essential.
- Crew members often communicate with family and friends using email.
- The most popular recreational activity is Earth-watching.

Sleeping

- Bunks are provided for crew members, though some choose to sleep in other parts of the orbiter, such as in a crew seat on the flight deck or in the airlock.
- At least one crew member must have his or her communications unit and headset switched on at all times in case there is an emergency communication from ground control.

Working

Key words

de-orbit	orbiter
extravehicular	payload
activity (EVA)	re-entry
flight deck	satellite
orbit	

Workload

- The workload during a Space Shuttle mission is intense.
- NASA is answerable to Congress and must justify the expense of putting a crew into orbit by achieving useful scientific results, deploying satellites for paying customers, and developing other possible commercial applications.
- Work is carried out according to a carefully planned mission schedule.
- Problems and delays must be dealt with and time may be cut from recreation and sleep periods to ensure that everything gets done.
- Mission specialists and payload specialists have to carry out specific work tasks during each mission.
- The pilot's and commander's main jobs are getting the Shuttle into orbit, maneuvering it in orbit, and returning it to Earth, but they will also help with other tasks on the mission.
- Much of the work related to modules, satellites, or experiments in the payload bay is carried out from the aft workstations on the flight deck.

Flight deck

pilot's seat

workstations

other crew seats

interdeck access

commander's seat

Types of work

- Launch and ascent
- Post-orbit activities: making the orbiter ready for work
- Monitoring orbiter systems
- Carrying out routine maintenance
- Maneuvering in orbit
- Retrieving, servicing, and deploying satellites (EVA)
- Other EVAs
- Operating modules or experiments in the payload bay
- Operating experiments in the crew compartment
- Earth observation and recording
- TV conferences with ground control, media, or government officials
- Deactivating experiments
- Preparing for de-orbit and re-entry

Aft flight deck work stations

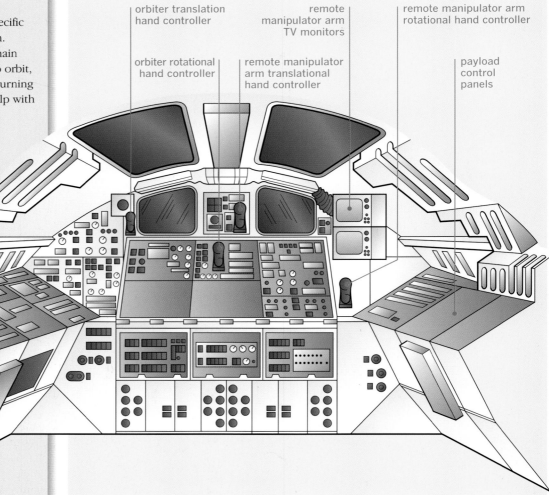

orbiter translation hand controller

remote manipulator arm TV monitors

remote manipulator arm rotational hand controller

orbiter rotational hand controller

remote manipulator arm translational hand controller

payload control panels

Launching satellites

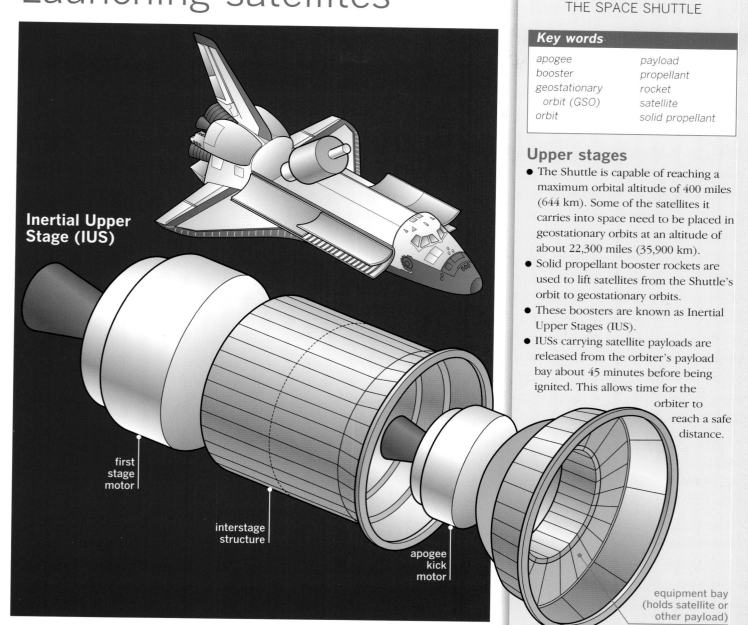

Inertial Upper Stage (IUS)

first stage motor

interstage structure

apogee kick motor

equipment bay (holds satellite or other payload)

Key words

apogee	payload
booster	propellant
geostationary orbit (GSO)	rocket
	satellite
orbit	solid propellant

Upper stages

- The Shuttle is capable of reaching a maximum orbital altitude of 400 miles (644 km). Some of the satellites it carries into space need to be placed in geostationary orbits at an altitude of about 22,300 miles (35,900 km).
- Solid propellant booster rockets are used to lift satellites from the Shuttle's orbit to geostationary orbits.
- These boosters are known as Inertial Upper Stages (IUS).
- IUSs carrying satellite payloads are released from the orbiter's payload bay about 45 minutes before being ignited. This allows time for the orbiter to reach a safe distance.

IUS release

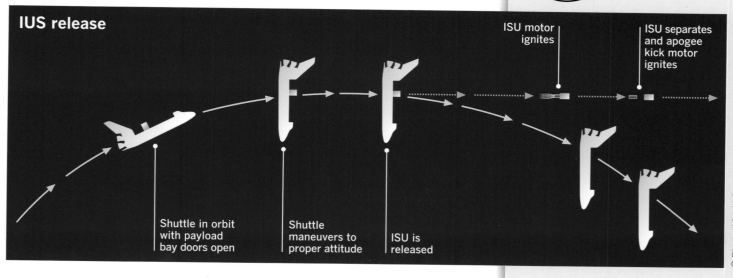

Shuttle in orbit with payload bay doors open

Shuttle maneuvers to proper attitude

ISU is released

ISU motor ignites

ISU separates and apogee kick motor ignites

© Diagram Visual Information Ltd.

Key words

abort	liftoff
attitude	mission control
booster	orbit
countdown	orbiter
launch control	

Countdown

- For a Shuttle to reach orbit successfully, hundreds of discrete events have to take place in the correct order and at the correct time. The schedule that organizes these events is known as a *countdown*.
- A typical countdown may begin up to two days before the actual launch, but the most critical phase of a Shuttle countdown is the two hour period before the launch and the 45–60 minutes after the launch.
- A Shuttle countdown can be halted at any time before the Solid Rocket Boosters are ignited.
- All Shuttle countdowns include certain essential elements, but details may vary depending on the nature of the mission being flown.
- Time before launch is referred to by the prefix "T minus" (T–), so T–0:30:00 means 30 minutes before launch.
- Time after launch is referred to by the prefix "T plus" (T+).

Launch totals

- The Space Shuttle (*Columbia*) was first launched on April 12, 1981.
- By January 2005 there had been 112 successful Space Shuttle launches.
- Only one Space Shuttle launch has failed. Mission STS 51-L (*Challenger*) exploded 73 seconds after liftoff on January 28, 1986. All seven crew members were killed.
- One other mission has failed to land safely. Mission STS 107 (*Columbia*) exploded about 16 minutes before scheduled touchdown on February 1, 2003. All seven crew members were killed.

Launch

A typical Space Shuttle countdown

T–5:00:00	Final countdown begins
T–4:30:00	Liquid oxygen pumped into External Tank liquid oxygen tank
T–2:50:00	Liquid hydrogen pumped into External Tank liquid hydrogen tank
T–1:50:00	Crew enter orbiter
T–1:30:00	Communications check with launch control
T–1:25:00	Communications check with mission control
T–1:10:00	Crew access hatch is closed and secured by ground crew
T–1:05:00	Crew carry out orbiter cabin leak check
T–0:30:00	Ground crew retires to secure area
T–0:25:00	Commander and pilot carry out voice communications check with mission control and receive updated abort data
T–0:20:00	Countdown held for ten minutes to allow any behind-schedule activities to be completed
T–0:16:00	Main propulsion system pressurized
T–0:09:00	Countdown held for another ten minutes to allow any behind-schedule activities to be completed
T–0:07:00	Crew access arm retracts
T–0:06:00	Orbiter's hydraulic system powered-up
T–0:04:30	Orbiter switches to internal power
T–0:03:45	Orbiter aero surfaces tested
T–0:03:00	Orbiter main engines gimbal to launch positions
T–0:02:55	External Tank oxygen vents close; liquid oxygen tank begins pressurization for launch
T–0:01:57	External Tank hydrogen vents close; liquid hydrogen tank begins pressurization for launch
T–0:00:25	Countdown management switches to orbiter computers
T–0:00:03.46	First Space Shuttle Main Engine (SSME) ignites
T–0:00:03.34	Second SSME ignites
T–0:00:03.22	Third SSME ignites
T–0:00:00	Solid Rocket Booster ignition timer starts
T+0:00:02.64	Solid Rocket Boosters ignite
T+0:00:03	Liftoff
T+0:00:06.50	Launch tower cleared
T+0:00:11	Begin 120° roll into "heads down" attitude
T+0:00:44	At speed of Mach 1, SSMEs reduce thrust to 65%
T+0:01:06	SSMEs increase thrust to 100%
T+0:02:00	Solid Rocket Boosters burn-out
T+0:02:07	Solid Rocket Booster separation
T+0:04:20	Last point at which a Return To Launch Site abort is possible
T+0:08:28	SSMEs reduce thrust to 65%
T+0:08:38	SSMEs shut down
T+0:08:54	External Tank separation
T+0:10:39	Orbital Maneuvering System (OMS) burns to raise orbit
T+0:12:24	OMS burn ends
T+0:12:30	Auxiliary power unit shut down
T+0:45:58	Second OMS burn
T+0:46:34	Second OMS burn ends

Landing

KSC Shuttle Landing Facility

rescue vehicle station
meteorological equipment
rescue vehicle station
television tower
landing aids control building
RF communications tower
airfield lighting
tow-way to Vehicle Assembly Building
parking apron
meteorological equipment
rescue vehicle station
runway 15/33
MSBLS runway 15
MSBLS runway 33
television tower

Key words

atmosphere
de-orbit
orbit
orbiter
re-entry

From orbit to Earth

- The orbiter has no engines for flight in the atmosphere: it approaches and lands like a glider.
- The commander of a mission pilots the orbiter during approach and landing: only one attempt is possible.
- The orbiter's descent rate is seven times steeper than that of an airliner.
- Landings at Kennedy Space Center are made at the Shuttle Landing Facility. The runway is designated Runway 15 for landings from the northwest and designated Runway 33 for landings from the southeast.

Time to touchdown	Event	Distance from runway
60 minutes	**De-orbit burn** The orbiter is turned so that it is flying tail first and the OMS engines are fired to slow the orbiter and lower its orbit into Earth's atmosphere. The orbiter is traveling at about 16,465 miles per hour (26,876 kmph).	175 miles (282 km)
25 minutes	**Entry interface** The orbiter begins to enter Earth's atmosphere. Vehicle exterior quickly heats up and communications with the ground are cut off by ionization of the air around the orbiter.	50 miles (80.5 km)
20 minutes	**Maximum heating** The exterior of the orbiter reaches its maximum temperatures. During re-entry the orbiter performs a series of wide S-shaped turns to help reduce velocity.	43.5 miles (70 km)
12 minutes	**Exit blackout** Communications with the ground are re-established. The orbiter is now traveling at about 8,275 miles per hour (13,317 kmph).	34 miles (55 km)
5 minutes 30 seconds	**Terminal Area Energy Management** Following a pre-planned descent trajectory, the orbiter glides toward landing. The commander must follow the trajectory precisely: there is only one chance of making a landing.	15.7 miles (25.3 km)
1 minute 16 seconds	**Autoland** The Microwave Scanning Beam Landing System (MSBLS) on the ground provides landing data for the final approach. The angle of descent of the orbiter is reduced from 22° to 1.5°. Its speed is now about 425 miles per hour (682 kmph).	7.5 miles (12 km)
14 seconds	**Wheels down** At an altitude of just 90 feet (27 m) the orbiter's landing gear is lowered.	1,100 feet (335 m)
0 seconds	**Touchdown** The rear wheels touchdown followed by the nosewheel five seconds later. The orbiter is traveling at about 215 miles per hour (346 kmph). Landing gear brakes, aerodynamic brakes, and a drag chute slow the orbiter to a halt.	2,760 feet (689 m) from end of runway

Television satellites

Key words

communications
  satellite
footprint
orbit
satellite

Satellite functions

- Many modern communications satellites combine telephone and television service provision.
- Combined service satellites may have over 100,000 voice circuits and three to six television channels.
- Dedicated television satellites can handle more than 30 channels.
- The area of Earth's surface that receives a usable signal from a satellite is known as the satellite's footprint.
- Commercial communications satellites are positioned in orbits that give them a footprint covering a specific market area, such as Europe or North America.
- Communications companies such as Eutelsat and Intelsat maintain large fleets of satellites allowing them to provide data networks for communications companies all over the world.
- Communications satellite fleets must be constantly upgraded with more advanced, higher capacity satellites representing an ongoing investment of billions of dollars.

Communications satellites

Services

- Voice/data networks for a variety of applications
- Internet and other data services
- Broadcast and direct-to-home video
- High data rate telephony
- Telemedicine, tele-education, video conferencing
- Interactive video and multimedia

Multimedia satellites

Multimedia communications

- High speed internet access
- Online service applications
- Video telephony
- Video conferencing
- Electronic commerce
- Telecommuting through access to various servers
- Distance learning
- Telemedicine
- Live entertainment, such as interactive video

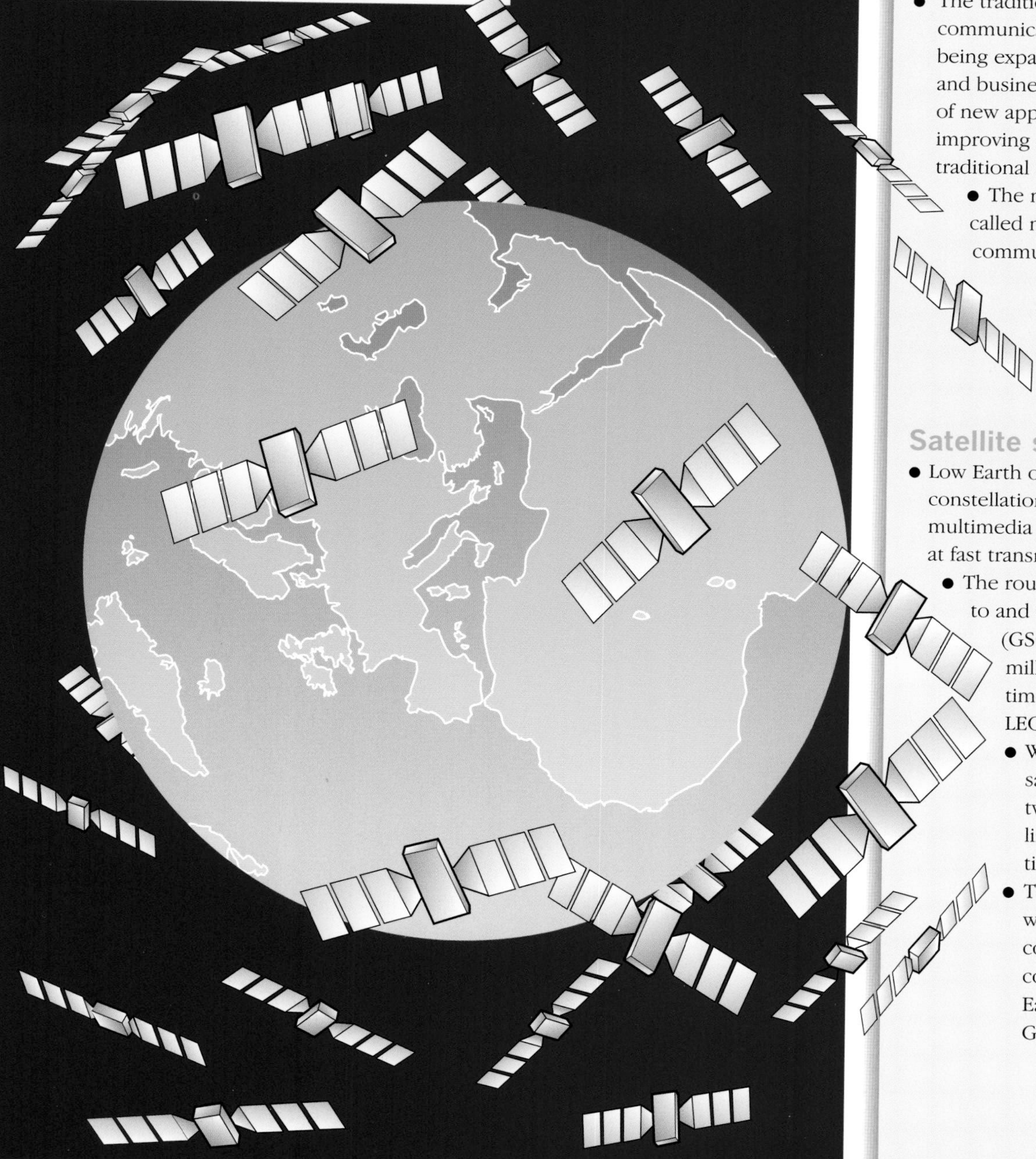

Key words

communications
  satellite
constellation
geostationary
  orbit (GSO)

low Earth orbit
  (LEO)
satellite

Multimedia communications

- The traditional TV and telephony communications satellite business is being expanded to provide private and business users with a wide range of new applications as well as improving and expanding access to traditional telephony applications.
  - The new business is generally called multimedia communications.

Satellite systems

- Low Earth orbit (LEO) satellite constellations provide continuous multimedia communications coverage at fast transmission rates.
  - The round trip for transmissions to and from a geostationary orbit (GSO) satellite takes 500 milliseconds, whereas the time taken by a satellite in LEO is only 30 milliseconds.
  - With a constellation of satellites in orbit, at least two satellites will be within line-of-sight of a user at any time.
  - The satellites also provide worldwide coverage compared with the coverage of one third of Earth by a single GSO satellite.

The Skybridge multimedia satellite constellation
Eighty satellites in 913-mile (1,469 km) circular orbits on 20 orbital planes (each with four satellites) provide users with continuous access to high data rate multimedia services.

Mobile communications satellites

Key words

communications
  satellite
low Earth orbit
  (LEO)
satellite

Mobile communications

- The first mobile communications satellites provided communications services to ships at sea.
- The improved transmission power of satellites and microelectronics has allowed mobile communications terminals to be reduced in size to that of the satellite phone.
- Mobile communications satellites compete with cellular mobile communications networks that rely on ground-based reception and transmission antennas.
- Mobile communications satellites have the advantage of allowing a user access to the network from anywhere in the world—even in remote areas where no cellular network exists.
- The low cost of cellular communications systems and the rapidly increasing area of their global coverage threatens to make the more expensive satellite networks redundant for civilian use.

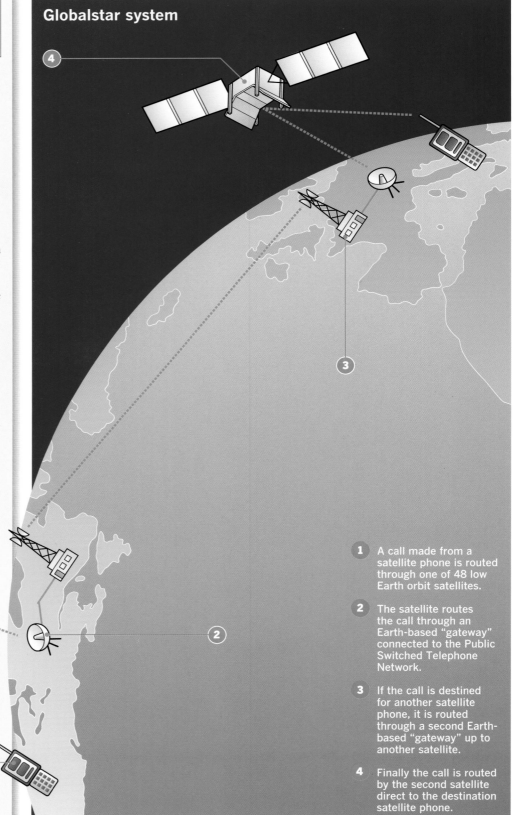

Globalstar system

1 A call made from a satellite phone is routed through one of 48 low Earth orbit satellites.

2 The satellite routes the call through an Earth-based "gateway" connected to the Public Switched Telephone Network.

3 If the call is destined for another satellite phone, it is routed through a second Earth-based "gateway" up to another satellite.

4 Finally the call is routed by the second satellite direct to the destination satellite phone.

Navigation satellites

Orbits of the GPS satellite constellation

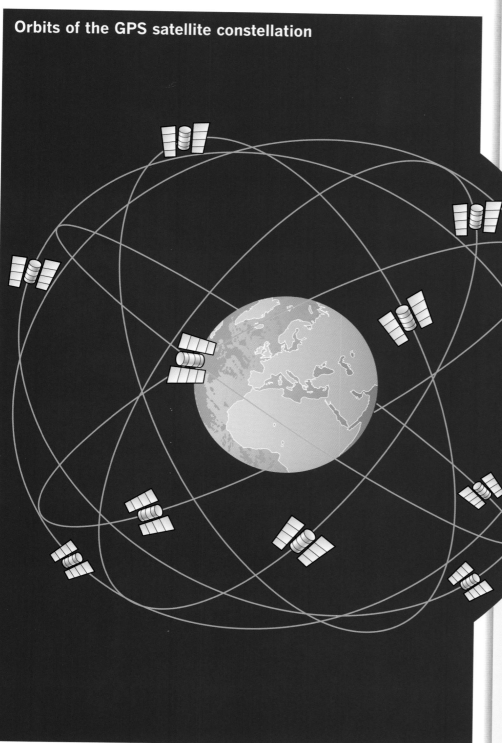

Key words

constellation   orbit
Global
  Positioning
  System (GPS)
inclination

Global Positioning System

- The *Global Positioning System* (GPS) is funded and operated by the Department of Defense.
- GPS was initially developed as a positioning system for use by the military. Today it is widely used by civilian organizations and private individuals.
- GPS allows users to pinpoint their location within 65 feet (20 m). In most cases accuracy is even better and some techniques allow specialist users, such as the military, to achieve accuracies of 4 inches (10 cm).

Satellites

- To operate properly the GPS requires a "constellation" of 24 satellites to be in orbit at the same time.
- Six groups of four equally spaced GPS satellites are maintained in circular orbits with a period of 12 hours. Each of these orbits is spaced 60 degrees apart and has an inclination of 55°.
- From any point on Earth's surface, between five and eight GPS satellites are in line of sight.
- GPS satellites are regularly replaced as they reach the end of their operational lifetimes, so that there may be more than the required 24 GPS satellites in orbit at any one time.

Control system

- The position and status of all GPS satellites is monitored by Earth-based tracking stations all over the world.

GPS users

- Aircraft, ships, ground vehicles, and individuals may be equipped with GPS receivers.
- The GPS receiver registers transmissions from four GPS satellites in line of sight and uses these transmissions to calculate the precise time and its current location in three dimensions.
- Positional information is given in terms of degrees, minutes, and seconds north or south, and east or west.

Earth-watching satellites

Key words

atmosphere
ozone layer
remote sensing
satellite

Observing the Earth

- One of the most important areas of satellite technology is the observation and study of Earth, especially its weather and climate.
- Hundreds of satellites have been used to study Earth and there are more in place today than ever before.
- There are three main areas of observation: meteorology, environmental monitoring, and commercial remote sensing.
- Much scientific effort has gone into environmental monitoring including observations of land use, pollution, floods, sea surface temperature, and ozone concentrations in the atmosphere.

TIROS

- The first Earth observation satellites were elements of the Television Infrared Observation Satellite program (TIROS), which was designed to provide regular images of global cloud cover.
- Launched in 1960, the TIROS satellites were the precursors of the sophisticated weather, or meteorological, satellites in use today.
- TIROS satellites provided data for the first Worldwide Weather Watch system.

TIROS in operation

1 A ground station transmits instructions to a TIROS satellite.

2 The TIROS satellite takes pictures of cloud cover over the specified area. On command the satellite transmits its pictures to a ground station.

3 Images are sent to the NASA weather bureau and other agencies for analysis.

4 Updated weather reports are sent to ships, planes, and other users.

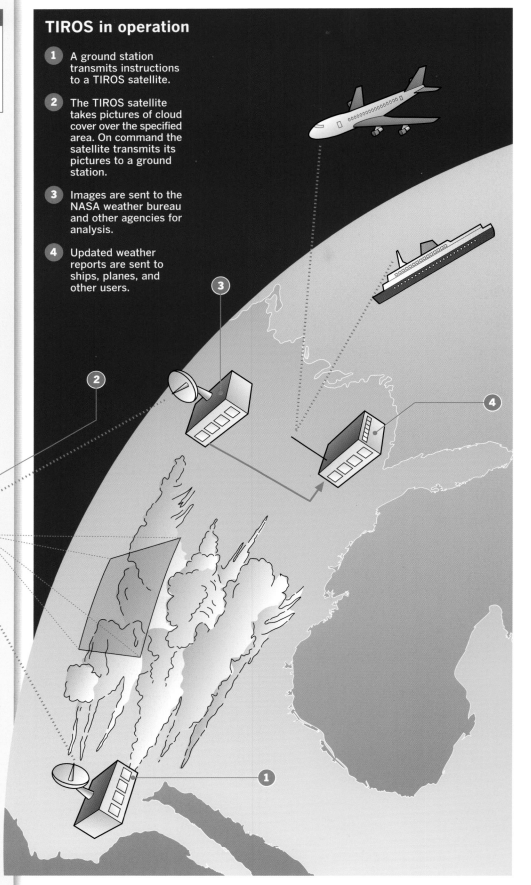

Weather satellites

Geostationary Environmental Satellites (GEOS)

trim tab

solar array

Key words

geostationary
*   *orbit (GSO)*
satellite
solar radiation
weather satellite

World Weather Watch

- The US, Europe, India, Japan, and Russia operate fleets of geostationary weather satellites as part of the World Weather Watch cooperative program.
- U.S. weather satellites are operated by the National Oceanic and Atmospheric Administration (NOAA).
- Standard NOAA weather satellites are known as Geostationary Environmental Satellites (GEOS).
- The instruments carried by GEOS are very similar to those carried by the dedicated meteorological satellites of other nations.

tracking and telemetry antenna

Earth sensors

S-band receiving antenna

S-band transmitting antenna

sounder cooler

sounder

Sun shields

imager

solar sail

X-ray sensor

UHF antenna

imager cooler

magnetometers

communications antenna

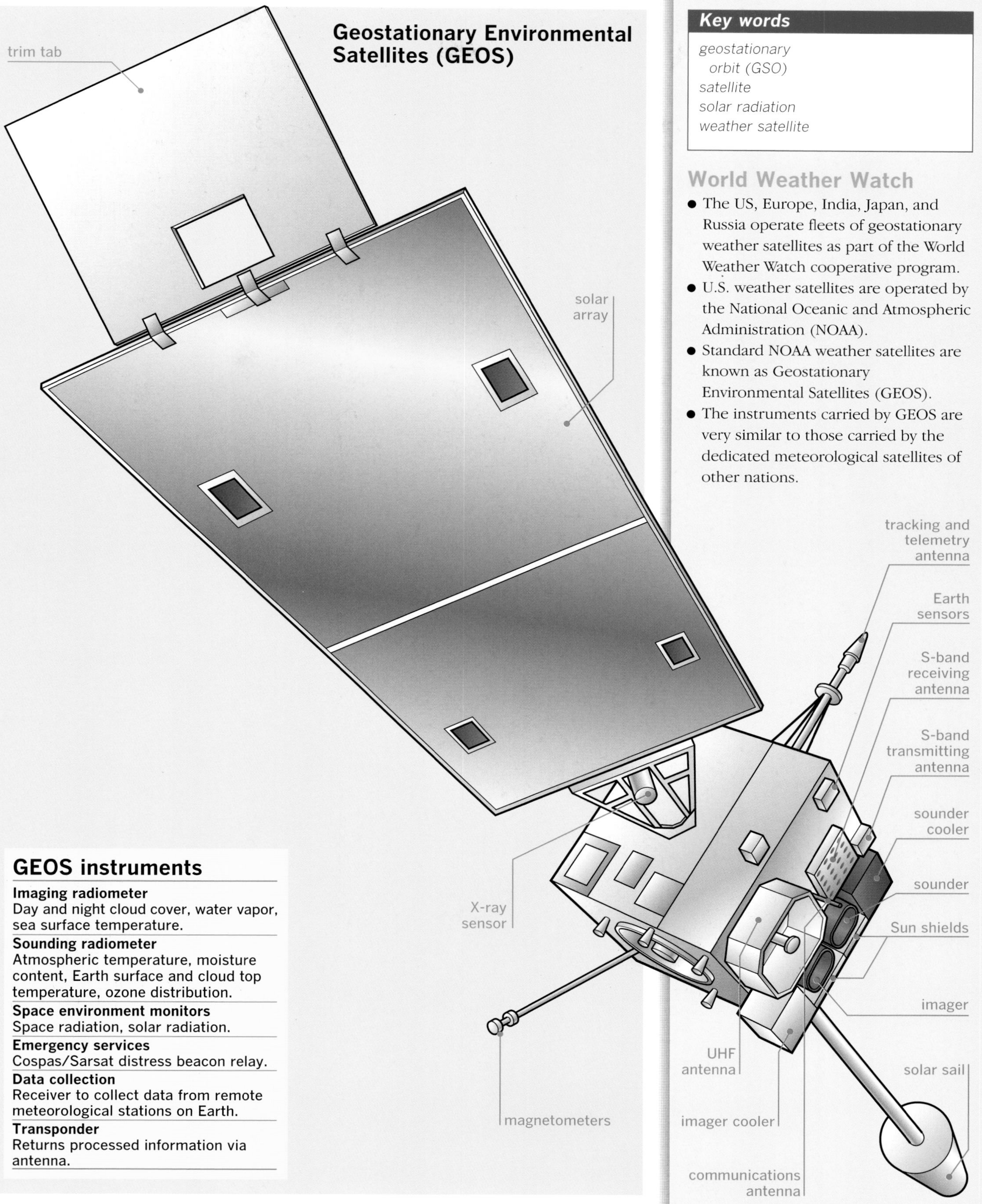

GEOS instruments

Imaging radiometer
Day and night cloud cover, water vapor, sea surface temperature.

Sounding radiometer
Atmospheric temperature, moisture content, Earth surface and cloud top temperature, ozone distribution.

Space environment monitors
Space radiation, solar radiation.

Emergency services
Cospas/Sarsat distress beacon relay.

Data collection
Receiver to collect data from remote meteorological stations on Earth.

Transponder
Returns processed information via antenna.

Key words

atmosphere	pole
bus	satellite
Earth	solar array
observation	solar radiation
satellite (EOS)	spacecraft
orbit	troposphere

Mission to Planet Earth

- A NASA program known as Mission to Planet Earth aims to collect comprehensive data about Earth's environment over a twenty-year period.
- Satellites from the US, Europe, and other space nations are involved in the program.
- The flagship of the program is the Earth observation satellite (EOS) *Terra* launched on December 18, 1999.
- *Terra* has an expected operational life span of six years, after which it will be replaced by more advanced satellites.
- Like many EOSs, *Terra* operates in a polar orbit that allows it to compile complete global surveys in regular cycles.

Environmental satellites

Terra instruments

Five instruments carried by Terra, and the phenomena they measure are:

Advanced Spaceborne Thermal Emission and Reflection (ASTER)
Surface spectral radiance; surface temperature; digital elevation maps; surface composition; vegetation maps; cloud; sea/polar ice; natural hazards.

Cloud/Earth's Radiant Energy System (CERES)
Cloud radiation forcing and feedbacks; radiant input to atmosphere and ocean energetics.

Multi-angle Imaging Spectro-Radiometer (MISR)
Cloud effects on solar radiation budget; influence of tropospheric aerosols on solar radiation budget; climate impact of land processes; biochemical cycle.

Moderate Resolution Imaging Spectrometer (MODIS)
Land and ocean surface temperature; ocean color (sediment, photoplankton); global vegetation maps; deforestation; clouds; aerosols; temperature and moisture soundings.

Measurements of Pollution in the Troposphere (MOPITT)
Upwelling and reflected infrared radiance in three carbon monoxide and methane absorption bands to model gases in the troposphere.

Terra (exploded view)

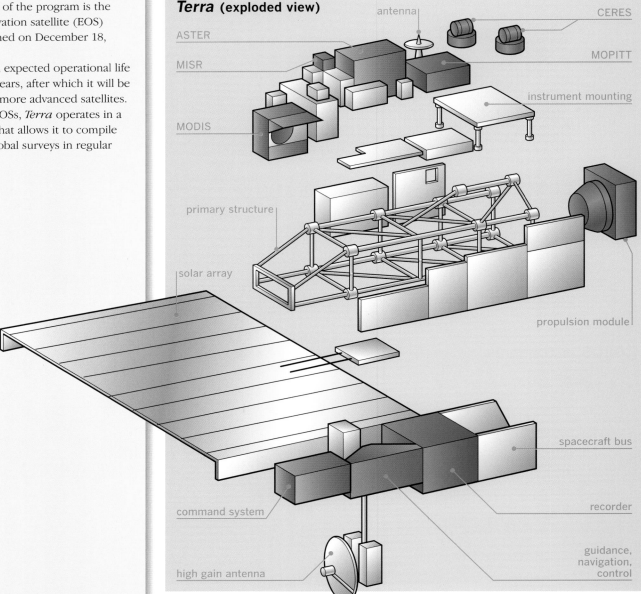

Atmospheric satellites

Upper Atmosphere Research Satellite (UARS) instruments

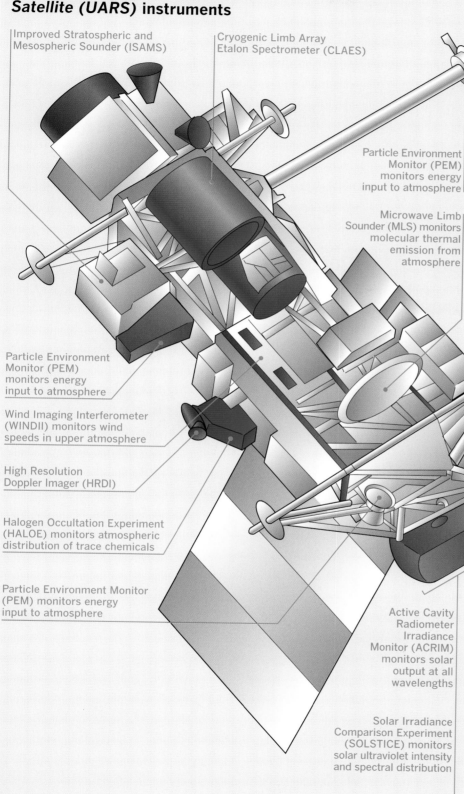

Improved Stratospheric and Mesospheric Sounder (ISAMS)

Cryogenic Limb Array Etalon Spectrometer (CLAES)

Particle Environment Monitor (PEM) monitors energy input to atmosphere

Microwave Limb Sounder (MLS) monitors molecular thermal emission from atmosphere

Particle Environment Monitor (PEM) monitors energy input to atmosphere

Wind Imaging Interferometer (WINDII) monitors wind speeds in upper atmosphere

High Resolution Doppler Imager (HRDI)

Halogen Occultation Experiment (HALOE) monitors atmospheric distribution of trace chemicals

Particle Environment Monitor (PEM) monitors energy input to atmosphere

Active Cavity Radiometer Irradiance Monitor (ACRIM) monitors solar output at all wavelengths

Solar Irradiance Comparison Experiment (SOLSTICE) monitors solar ultraviolet intensity and spectral distribution

Solar UV Spectral Irradiance Monitor (SUSIM)

Key words

atmosphere	stratosphere
magnetosphere	troposphere
pole	upper
satellite	atmosphere
solar radiation	

Atmosphere observation

- Earth's atmosphere is a highly complex system involving interactions between chemical, dynamic physical, and radiation processes.
- Satellites have been used to study the temperature, pressure, wind dynamics, and chemical composition of Earth's atmosphere—particularly the upper atmosphere.
- A major concern is the relationship between ozone levels in the stratosphere and man-made gases as well as gases from biological processes.
- The ozone layer protects life on Earth from the harmful effects of solar radiation.
- Since the 1960s scientists have been monitoring a steady reduction in the concentration of ozone in the upper atmosphere, particularly over the polar regions.

Upper Atmosphere Research Satellite (UARS)

- *UARS* was deployed from the Space Shuttle in September 1991 as the flagship of atmospheric research by satellites.
- *UARS* provides a continuous global look at the upper atmosphere.
- It provides data about the atmosphere's internal structure: trace constituents, physical dynamics, radiative emissions, thermal structure, density; and about external influences: solar radiation, tropospheric conditions, magnetospheric particles, and electric fields.

Radiation satellites

© Diagram Visual Information Ltd.

Key words

magnetosphere
solar wind
Van Allen belt

Radiation belts

- *Explorer 1*, America's first satellite, discovered radiation belts around Earth in 1958.
- Earth's radiation belts are one part of a system called the *magnetosphere*.
- The magnetosphere is a region surrounding Earth where the planet's magnetic field interacts with the flow of ionized particles in the *solar wind*—the radiation coming from the Sun.
- The radiation belts are made up of electrons, protons, and heavier sub-atomic particles such as alpha particles. These particles become trapped in Earth's magnetic field.
- The radiation belts are doughnut-shaped, with an inner and outer belt.
- These belts of trapped radiation are called the Van Allen belts.
- James Van Allen (1914–) designed the cosmic ray package on *Explorer 1* that discovered the existence of these belts.
- *Pioneer 3*, an American spacecraft that attempted but failed to make a flight to the Moon in 1958, also assisted in the discovery of the Van Allen belts.
- Several Explorer series and other satellites have flown through the belts to study them further.

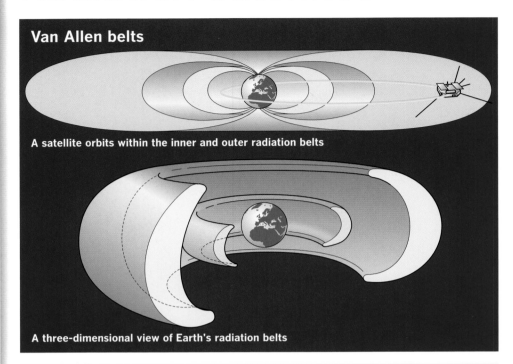

Van Allen belts

A satellite orbits within the inner and outer radiation belts

A three-dimensional view of Earth's radiation belts

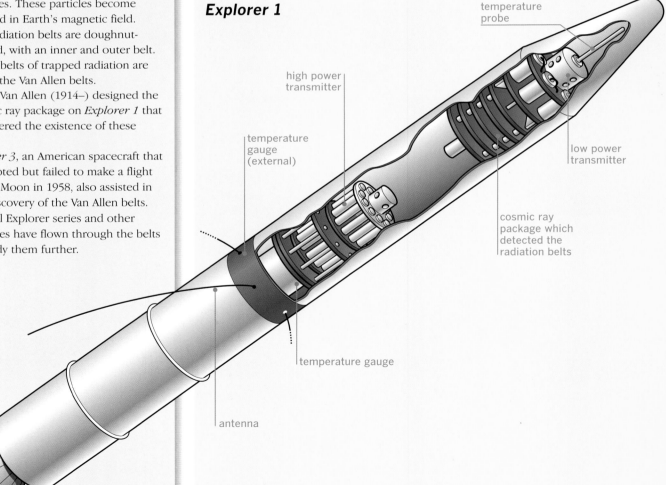

Explorer 1

temperature probe

high power transmitter

temperature gauge (external)

low power transmitter

cosmic ray package which detected the radiation belts

temperature gauge

antenna

Data satellites

Earth Probe/TOMS

deployed
solar array

thrusters

antenna

orbital adjust module

propellant tanks

battery

avionics

scanner

equipment module

Sun sensor

stowed solar array

Total Ozone
Mapping Spectrometer

antenna

Key words

Earth	radar
observation	satellite
satellite (EOS)	solar array
ozone layer	
propellant	

Earth observation satellite instruments

- Most Earth observation satellites (EOSs) are equipped with a range of instruments allowing them to gather data about different targets.
- A typical EOS will be equipped with a multispectral, panchromatic or radar imaging system, a radiometer, an altimeter, and sounders.

Total Ozone Mapping Spectrometer

- The Mission to Planet Earth program is an ongoing NASA program to study every aspect of Earth's atmosphere, water cycles, biological cycles, and geology using instruments in orbit.
  - The Total Ozone Mapping Spectrometer (TOMS) is an instrument for measuring the quantity of ozone in the atmosphere. It was first developed in the 1970s and variants of it have been mounted on a number of satellites in the Mission to Planet Earth program.
  - The *Earth Probe/TOMS* satellite (launched 1994) is an example of the kind of EOS that has carried the TOMS instrument.
  - In conjunction with other spacecraft, such as *Meteor 3/TOMS* and *Advanced Earth Observing System/TOMS*, *Earth Probe/TOMS* has enabled scientists to gather data over many years and led to a better understanding of the condition of Earth's ozone layer.
- *Aura* is a recent EOS (launched July 2004) operating as part of the Mission to Planet Earth program. *Aura*'s instruments are designed to measure atmospheric concentrations of ozone, water vapor, CFCs, methane, and nitrogen compounds.

Earth observation satellites

© Diagram Visual Information Ltd.

Key words

atmosphere
gravity
infrared
satellite
solar radiation

Earth observation satellites today

- Concerns about climate change have prompted scientists to conduct in-depth studies of Earth's atmosphere and the effects of solar radiation on it.
- NASA alone is currently operating more than 20 Earth observation satellites that are investigating everything from cloud formation to Earth's gravity field.
- Satellites are able to collect large quantities of global data very rapidly.

Earth observation satellite	Tasks	Launch date
Active Cavity Radiometer Irradiance Monitor Satellite (ACRIMSAT)	Solar radiation reaching Earth	December 1999
Aqua (EOS PM 1)	Earth's water cycle	May 2002
Aquarius	Sea surface salinity	September 2008
Aura	Earth's atmosphere	July 2004
Cloud-Aerosol Lidar and Infrared Pathfinder Satellite Observations (CALIPSO)	Effects of clouds and particles on Earth's climate	May 2005
Challenging Mini-Satellite Payload for Geo-scientific Research and Applications Program (CHAMP)	Earth's gravitational and magnetic fields	July 2000
CloudSat	Vertical structure of Earth's clouds	May 2005
Geostationary Operational Environmental Satellite (GOES) N series	Meteorological research	April 2005–October 2008
Global Precipitation Measurement (GPM)	Earth's precipitation	2010
Gravity Recovery and Climate Experiment (GRACE)	Effects of the water cycle on Earth's gravitational field	March 2002
Hydrosphere State Mission (Hydros)	Freezing and thawing of Earth's soil moisture	2010
Ice Clouds and Land Elevation Satellite (ICESat)	Earth's ice sheets	January 2003
JASON 1	Earth's ocean circulation	December 2001
LANDSAT 7	Earth imagery	April 1999
New Millenium Program Earth Observing 1 (NMP EO 1)	Earth imagery instruments	November 2000
NOAA Polar Operational Environmental Satellites (POES)	Meteorological observations	March 2005–2007
Orbiting Carbon Observatory (OCO)	Carbon dioxide in Earth's atmosphere	October 2007
Ocean Surface Topography Mission (OSTM)	Sea surface heights	April 2008
Quick Scatterometer (QuikSCAT)	Sea surface wind speeds	June 1999
Solar Radiation and Climate Experiment (SORCE)	Solar radiation reaching Earth	January 2003

Optical spy satellites

Big Bird KH-9

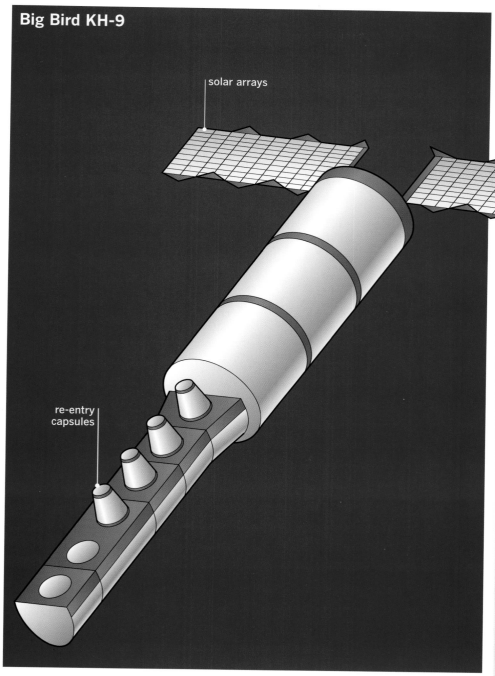

solar arrays

re-entry
capsules

Key words

bus   spy satellite
orbit
re-entry
satellite
spacecraft

Spy satellite development

- The first spy satellites took high-resolution optical images on film, which was then returned to Earth in a re-entry capsule.
- Later craft transmitted high-resolution digital images direct from orbit either to the ground or through data relay satellites.
- Images with a resolution down to a few inches can now be obtained.
- Spy satellites are maneuvered into specific orbits to image areas of special interest.
- Modern multispectral imaging systems can view objects—even individuals—at night.

United States

- Project Corona, disguised under the name Discoverer, was also designated Key Hole (KH-1) in 1958, though the first successful mission did not take place until 1960.
- These early spy satellites had a life span of only a few days in orbit.
- Successive generations of KH-2 to KH-8 series flew until 1984.
- The KH-9 series (also called Big Bird) was equipped with four re-entry film capsules and also transmitted digital images to Earth.
- The KH-11 series (there was no KH-10) were uprated Big Birds with re-entry capsules and multispectral imaging capability.
- The KH-12 (also called Crystal) was based on the *Hubble Space Telescope* spacecraft bus.
- These were all equipped with a full suite of multispectral instruments, including those that could even detect body heat at night, and also other reconnaissance applications, such as electronic intelligence.

USSR/Russia

- The first Soviet spy satellite was launched in 1962 and was based on the crewed Vostok craft and its spherical re-entry capsule.
- The series of eight types of craft were code-named Zenit and the program ran until about 1974.
- Systems called Yantar and Kometa were introduced in 1974 and 1981 and were based on crewed Soyuz spacecraft.
- The first digital imaging spy satellite was launched in 1982.

France/Germany/Italy/Spain

- *Helios 1* is a digital imaging spy satellite based on the commercial remote sensing satellite *Spot*. It was launched in 1995.
- A second Helios is under development.

Radar spy satellites

Radar imaging

- Unlike optical spy satellites, radar spy satellites are able to see through cloud cover.
- Radar signals emitted from the satellite bounce off ground targets and are picked up again by the satellite's large dish antenna.
- The height and profile of an object on the ground can be determined from these reflected pulses and the digital images produced.
- *Indigo*, a U.S. prototype radar reconnaissance satellite, was launched in 1982.
- The currently operational radar reconnaissance satellite series is known as Lacrosse.
- Lacrosse is thought to be able to obtain images with a resolution of about 3 feet (1 m).

Lacrosse

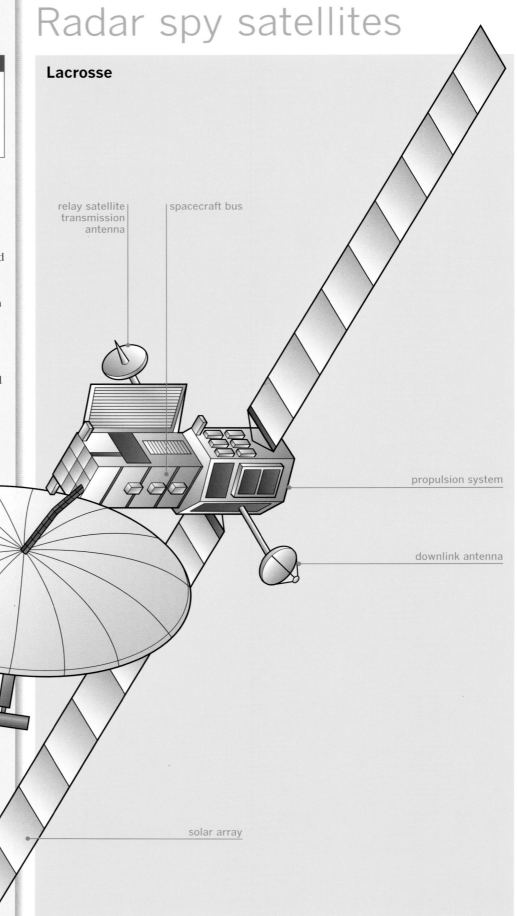

relay satellite transmission antenna

spacecraft bus

propulsion system

downlink antenna

receiving dish antenna

imaging radar antenna

solar array

Radio spy satellites

Jumpseat

U.S. SIGINT satellites (year introduced)	
Solrad	1960
Ferret and Canyon	1962
Rholite/Aquacade	1970
Jumpseat	1970s
Chalet/Vortex	1978
Magnum/Orion	1985
Mercury	1994
Trumpet	1994
Soviet SIGINT satellites (year introduced)	
Tselina	1970
Tselina 2	1984

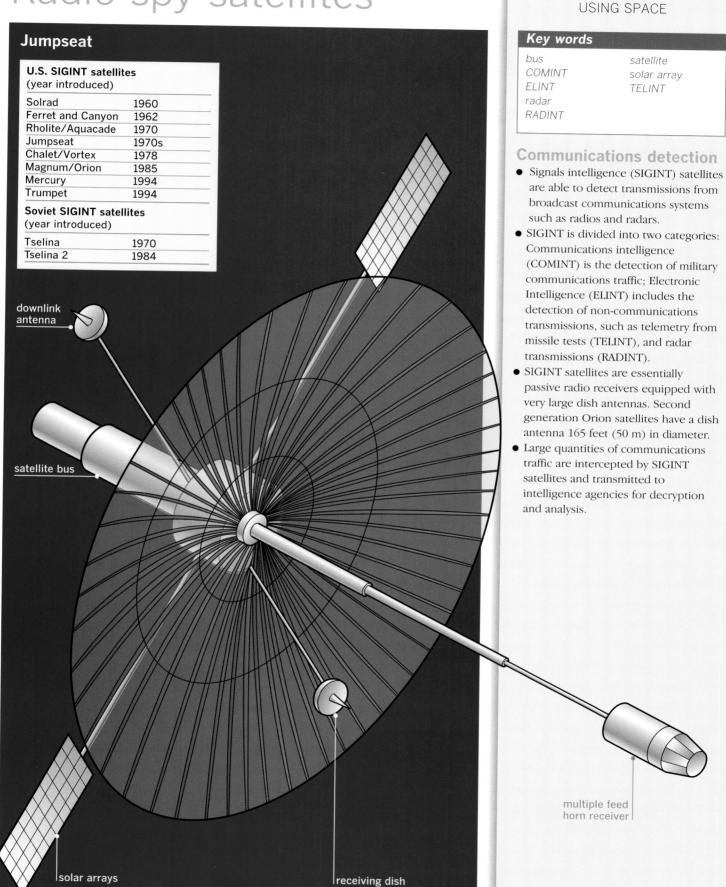

downlink antenna

satellite bus

solar arrays

receiving dish

multiple feed horn receiver

Key words

bus	satellite
COMINT	solar array
ELINT	TELINT
radar	
RADINT	

Communications detection

- Signals intelligence (SIGINT) satellites are able to detect transmissions from broadcast communications systems such as radios and radars.
- SIGINT is divided into two categories: Communications intelligence (COMINT) is the detection of military communications traffic; Electronic Intelligence (ELINT) includes the detection of non-communications transmissions, such as telemetry from missile tests (TELINT), and radar transmissions (RADINT).
- SIGINT satellites are essentially passive radio receivers equipped with very large dish antennas. Second generation Orion satellites have a dish antenna 165 feet (50 m) in diameter.
- Large quantities of communications traffic are intercepted by SIGINT satellites and transmitted to intelligence agencies for decryption and analysis.

Key words

bus
constellation
geostationary
  orbit (GSO)
infrared
low Earth orbit
  (LEO)
orbit
satellite
solar array
spacecraft
telescope

Early warning mission

- Following the 1963 Nuclear Test Ban Treaty, which banned the use or testing of nuclear weapons in space, the U.S. Vela monitoring program was initiated.
- Vela satellites were initially capable of detecting nuclear explosions in space.
- Later Vela satellites were also able to detect nuclear explosions in the atmosphere and on the ground.
- The Vela program ended in 1984.
- The U.S. Defence Support Program (DSP) was initiated in 1970 to provide early warning of missile launches as well as the ability to detect nuclear explosions.
- Modern DSP satellites are able to detect heat from long and short range missile launches, aircraft engines using afterburners, as well as nuclear explosions.
- Several DSP satellites are maintained on station in geostationary orbits to provide global coverage. New satellites are inserted into the constellation as on-station satellites reach the end of their operational life.
- The latest generation of early warning satellites, Space Based Infrared System (SBIRS), uses low Earth orbit satellites with the ability to detect missile launches to track missiles throughout their flight.
- The Soviet Union operated a fleet of Oko early warning satellites and a later series known as Prognoz.

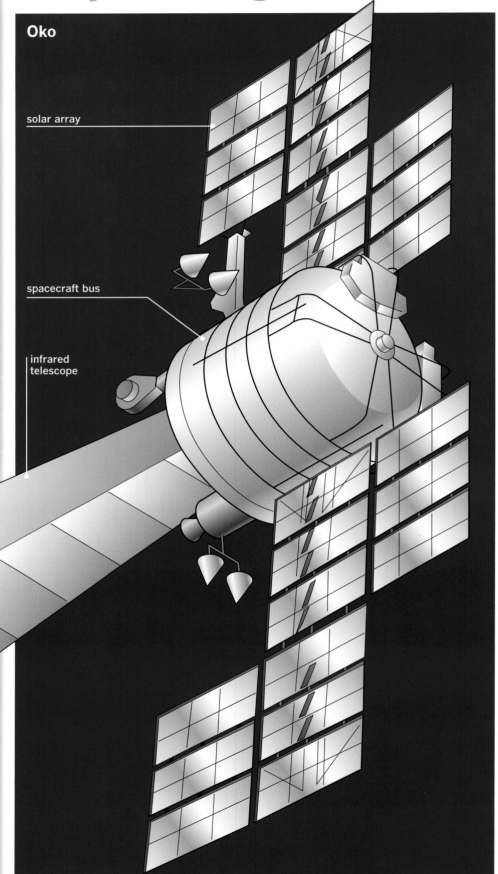

Oko

solar array

spacecraft bus

infrared telescope

Research satellites

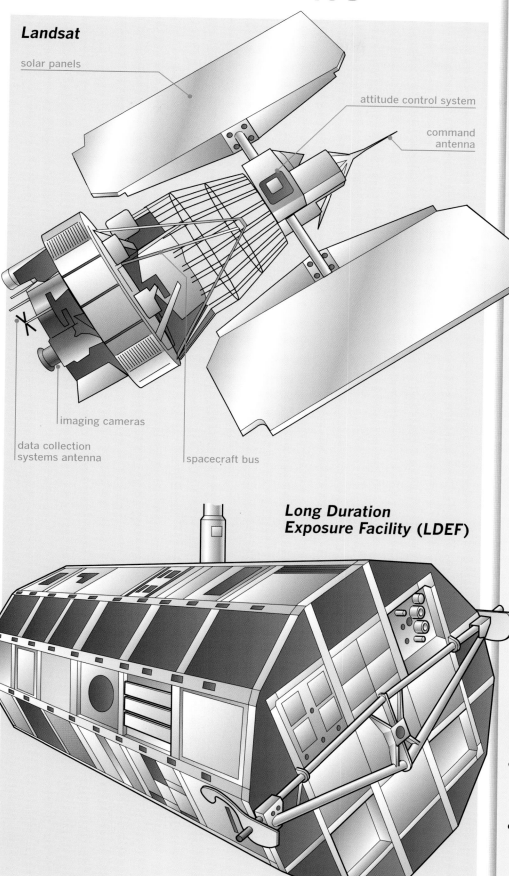

Landsat

solar panels

attitude control system

command antenna

imaging cameras

data collection systems antenna

spacecraft bus

Long Duration Exposure Facility (LDEF)

Key words

bus	satellite
gravity	solar panel
micrometeoroid	spacecraft
orbit	
remote sensing	

Research and development

- Many satellites are launched to test technologies, materials, and equipment before operational satellites can be placed in orbit.
- Several research and technology spacecraft opened the way for the communications, Earth observation, and scientific satellites of today.

Applications Technology Satellite program

- The Applications Technology Satellite program consisted of five research satellites (ATS 1, 2, 3, 4, and 5) launched between 1966 and 1969.
- The five satellites carried a variety of experimental weather observation, space environment sensing, and communications equipment.

Long Duration Exposure Facility (LDEF)

- Launched in 1984, the LDEF was retrieved from orbit and returned to Earth by the Space Shuttle in 1990.
- Initially intended to remain in space for one year, its retrieval was delayed by the *Challenger* disaster in 1986.
- Fifty-seven experiments onboard the LDEF provided data about the effects of long-term exposure to the environment of space, including the incidence of impacts with micrometeoroids.

Earth Resources Technology Satellite (ERTS)

- Now known as *Landsat*, the ERTS was launched in 1972 to demonstrate the usefulness of remote sensing from space.
- It determined what type of data could be obtained and how useful it would be in monitoring Earth systems.

Key words

constellation	polar orbit
heliosphere	pole
Lagrange point	satellite
latitude	solar radiation
magnetosphere	

Solar observation

- Solar radiation is the most critical factor in determining conditions on Earth.
- It is the driving force behind Earth's climate and also has a significant impact on communications and even the functioning of electronic devices.
- Satellites observing the Sun help scientists to better understand Earth's climate and to predict the effects of solar storms.
- Several satellites maintain a constant watch on the Sun.

Solar and Heliospheric Observatory (SOHO)

- The Solar and Heliospheric Observatory (SOHO) is a European Space Agency (ESA) and NASA satellite that constantly monitors the Sun and the heliosphere.
- It orbits the first Lagrange point between Earth and the Sun.

Cluster

- Cluster is a constellation of four identical ESA satellites designed to study interactions between solar radiation and Earth's magnetosphere.
- The four satellites were placed in a high Earth polar orbit and fly in a pyramid formation in order to provide data for a three-dimensional model of the environment they are investigating.

Ulysses

- Ulysses is an ESA Sun orbiting probe designed to investigate the Sun and the heliosphere.
- It was placed in a unique solar polar orbit that allows it to investigate the Sun at all latitudes including the polar regions that are unobservable from Earth.

Sun-watching satellites

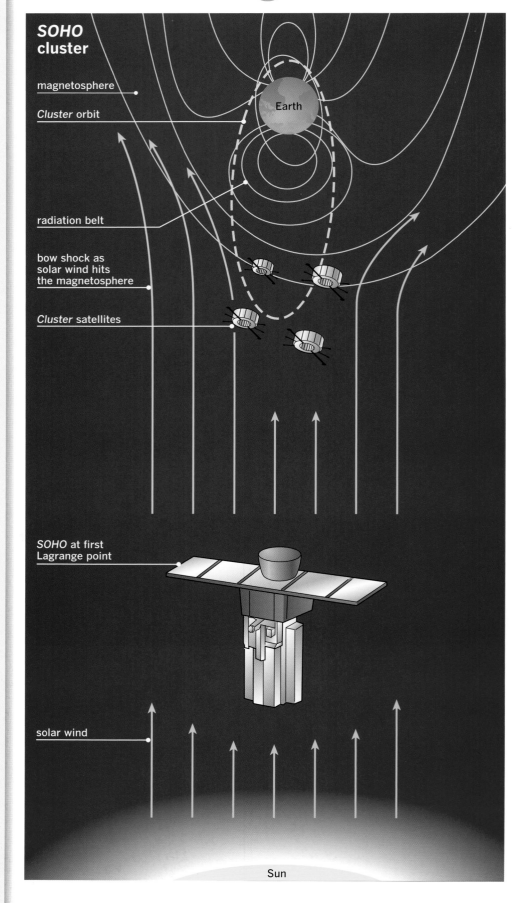

SOHO cluster

- magnetosphere
- Cluster orbit
- radiation belt
- bow shock as solar wind hits the magnetosphere
- Cluster satellites
- Earth
- SOHO at first Lagrange point
- solar wind
- Sun

Microgravity satellites

Eureca

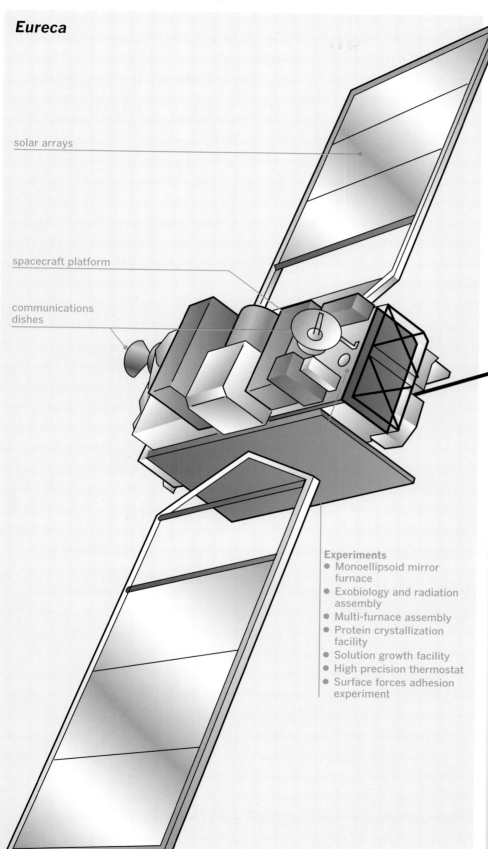

solar arrays

spacecraft platform

communications dishes

Experiments
- Monoellipsoid mirror furnace
- Exobiology and radiation assembly
- Multi-furnace assembly
- Protein crystallization facility
- Solution growth facility
- High precision thermostat
- Surface forces adhesion experiment

Microgravity

- A satellite or other spacecraft in Earth orbit is in continuous free fall.
- Conditions onboard a craft in free fall are described as weightless or, more accurately, *microgravity* conditions.
- A sustained microgravity environment offers unique laboratory conditions for scientists to study a range of phenomena that are masked or altered by the gravity conditions on Earth's surface.
- The main areas of microgravity research that are of interest to scientists are biotechnology, combustion science, fluid physics, fundamental physics, and materials science.

Microgravity experiments

- Crews on the Space Shuttle and on space stations conduct several microgravity experiments as part of wide-ranging scientific studies. These experiments are then returned to Earth for analysis.
- Several recoverable uncrewed orbital spacecraft have been used by different countries for microgravity research:
- China: FSW series satellites, first launched in 1975;
- Russia: Photon spacecraft, based on the manned Vostok spacecraft, first launched in 1985;
- Europe: *Eureca* free flying platform deployed from the Space Shuttle in 1992 and retrieved from orbit by the Space Shuttle in 1993;
- USA/Germany: *Astro-SPAS* platforms deployed from the Space Shuttle and retrieved before its return to Earth, first launched in 1983;
- USA: GAS and Hitchhiker payloads in the Space Shuttle's payload bay, first launched in 1981 and 1986 respectively.

Radio astronomy

Key words

atmosphere   solar panel
galaxy
interferometry
orbit
radio wave

History

- Satellites equipped with radio antennas are used to intercept long wavelength radio waves, which cannot penetrate Earth's atmosphere, and to extend the use of interferometer technique observations.

Explorer 38 and 49

- These are two similar radio astronomy spacecraft launched by NASA.
- *Explorer 38* was launched in 1968 and *Explorer 49* in 1973.
- *Explorer 38* was placed in Earth orbit.
- *Explorer 49* was placed in orbit around the Moon.
- Both craft monitored radio emissions from Jupiter, the Sun, and from sources outside our galaxy.

Very Long Baseline Interferometer (VLBI) radio satellite

- The *VLBI* radio satellite is a Japanese spacecraft designed to extend interferometer techniques into space.
- It was launched in 1997.
- Together with Earth-based radio telescopes, it creates a virtual dish with a diameter two-and-a-half times that of Earth (19,800 miles, 31,900 km).
- Up to 40 radio telescopes can co-observe with the *VLBI* satellite.

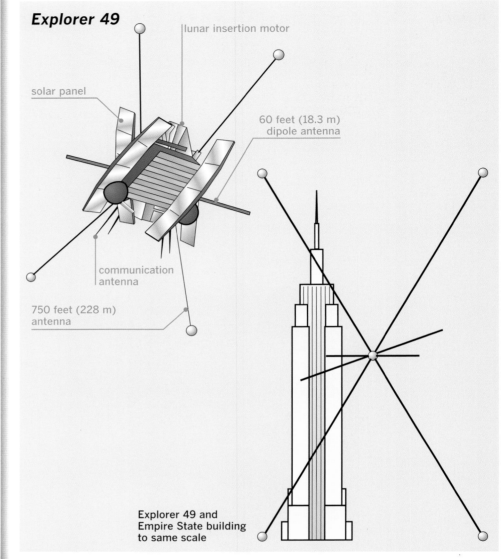

Explorer 49

lunar insertion motor

solar panel

60 feet (18.3 m) dipole antenna

communication antenna

750 feet (228 m) antenna

Explorer 49 and Empire State building to same scale

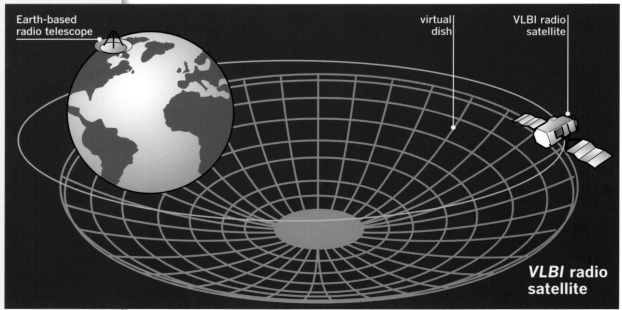

Earth-based radio telescope

virtual dish

VLBI radio satellite

VLBI radio satellite

Infrared astronomy

Key words

infrared	telescope
orbit	
satellite	
solar orbit	
spacecraft	

Infrared Space Observatory (ISO)

Data

Weight:	5,507 pounds (2,498 kg)
Length:	17.37 feet (5.3 m)
Maximum diameter:	11.8 feet (3.6 m)
Orbit:	600 by 43,000 miles (1,000 by 71,000 km)

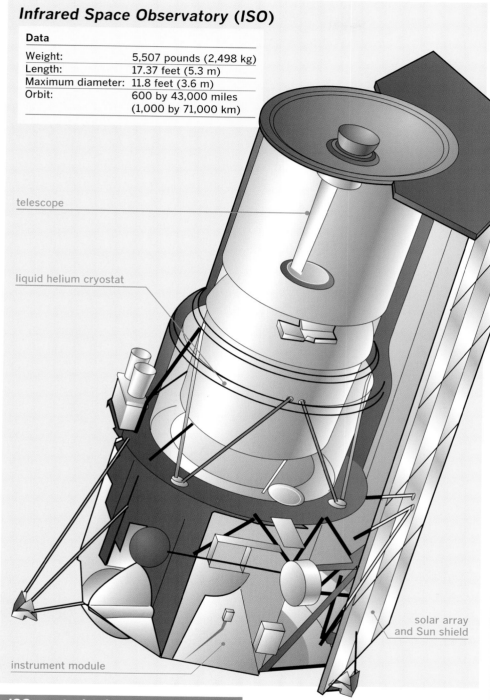

telescope

liquid helium cryostat

solar array and Sun shield

instrument module

History

- *Infrared Astronomical Satellite (IRAS)*, was a joint U.S., Dutch, and British satellite launched in 1983.
- It mapped 250,000 infrared sources.
- *Infrared Space Observatory (ISO)*, was an ESA satellite launched in 1995.
- *ISO* had 1,000 times the sensitivity of IRAS.
- *ISO* ceased operating in 1998, having made 26,000 observations.

Spitzer Space Telescope

- The *Spitzer Space Telescope* is a NASA spacecraft designed to perform infrared astronomy.
- Originally known as the *Space Infrared Telescope Facility (SIRTF)*, the spacecraft was renamed for U.S. astronomer Lyman Spitzer.
- The spacecraft was launched in August 2003 by Delta rocket.
- It was placed in an Earth-trailing solar orbit at a distance sufficient to avoid interference from infrared radiation emitted from Earth. This reduced the need to carry large quantities of coolant liquid.

ISO cryotechnology

- In order to sense weak infrared waves the telescope had to be supercooled.
- A Sun shield kept the instruments out of the warmth of the Sun.
- A flask containing 620 gallons (2,250 l) of liquid helium at −459°F (−273°C) kept the telescope supercooled.
- Once the liquid helium had been used up the telescope became unusable.

ISO instruments

- Infrared camera
- Photo polarimeter
- Shortwave spectrometer
- Longwave spectrometer

Ultraviolet astronomy

International Ultraviolet Explorer (IUE)

- Launched in 1976, the *International Ultraviolet Explorer (IUE)* was a joint NASA/ESA spacecraft designed to perform ultraviolet astronomy.
- *IUE* was the first specialized ultraviolet astronomy spacecraft and the first astronomy platform of any kind to be placed in high Earth orbit (HEO).
- Its main mission was to obtain high-resolution spectra of all star types and of gas streams around binary star systems. It also measured the effects of interstellar dust on starlight.

Extreme Ultraviolet Explorer (EUVE)

- *Extreme Ultraviolet Explorer (EUVE)* was a NASA spacecraft designed to perform ultraviolet astronomy at wavelengths of 7–76 nanometers (nm).
- *EUVE* was launched in June 1992 and operated until January 2001.
- *EUVE* was the first ultraviolet astronomy spacecraft to carry out an all-sky survey.

Far Ultraviolet Spectroscopic Explorer (FUSE)

- *Far Ultraviolet Spectroscopic Explorer (FUSE)* is a NASA spacecraft designed to perform ultraviolet astronomy at wavelengths of 90–120 nm.
- *FUSE* was launched in June 1999 and continues to operate to date.
- Its main mission is to study the relative quantities of hydrogen and deuterium in the interstellar medium and to determine the makeup and quantities of hot gases in our galaxy.

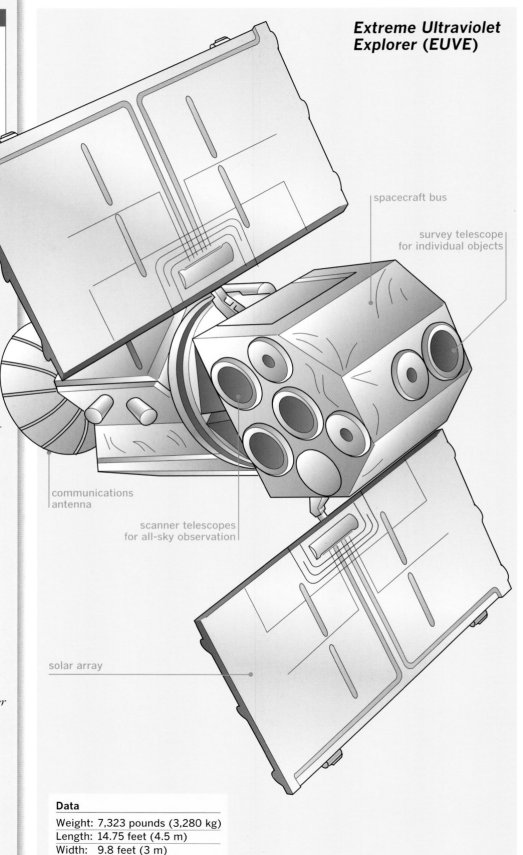

Extreme Ultraviolet Explorer (EUVE)

spacecraft bus

survey telescope for individual objects

communications antenna

scanner telescopes for all-sky observation

solar array

Data

Weight:	7,323 pounds (3,280 kg)
Length:	14.75 feet (4.5 m)
Width:	9.8 feet (3 m)

X-ray astronomy

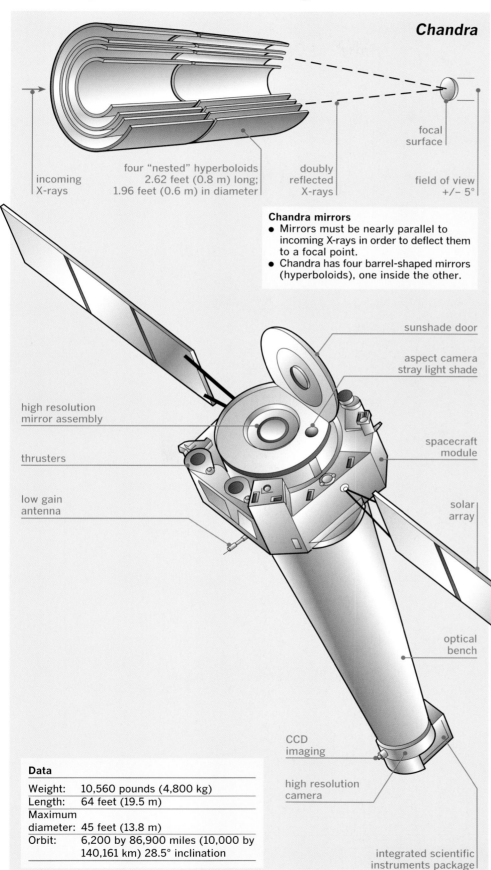

Chandra

incoming X-rays

four "nested" hyperboloids 2.62 feet (0.8 m) long; 1.96 feet (0.6 m) in diameter

doubly reflected X-rays

focal surface

field of view +/– 5°

Chandra mirrors
- Mirrors must be nearly parallel to incoming X-rays in order to deflect them to a focal point.
- Chandra has four barrel-shaped mirrors (hyperboloids), one inside the other.

sunshade door

aspect camera stray light shade

high resolution mirror assembly

thrusters

low gain antenna

spacecraft module

solar array

optical bench

CCD imaging

high resolution camera

integrated scientific instruments package

Data

Weight:	10,560 pounds (4,800 kg)
Length:	64 feet (19.5 m)
Maximum diameter:	45 feet (13.8 m)
Orbit:	6,200 by 86,900 miles (10,000 by 140,161 km) 28.5° inclination

Key words

Geiger counter	X-ray
pulsar	
solar array	
spacecraft	
supernova	

Uhuru

- *Uhuru*, also known as *Small Astronomical Satellite 1* (*SAS 1*), was a NASA spacecraft with a simple X-ray detector similar to a Geiger counter.
- It was launched in December 1970 and was the first spacecraft dedicated to X-ray astronomy.

Einstein

- *Einstein*, also known as *High Energy Astrophysical Observatory 2* (*HEAO 2*), was a NASA spacecraft designed to perform X-ray astronomy.
- It was launched in November 1978 and its observations revolutionized astronomers' understanding of X-ray sources in the universe.

ROSAT

- *ROSAT*, also known as *Roentgen Satellite*, was a joint U.S., British, and German spacecraft designed to perform X-ray astronomy.
- It was launched in June 1990 and made the first X-ray all-sky survey.
- *ROSAT*'s sensitivity was about 1,000 times greater than *UHURU*'s.

Chandra

- *Chandra X-ray Observatory* is NASA's latest X-ray astronomy spacecraft.
- *Chandra* was formerly known as *Advanced X-ray Astrophysics Facility* (*AXAF*) and was renamed for the Indian-U.S. astronomer Subrahmanyan Chandrasekhar.
- It was launched in July 1999 aboard the Space Shuttle *Columbia*.
- *Chandra*'s main mission is to image high-energy targets such as supernova remnants and pulsars.
- It is able to provide images with a resolution 50 times better than *ROSAT* managed.

Gamma ray astronomy

**Compton Gamma Ray
Observatory (CGRO)**

Key words

atmosphere	pulsar
blazar	re-entry
de-orbit	telescope
gamma ray	
gamma ray burst	

Compton Gamma Ray Observatory (CGRO)

- *Compton Gamma Ray Observatory (CGRO)* was a NASA spacecraft designed to perform gamma ray astronomy.
- *Compton* was launched aboard the Space Shuttle *Atlantis* in April 1991 and was the first spacecraft dedicated to gamma ray astronomy.
- It was named for U.S. physicist Arthur Compton.
- The spacecraft operated until June 2000 when it was deliberately de-orbited and destroyed as it re-entered Earth's atmosphere.
- *Compton's* mission was to observe the most energetic phenomena in the universe, including pulsars, gamma ray bursts, and quasars.
- *Compton's* instruments discovered a new class of extremely energetic quasars known as *blazars*.
- *Compton* detected more than 2,500 gamma ray bursts and showed that they are distributed isotropically throughout the sky.

Gamma Ray Large Area Space Telescope (GLAST)

- *Gamma Ray Large Area Space Telescope (GLAST)* is the next generation of NASA gamma ray astronomy spacecraft.
- It is due to be launched in 2007 and will carry more sensitive instruments than *Compton*.

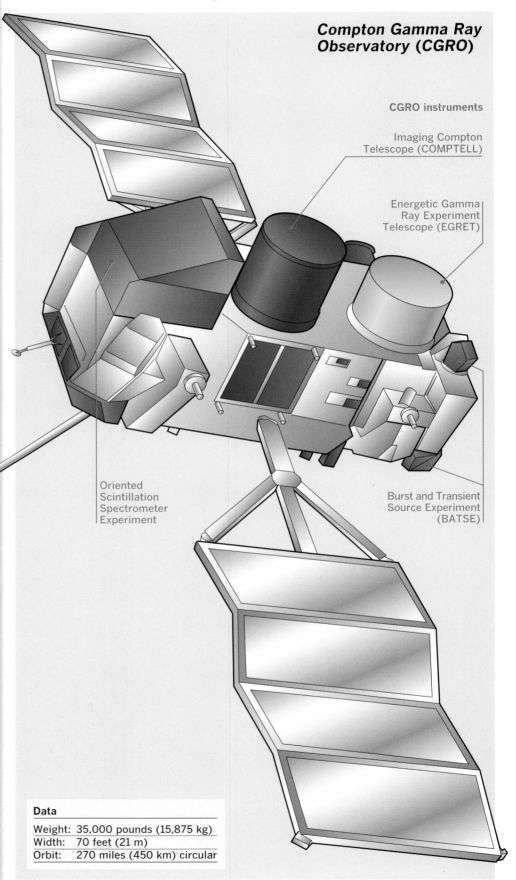

CGRO instruments

Imaging Compton Telescope (COMPTELL)

Energetic Gamma Ray Experiment Telescope (EGRET)

Oriented Scintillation Spectrometer Experiment

Burst and Transient Source Experiment (BATSE)

Data

Weight:	35,000 pounds (15,875 kg)
Width:	70 feet (21 m)
Orbit:	270 miles (450 km) circular

Cosmic Background Explorer

Cosmic Background Explorer (COBE)

Data

Weight: 4,993 pounds (2,265 kg)
Length: 19 feet (5.8 m)
Diameter: 8 feet (2.45 m)
Orbit: 562 miles (900 km) circular

Key words

big bang
cosmic
  microwave
  background
  radiation (CMB)

infrared
microwave
solar array
spacecraft

Cosmic Background Explorer (COBE)

- *Cosmic Background Explorer (COBE)*, also known as *Explorer 66*, was a NASA spacecraft designed to observe the *cosmic microwave background radiation (CMB)* of the universe.
- The CMB is essentially radiant energy left over from the big bang. Its temperature and distribution provide information about processes during the birth of the universe.
- *COBE* conducted the first all-sky survey of the CMB.
- *COBE*'s survey showed for the first time that the CMB is not uniform, revolutionizing astronomers' understanding of the origins of the universe.
- Measurements of the temperature of the CMB (about 2.725 kelvins) closely correspond with predictions of the big bang theory.

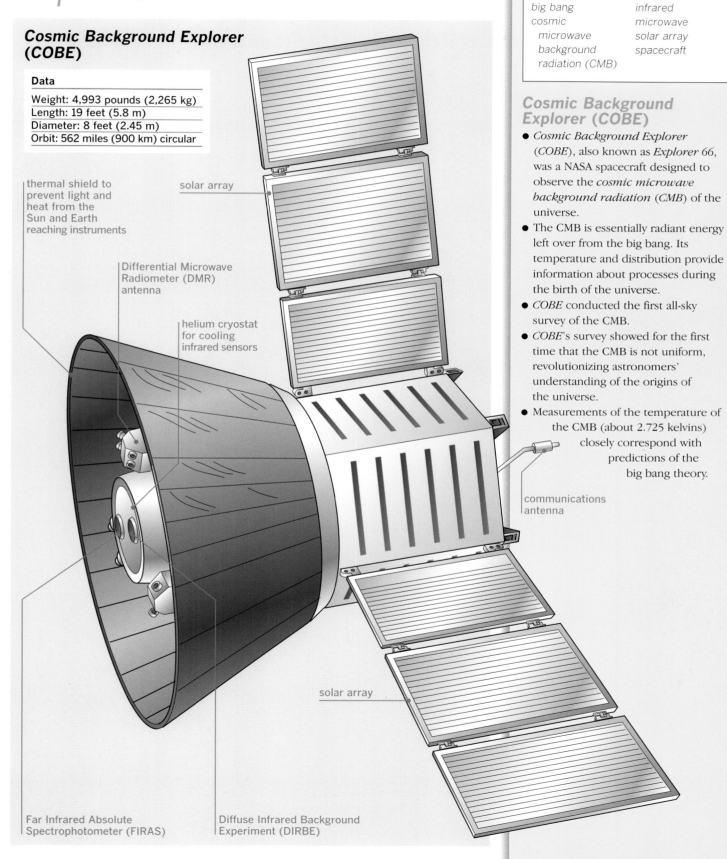

thermal shield to prevent light and heat from the Sun and Earth reaching instruments

solar array

Differential Microwave Radiometer (DMR) antenna

helium cryostat for cooling infrared sensors

communications antenna

solar array

Far Infrared Absolute Spectrophotometer (FIRAS)

Diffuse Infrared Background Experiment (DIRBE)

Key words

astronaut	ultraviolet
infrared	
solar array	
spacecraft	
telescope	

Hubble Space Telescope (HST)

- The *Hubble Space Telescope* (*HST*) is a joint NASA/ESA spacecraft designed to perform observations in the visible, near-ultraviolet, and near-infrared spectrums.

- *HST* was launched aboard the Space Shuttle *Discovery* in April 1990.

- *HST* was named for U.S. astronomer Edwin Hubble (1889–1953).

- A manufacturing fault in *HST*'s main mirror and problems with the solar panels meant that the spacecraft had to be repaired and upgraded by astronauts aboard the Space Shuttle *Endeavour* in December 1993.

- *HST* was designed to be easily upgraded. There have been four Space Shuttle missions to date, during which *HST* instruments have been replaced with newer and better versions.

- The spacecraft has made more than 330,000 observations of more than 25,000 astronomical targets to date.

- *HST* has revolutionized astronomers' understanding of the universe by providing images of processes, such as star formation, that were previously unobtainable.

Hubble Space Telescope (HST)

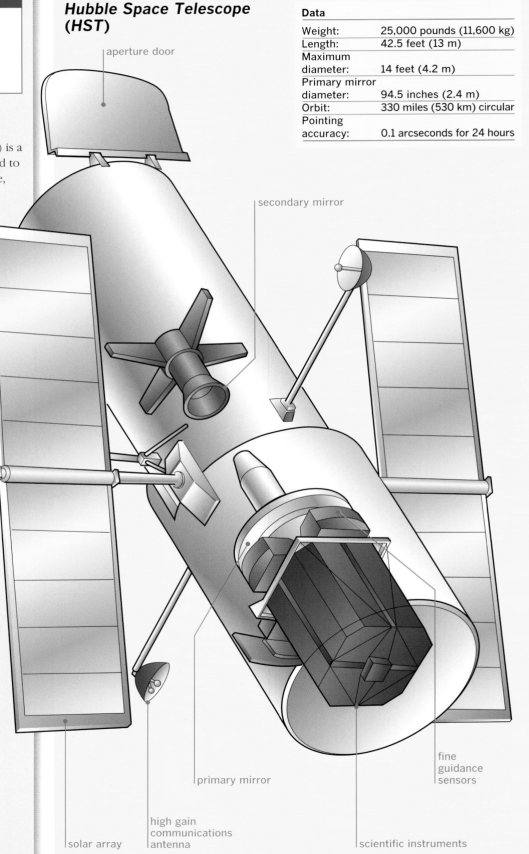

aperture door

secondary mirror

primary mirror

high gain communications antenna

solar array

fine guidance sensors

scientific instruments

Data	
Weight:	25,000 pounds (11,600 kg)
Length:	42.5 feet (13 m)
Maximum diameter:	14 feet (4.2 m)
Primary mirror diameter:	94.5 inches (2.4 m)
Orbit:	330 miles (530 km) circular
Pointing accuracy:	0.1 arcseconds for 24 hours

Launch totals

Annual spacecraft launches 1957–2005

Number of launches

(y-axis values: 250, 240, 230, 220, 210, 200, 190, 180, 170, 160, 150, 140, 130, 120, 110, 100, 90, 80, 70, 60, 50, 40, 30, 20, 10)

(x-axis years: 1957 1960, 1970, 1980, 1990, 2000, 2005)

Year

Key words

orbit
probe
satellite

History of spaceflight

- Since the launch of the world's first artificial satellite, *Sputnik 1* in October 1957, there have been more than 5,000 successful flights by launch vehicles. The exact number of launches since that time is unclear because of secrecy during the Cold War period.

- Of those thousands of launch vehicles, only about 250 have carried humans into space. The rest have transported commercial, scientific, and military satellites, as well as a few interplanetary probes.

- Some launch vehicles, especially more modern ones such as the Space Shuttle or the commercial European Ariane rocket, routinely carry multiple satellites into orbit in a single flight. Consequently, the number of spacecraft (including all satellites) that have been launched is much greater than the number of launch vehicles.

- The year with the highest number of recorded successful launch vehicle flights was 1965, with a total of 225.

- Since 1965, the annual total of flights has fallen steadily. There are three main reasons for this decline. Since the collapse of the USSR, Russia has severely reduced its spending on scientific and military spaceflights, resulting in a dramatic decrease in the number of launches it is able to carry out. The end of the Cold War has also decreased U.S. spending on military space applications. Finally, the development of commercial launch vehicles capable of delivering several satellites to Earth orbit in a single trip, coupled with the development of lighter satellites, has meant that more spacecraft can be taken into space with fewer launches.

Key words

abort To cancel or stop a pre-planned maneuver or operation, usually because of equipment failure.

absolute magnitude A measure of the intrinsic brightness of a star or other celestial object.

accelerometer An instrument for measuring changes in acceleration.

accretion disc A flat disc of tightly packed gas and material in orbit around a massive celestial body, such as a star or a black hole.

active galaxy A galaxy with a very compact and very luminous core.

aerobraking The process of slowing a spacecraft by temporarily allowing it to enter the upper layers of a planet's atmosphere, thereby creating drag.

aerodynamic heating The heating of an object passing through the atmosphere of a planet at high speed caused by friction with atmospheric gases.

airlock A chamber that allows access between two environments with differing air pressures. In a spacecraft an airlock enables access between the pressurized interior of the craft and space.

albedo The ratio of the amount of light reflected by an object and the amount of incident light. It is a measure of the reflectivity or intrinsic brightness of an object.

Amor A member of the class of Near Earth Asteroids with orbits that approach or cross the orbit of Mars.

annular solar eclipse An eclipse of the Sun by the Moon when the Moon is at perigee so that a thin ring of the Sun remains visible.

apastron For an orbit around a star, the point on that orbit that is most distant from that star.

aphelion For an orbit around the Sun, the point on that orbit that is most distant from the Sun.

apoapsis For an orbit around any body, the point on that orbit that is most distant from that body.

apogee For an orbit around Earth, the point on that orbit that is most distant from Earth.

apolune For an orbit around the Moon, the point on that orbit that is most distant from the Moon.

apparent magnitude A measure of the apparent brightness of a star or other celestial object that disregards the effects of distance on brightness.

apparition The period of time in which a comet is observable.

Apollo A member of the class of Near Earth Asteroids with orbits that approach or cross the orbit of Earth.

asteroid Any natural body in space that is larger than about 160 feet (50 m) in diameter, smaller than a moon, and mostly composed of rock rather than icy material.

asteroid belt A concentration of asteroids orbiting the Sun between the orbits of Mars and Jupiter. Also known as the main belt.

astrometric binary A binary star system in which only one member of the system is bright enough to be observed. The existence of the other member is implied by astrometric measurements.

astrometry The accurate determination of the positions and motions of celestial objects.

astronaut A person trained to travel in space.

astronomical unit (au) The mean distance between Earth and the Sun; about 93 million miles (149.6 million km).

Aten A member of the class of Near Earth Asteroids with orbits that are closer to the Sun than Earth's orbit most or all of the time.

atmosphere The envelope of gases surrounding a planet or other celestial body.

attitude A description of a spacecraft's orientation in space relative to a fixed frame of reference.

axis The imaginary line through the poles about which a celestial body rotates.

ballistic missile A missile that is guided and powered in the first part of its flight but falls freely as it approaches its target.

barred spiral galaxy A spiral galaxy in which the arms of the spiral originate from the ends of a bar through the galactic core.

big bang The hypothetical point in space and time at which all matter and energy came into existence.

big crunch The hypothetical point in space and time at which all matter and energy will cease to exist.

binary planet system Two planets of similar mass that orbit each other around a center of mass that is located outside the sphere of either planet. Pluto and its moon Charon are sometimes described as a binary planet system.

binary star system Two stars orbiting each other around a common center of mass.

black dwarf The final stage of stellar evolution for a star with a mass close to the mass of the Sun in which it no longer emits radiation of any kind.

black hole A region of space with a gravity field so strong that it has an escape velocity greater than the speed of light. Black holes cannot be observed directly, but their presence may be inferred from associated phenomena.

blazar A type of active galaxy that exhibits rapid and unpredictable variations in brightness.

blue shift An increase in the measured frequency of light from an approaching source or from a source that is being approached by an observer.

booster A rocket that supplements the thrust supplied by the main propulsion system of a spacecraft.

brown dwarf A massive celestial object with a starlike composition but with insufficient mass to support sustained nuclear fusion.

bus The main structural body of an uncrewed spacecraft or satellite that houses or supports instruments or other active components.

calendar A method of dividing time into discrete units according to repeating astronomical cycles such as the sidereal and rotational periods of Earth.

Cassini Division A 300-mile (500 km) wide gap between the inner and outer rings of Saturn.

celestial equator The projection of the equator of a planet onto the celestial sphere.

celestial north pole The projection of the north pole of a planet onto the celestial sphere.

celestial south pole The projection of the south pole of a planet onto the celestial sphere.

celestial sphere An imaginary sphere concentric with the center of Earth on which all celestial objects appear to be projected. It is referred to by astronomers as a way of describing the position of objects in the sky.

central duration The period of time during which the total or annular phase of solar eclipse takes place.

Cepheid variable A member of a class of variable stars with very predictable variation in luminosity that results from periodic expansion and contraction.

chemical rocket A rocket that provides thrust produced by chemical reactions.

chromosphere The lowest layer of the Sun's atmosphere above the photosphere.

closed universe A hypothetical universe in which there is enough matter to eventually halt and reverse the expansion that began with the big bang.

coma The haze of dust and gas surrounding the nucleus of an active comet.

comet An irregular agglomeration of water ice, frozen gases, and small amounts of rocky material in orbit around the Sun.

comet nucleus The rocky and icy core of a comet.

COMINT An acronym for Communications Intelligence.

communications satellite An artificial satellite designed primarily to facilitate communications.

Congreve rocket A British 19th-century solid propellant rocket used as artillery.

conjunction When two or more celestial bodies are very close together on the celestial sphere.

constellation (1) One of 88 named regions of the celestial sphere containing stars in a specific configuration. (2) A group of identical or similar artificial satellites in orbit.

contact binary A binary star system in which both stars fill their Roche lobes so that their upper atmospheres form a common envelope.

core The central region of a planet, star, or other celestial body.

corona The outermost layer of the Sun's atmosphere.

cosmic microwave background radiation (CMB) Low-level microwave radio emissions that emanate in almost equal intensity from across the entire sky. It is thought to be radiation left over from the big bang.

cosmic ray Electromagnetic rays of extremely high frequency and energy.

cosmonaut The Russian term for a person trained for space travel.

countdown The period before a significant event in space travel (such as the launch of a spacecraft), in which a preplanned series of activities is carried out in preparation for that event.

crater A depression in the surface of a celestial body formed by a meteorite impact or by volcanic activity.

crust The outermost solid layer of a planet, moon, or other celestial body.

cryogenic liquid propellant A liquid propellant that has a boiling point lower than −130°F (−90°C).

cubewano A class of Kuiper belt object that is not in resonance with the orbits of the outer planets.

dark matter Hypothetical material that neither emits nor reflects electromagnetic radiation (making it impossible to observe directly). Some theories maintain this composes the missing mass of the universe.

de-orbit To change a spacecraft's velocity so that it no longer has sufficient speed to maintain an orbit.

detached binary A binary star system in which neither member exceeds its Roche limits, and so has no significant effect on the other's evolution.

docking The sustained joining together of two spacecraft or of a spacecraft and a space station.

Doppler effect The apparent change in the wavelength of electromagnetic radiation caused by the motion of a source, an observer, or both.

Doppler method A method of detecting exoplanets that uses observations of the spectral lines of stars to find small Doppler effect shifts.

dust cloud A concentration of interstellar dust.

dust tail The visible stream of dust particles driven off an active comet's nucleus by escaping gases.

Earth Observation Satellite (EOS) An artificial satellite designed to perform active or passive sensing of Earth.

eccentricity The deviation of an orbit from a circle.

eclipse The obscuring of one celestial body by another, usually the Moon or Earth obscuring the Sun.

eclipse magnitude A measure of how much of the Sun is covered by the Moon during a solar eclipse.

eclipsing binary A binary star system in which, from the point of view of an observer, one member periodically passes in front of the other.

ecliptic (1) The plane of Earth's orbit around the Sun. (2) The plane of the solar system's orbit around the galactic center.

ejection seat A crew member's seat equipped with a rocket motor or other propulsion system that is capable of safely propelling a person from a damaged vehicle.

electromagnetic spectrum The entire range of wavelengths and frequencies of electromagnetic radiation.

element One of the 92 naturally occurring substances that are not a combination of other substances.

ELINT An acronym for Electronic Intelligence.

elliptical galaxy A galaxy with a smooth, rounded appearance.

EMU An acronym for Extravehicular Mobility Unit.

entropy The tendency for a system to lose energy and order over time.

equator An imaginary line around the diameter of a planet or other celestial body halfway between that body's north and south poles.

equinox One of two occasions in every year when the Sun crosses the celestial equator.

eruptive prominence An energetic eruption of material from the Sun that forms a persistent arch in the Sun's chromosphere.

escape tower Rockets attached to the crew compartment of a spacecraft that are capable of propelling the compartment safely away from the launch vehicle in the event of an emergency.

escape velocity The initial velocity that an object needs to escape from the gravitational attraction of a massive object such as a planet permanently.

event horizon The boundary around a black hole at which the escape velocity is exactly equal to the speed of light. Information about events beyond the event horizon can never reach the universe outside.

exoplanet A planet not in the solar system.

extravehicular activity (EVA) Any activity conducted in space outside of the pressurized confines of a spacecraft or space station.

extrinsic variable A variable star in which changes in luminosity are due to phenomena extrinsic to that star.

flight deck The area of a crewed spacecraft that contains the critical instruments and controls needed to pilot it.

flyby A spacecraft passing relatively close to a celestial body.

footprint The area of a planet's surface (usually Earth) in which an artificial satellite's signals can be received.

free fall A state where gravity is the only force acting on a body.

fuel cell An electrochemical device that converts hydrogen and oxygen into electricity and heat.

full Moon The phase of the Moon during which the maximum extent of the illuminated surface is visible.

galactic center The central region of a galaxy.

galactic plane The plane of the orbit of the majority of material in a galaxy around that galaxy's center.

galaxy A collection of stars, gas, and dust bound together by gravity.

galaxy cluster A group of about 50 to 1,000 galaxies bound together by gravity.

galaxy group A group of fewer than 50 galaxies bound together by gravity.

galaxy supercluster A group of thousands of galaxy groups and clusters bound together by gravity.

galley The area in a spacecraft where food is prepared.

gamma ray Short-wavelength electromagnetic radiation, similar to X-rays but of nuclear origin, with a wavelength range of about 10^{-14} to 10^{-10} m.

gamma ray burst Very powerful bursts of gamma rays lasting from fractions of a second to a few minutes, and emanating from all regions of the sky.

gas cloud A concentration of interstellar gas.

gas giant A large planet that is composed mostly of elements that are gases on Earth (hydrogen and helium) rather than rocky material.

Geiger counter An instrument for detecting and measuring ionizing radiation.

geostationary orbit (GSO) A geosynchronous orbit that matches Earth's direction and rate of rotation so that a satellite remains above a fixed point on the surface.

geostationary transfer orbit (GTO) A class of Hohmann transfer orbit that is a transitional orbit between low Earth orbit and geostationary orbit.

geosynchronous orbit (GEO) A class of orbit that has the same orbital period as Earth's rotational period.

Global Positioning System (GPS) A navigation system that utilizes signals from a constellation of artificial satellites.

globular cluster A spherical grouping of between 10,000 and one million old stars associated with a galaxy.

gravitational attraction The tendency for all objects with mass to be attracted to each other. Modern theories maintain that gravity is not a force but the result of space curvature and time dilation.

gravitational lensing The distortion of light by massive celestial objects.

gravitational slingshot The use of the motion of a planet to alter the course and speed of a spacecraft.

gravity The quality of an object with mass that results in gravitational attraction.

greenhouse effect An increase in a planet's temperature caused by its atmosphere trapping heat.

greenhouse gas A gas that creates a greenhouse effect.

ground track The path on the surface of a planet that is directly below the path of an orbiting satellite.

gyroscope An instrument that has a stable spin in all three planes used to measure changes in orientation.

halo orbit An orbit around a Lagrange point.

heat death The state of maximum entropy.

heat shield A protective covering that prevents a spacecraft from aerodynamic heating.

heliocentric Centered on the Sun.

heliopause The boundary where the solar wind is slowed to a standstill by the interstellar medium.

heliosphere The space within the heliopause.

hemisphere Half of a planet.

Hertzsprung-Russell (H-R) diagram A diagram that shows the relationship between absolute magnitude, luminosity, star classification, and surface temperature for stellar evolution.

high Earth orbit (HEO) An orbit with an altitude greater than geosynchronous orbit.

Hohmann transfer orbit A transitional orbit that touches a starting orbit around one body and a final orbit around another.

Hubble's constant The actual ratio of the speed of recession of an object in the universe to the distance of that object from an observer.

Hubble's law The theory that the farther away an object in the universe is from an observer, the faster its rate of recession, and that this relationship is constant.

hybrid solar eclipse A solar eclipse that is total in some locations and annular in others.

hypergolic liquid propellant Propellants that spontaneously combust on contact with each other.

ICBM An acronym for Intercontinental Ballistic Missile.

impact crater A crater formed by the impact of a meteorite rather than by volcanic activity.

inclination The angle between the plane of an orbit and a reference plane. For spacecraft the reference plane is usually a planet's equator. For celestial bodies the reference plane is usually the ecliptic.

infrared Electromagnetic radiation that includes wavelengths from 0.7 to 1,000 microns.

inner planet One of the four planets closer to the Sun than the main belt of asteroids.

inner solar system All objects in the solar system closer to the Sun than Jupiter.

interferometry The technique of combining information gathered from separate telescopes.

intermediate circular orbit (ICO) An orbit with an altitude higher than low Earth orbit but lower than geosynchronous orbit.

interplanetary dust Very small (a fraction of a micron) particles of matter dispersed throughout the space between the planets of the solar system.

interstellar dust Very small (a fraction of a micron) particles of matter that make up about one percent of the interstellar medium.

interstellar medium The very low density (about 1 atom per cubic cm) material dispersed throughout the space between the stars.

intrinsic variable A variable star in which changes in luminosity are due to phenomena intrinsic to that star rather than the influence of other factors.

ion engine A propulsion system that generates thrust by accelerating a stream of positive ions.

ionosphere A layer of charged particles in Earth's upper atmosphere at an altitude of between about 25 and 250 miles (40–400 km).

ion tail The stream of plasma driven off an active comet nucleus by interactions with the solar wind.

IRBM An acronym for Intermediate Range Ballistic Missile.

irregular galaxy A galaxy with no regular shape or symmetrical features.

irregular variable A variable star that changes in luminosity at irregular and unpredictable intervals.

Jovian planet A planet that resembles Jupiter in size and composition.

Kepler's laws A description of the laws of planetary motion published by German astronomer Johannes Kepler between 1609 and 1619.

kiloparsec One thousand parsecs.

Kuiper belt A region of the solar system stretching from about 30 to 50 au from the Sun in a narrow band around the ecliptic. It is thought to contain thousands of objects similar to comet nuclei.

Kuiper belt object (KBO) Any Sun-orbiting object within the Kuiper belt.

Lagrange point One of five points in the plane of two massive bodies orbiting each other, where a third body of negligible mass can remain in equilibrium.

lander A spacecraft or part of a spacecraft that is designed to land on the surface of a celestial body.

latitude A measure of the angular distance north or south of the equator of a planet or other celestial body.

launch control The personnel and equipment needed to manage a spacecraft launch.

launch escape system Any equipment that allows a crew to escape from a spacecraft on the launch pad.

launch pad The structure that supports a spacecraft and provides communication and other links until the moment of liftoff.

launch window The time period in which a spacecraft must be launched in order for it to reach its intended destination.

life support The equipment on board a spacecraft or attached to a space suit that allows crew members to survive in space.

liftoff The moment a spacecraft leaves its launch pad.

light day The distance traveled by light in a vacuum in one day.

light month The distance traveled by light in a vacuum in one month.

light second The distance traveled by light in a vacuum in one second.

light year (ly) The distance traveled by light in a vacuum in one year.

liquid propellant Propellant that is in a liquid form when it is used.

Local Arm The arm of the Milky Way galaxy that contains the Sun and the solar system.

Local Group The galaxy group that includes the Milky Way galaxy.

Local Supercluster The galaxy supercluster that includes the Milky Way galaxy.

longitude A measure of the angular distance east or west of an arbitrary line connecting the north and south poles of a planet (on Earth the prime meridian).

long period comet A comet with an orbital period of more than 200 years.

low Earth orbit (LEO) An Earth orbit with an altitude between about 220 and 870 miles (350–1,400 km).

luminosity The rate at which an object (usually a star) emits energy.

lunar cycle The 28-day period during which the Moon completes one orbit of Earth.

lunar eclipse An occasion on which Earth blocks the Sun's direct light from reaching the Moon.

lunar phase One of the regular changes in the appearance of the Moon that are the result of more or less of the illuminated portion of the Moon's surface being visible from Earth.

lunar sea One of several large, relatively flat and crater-free areas of the Moon.

Mach The ratio of a speed to the speed of sound.

MACHO An acronym for Massive Compact Halo Object.

magnestar A pulsar with a magnetic field more than 1,000 times more powerful than Earth's.

magnetosphere The region within which a planet's magnetic field has a greater influence than the solar wind.

magnetotail The extension of the magnetosphere on the side of a planet facing away from the Sun.

magnitude The brightness of a celestial object.

main belt asteroid An asteroid that orbits in the main belt of asteroids between Mars and Jupiter.

main sequence A group of mature, stable stars that occupy a diagonal band across a Hertzsprung-Russell diagram.

mantle The layer of a planet that lies between the core and the crust.

mare (plural: **maria**) Another term for lunar sea.

mature star A star that has settled into an extended equilibrium state in which the energy produced by nuclear fusion balances gravitation contraction.

medium Earth orbit (MEO) Another term for intermediate circular orbit.

megaparsec (Mpc) One million parsecs.

meteor A meteoroid that enters an atmosphere.

meteorite A meteoroid that impacts a planet.

meteoroid Any naturally occurring cohesive lump of material in space that is larger than a molecule but smaller than about 160 feet (50 m) in diameter.

microgravity A state in which gravity is reduced to almost negligible levels, such as during free fall.

micrometeorite A meteorite between 5 μm and 15 cm in diameter.

micrometeoroid A meteoroid between 5 μm and 15 cm in diameter.

microwave A form of electromagnetic radiation with high frequencies and wavelengths of 1 mm to 50 cm.

midcourse correction A small change in the speed or path of a spacecraft during transit.

Milky Way The galaxy that contains our solar system.

millisecond pulsar A pulsar with a pulse period of less than 25 milliseconds.

Mira variable A variable star that expands and contracts over a period of 100 days or more.

missing mass Hypothetical matter making up 90 percent of the mass of the universe.

mission control The personnel and equipment needed to manage a spacecraft flight.

MMU An acronym for Manned Maneuvering Unit.

Molniya orbit A highly elliptical Earth orbit that allows a satellite to remain within the line-of-sight of the north or south polar region for a large part of its orbital period.

moon A natural satellite of a planet.

Moonwalk Extravehicular activity on the Moon's surface.

Morgan-Keenan classification A system for classifying stars according to their surface temperatures.

multiple star system A system of two or more stars orbiting around a common center of mass.

Near Earth Asteroid (NEA) A Near Earth Object that is classified as an asteroid.

Near Earth Object (NEO) Any object with an orbit that approaches Earth's orbit to within 0.3 au.

nebula A concentration of interstellar gas and dust.

neutron star A very dense, rapidly rotating object composed almost entirely of neutrons. Thought to be the remnants of massive stars that have undergone a supernova explosion.

new Moon The lunar phase in which the minimum of the Moon's illuminated surface is visible.

northern hemisphere The half of a planet or other celestial body north of its equator.

north pole The surface point of a celestial body's axis of rotation around which the surface appears to rotate in a clockwise direction.

nuclear fusion The process by which less-massive nuclei are fused together under extremely high temperatures and densities to form more-massive nuclei plus energy.

Oort cloud A roughly spherical shell of space that extends from about 50,000 to 100,000 au from the Sun and is thought to contain millions of comet nuclei.

Oort cloud object Any Sun-orbiting object within the Oort cloud.

open universe A universe in which there is insufficient matter to eventually halt and reverse the expansion that began with a big bang.

orbit The path taken by one body around another, usually more massive, body. It is determined by the mass of the orbited body and the velocity of the orbiting body.

orbital mechanics The study of the motions of artificial satellites and spacecraft moving under gravity, thrust, and other influences.

orbital period The time taken to complete one orbit.

orbital speed The average speed at which a body moves in its orbit.

orbiter A spacecraft designed to enter and operate in orbit around a celestial body.

ordnance Pyrotechnic or explosive materials.

outer planet One of the five planets farther from the Sun than the main belt of asteroids.

outer solar system All objects in the solar system farther from the Sun than the main belt of asteroids.

oxidizer A substance that promotes combustion.

ozone layer A layer in Earth's atmosphere at an altitude of between about 25 and 250 miles (40–400 km) that contains a higher than average proportion of oxygen in the form of ozone.

parallax An apparent shift in an object's position when observed from two different locations.

parsec (pc) A unit of distance equal to the distance from an observer on Earth at which an object would have a parallax of one arc second when viewed from opposite sides of Earth's orbit around the Sun.

partial lunar eclipse An occasion on which Earth blocks some of the Sun's light from reaching the Moon.

partial solar eclipse An occasion on which the Moon blocks some of the Sun's light from reaching Earth.

payload Anything carried by a spacecraft that is not essential for the operation of that spacecraft.

periapsis The point on an orbit that is closest to the body it is orbiting.

periastron The point on an orbit around a star that is closest to that star.

perigee The point on an orbit around Earth that is closest to Earth.

perihelion The point on an orbit around the Sun that is closest to the Sun.

perilune The point on an orbit around the Moon that is closest to the Moon.

planet Since the discovery of bodies in the Kuiper belt similar in size to Pluto there has been no internationally agreed definition for the term 'planet' among scientists. The most popular definitions include the requirement that a planet should have a diameter of more than 1,200 miles (2,000 km), that its shape should be stable due to its own gravity, or that it should be the dominant object in its immediate neighborhood.

planetary nebula An expanding shell of gases expelled from a star late in its stellar evolution.

plasma A state of matter consisting of a gas of positively charged and negatively charged particles in approximately equal concentrations.

plutino A Kuiper belt object that completes two solar orbits for every three solar orbits made by Neptune.

polar jet An energetic stream of matter emitted from the poles of a protostar.

polar orbit An orbit that passes over or close to both poles of a celestial body.

pole One of two points on a celestial body where its axis of rotation intersects its surface.

potentially hazardous object (PHO) Any object in the solar system with an orbit that approaches Earth's orbit to within 0.025 au.

precession of the equinoxes A circular motion of Earth's axis with respect to the position of the stars.

probe An uncrewed spacecraft designed to gather information about an environment.

propellant A fuel used with an oxidizer to provide propulsion.

protostar A star in the early stages of stellar evolution before sustained nuclear fusion has begun.

pulsar A rapidly rotating neutron star that emits beams of radiation from its poles.

pulsar timing A method of detecting exoplanets in orbit around pulsars by measuring irregularities in the pulse periods of pulsars.

quantum gravity An as yet unformulated theory that combines the theories of quantum mechanics and general relativity.

quasar A very distant object about the size of a solar system that emits many times more energy than a regular galaxy.

quasi-stellar object (QSO) Another term for a quasar.

quiescent prominence A patch or sheet of energized gas that forms in the Sun's chromosphere.

radar A method of determining the distance to an object by measuring the time taken for high frequency microwave pulses to reflect from it.

RADINT An acronym for Radar Intelligence.

radio loud The state in which a celestial object emits radio waves.

radio quiet The state in which a celestial object does not emit radio waves.

radio telescope A telescope designed to make observations in radio wavelengths.

radio wave An electromagnetic wave with a frequency between 100 MHz and 3,000,000 MHz.

reaction control A propulsion system on a spacecraft used to make small attitude changes.

red giant A star in a late stage of stellar evolution, when it has expanded and cooled.

red shift The lengthening of the wavelength of electromagnetic radiation caused when the source and the observer are moving apart.

red supergiant A very large star in a late stage of stellar evolution, when it has expanded and cooled.

re-entry The return of a spacecraft to Earth's atmosphere.

reflecting telescope A telescope that collects light by means of a concave mirror.

refracting telescope A telescope that uses a lens to gather and focus light from a distant object and a second lens to magnify further the image produced by the first.

remote sensing The collection of information about an object by the interception of electromagnetic radiation emitted by that object.

rendezvous The planned close approach of two spacecraft in space.

retrofire The act of igniting a retro rocket.

retrograde Orbiting or revolving in the opposite direction to that usually observed.

retro rocket A small rocket engine used to slow a spacecraft.

Roche lobe The area surrounding a body within which material is gravitationally bound to that body.

rocket An engine that expels gases at high velocity in order to generate a propulsion force.

rocky planet A planet largely composed of rock and metal rather than gases.

rotational period The time taken for a celestial body to complete one revolution on its axis.

rover A vehicle designed to travel across the surface of a celestial body other than Earth.

satellite Any object in orbit around a celestial body.

season A period of the year with a characteristic climate.

semiregular variable A variable star with luminosity variations that are usually regular.

short period comet A comet with an orbital period of less than 200 years.

sidereal period The time taken for a celestial body to complete one orbit of the Sun (or other star).

singularity A point with no dimensions at which gravity and mass are infinite.

solar array A connected set of solar cells.

solar cell A device that converts sunlight into electricity.

solar eclipse An occasion on which the Moon blocks the Sun's light from reaching part of Earth's surface.

solar flare An energetic eruption of material from the surface of the Sun.

solar orbit An orbit around the Sun.

solar panel A spacecraft structure that supports a solar array.

solar prominence A prominent structure of energetic material in the Sun's chromosphere.

solar radiation The complete range of electromagnetic radiation emitted by the Sun.

solar system A star and all the nonluminous bodies associated with it.

solar wind The outward flow of plasma and gas from the Sun.

KEY WORDS

solid propellant A propellant that is a solid when used.

southern hemisphere The region of a celestial body to the south of its equator.

south pole The surface point of a celestial body's axis of rotation around which the surface appears to rotate in a counterclockwise direction.

spacecraft An artificial device designed to travel at or beyond low Earth orbit.

space junk Any artificial defunct object in space.

space race The period of intense political and technological rivalry between the United States and the Soviet Union in the 1950s and 1960s.

space station A large spacecraft designed to stay in orbit around Earth and capable of supporting a crew for an extended period of time.

spacesuit Protective clothing worn by an astronaut outside of a spacecraft or space station in space.

spacewalk Another term for extravehicular activity.

spectral line A particular wavelength of light used by astronomers to infer the abundance of elements.

spectral type A star classification based on the analysis of spectral lines.

spiral galaxy A galaxy with a dense central disc surrounded by curved arms in the same plane.

splashdown Landing in water.

spy satellite An artificial satellite used to gather intelligence.

stage A portion of a launch vehicle that provides thrust for just one phase of a launch.

star A celestial body that emits radiation derived from nuclear fusion reactions.

stellar evolution The series of forms that a star passes through during its existence.

stellar mass black hole A black hole with a mass between about four and 15 times the mass of the Sun.

stratosphere A layer of Earth's atmosphere at altitudes between about 6 and 30 miles (10–50 km).

suborbital A flight or trajectory less than one orbit.

summer solstice The occasion on which the Sun is at its northernmost point above the celestial equator.

sunspot A cool region of the Sun's surface.

supermassive black hole A black hole with a mass billions of times the mass of the Sun.

supernova An explosion that ejects the majority of a star's mass following a gravitational collapse.

telemetry The transmission of data.

telescope An instrument designed to collect and focus electromagnetic radiation.

TELINT An acronym for Telemetry Intelligence.

terrae Uplands on the Moon.

terrestrial planet A planet similar in size and composition to Earth.

tidally locked A natural satellite or moon that has a rotational period that is exactly the same as its orbital period. The same side of the satellite is always facing the body it is orbiting.

tide The periodic rise and fall of sea level caused primarily by the gravitational influence of the Moon.

total duration The duration of an eclipse.

total lunar eclipse An occasion on which Earth blocks all direct sunlight from reaching the Moon.

total solar eclipse An occasion on which the Moon blocks all direct sunlight from part of Earth.

transit method A method of detecting exoplanets by observing the shadow of a planet in front of a star.

trans-Neptunian object (TNO) Any object in the solar system with an orbit generally beyond the orbit of Neptune.

Trojan An asteroid in either of the two clusters of asteroids found at two of Jupiter's Lagrange points.

troposphere The lowest level of Earth's atmosphere from the ground to an altitude of about 11 miles (17 km).

T-Tauri star A young star in which sustainable nuclear fusion is restricted to its core and that is still undergoing gravitational contraction.

twotino A Kuiper belt object that completes one solar orbit for every two solar orbits made by Neptune.

ultraviolet Electromagnetic radiation with wavelengths in the range 375–12.5 nanometers.

umbral magnitude The proportion of the Moon's surface obscured during a lunar eclipse.

upper atmosphere Earth's atmosphere above the troposphere.

vacuum The absence of all matter.

Van Allen belt A belt of charged particles around Earth held in place by its magnetic field.

variable star Any star that undergoes a relatively large change in luminosity over a short period of time.

vernier A small reaction control motor.

visual binary Two stars that appear to be part of a binary star system but which are in fact too distant to be gravitationally bound.

weather satellite A satellite that monitors weather.

white dwarf A star that has shed about 80 percent of its mass in the form of a planetary nebula.

WIMP An acronym for Weakly Interacting Massive Particle.

X-ray Electromagnetic radiation with wavelengths in the range of 0.00001–0.01 microns.

X-ray binary A binary star system that periodically emits powerful X-ray bursts.

X-ray burster A neutron star that periodically emits powerful X-ray bursts.

Internet resources

There is a lot of useful information on the internet. Information on a particular topic may be available through a search engine such as Google (http://www.google.com). Some of the sites that are found in this way may be very useful, others not. Below is a selection of Web sites related to the material covered by this book.

The publisher takes no responsibility for the information contained within these Web sites. All the sites were accessible in March 2006.

Amazing Space (Hubble Space Telescope Online)
Educational resources based on the discoveries of the Hubble Space Telescope.
> http://amazing-space.stsci.edu

Ames Research Center
NASA's space science and astrobiology division.
> http://www-space.arc.nasa.gov

An Atlas of the Universe
Attempts to convey astronomical distances and our place in the universe by visual scaling.
> http://anzwers.org/free/universe

Apollo Program
A record of the historic Moon missions.
> http://www.nasm.edu/APOLLO

Astronomy Picture of the Day
Features a new image from the universe daily.
> http://antwrp.gsfc.nasa.gov/apod/astropix.html

BBC Science and Nature: Space
An educational resource from the British Broadcasting Corporation.
> http://www.bbc.co.uk/science/space

European Space Agency (ESA)
Web site of the European Space Agency.
> http://www.esa.int/export/esaCP

European Space Agency (ESA) Eduspace
The European Earth observation Web site for high schools.
> http://www.eduspace.esa.int

Goddard Space Flight Center
A major NASA science center for the U.S. space program.
> http://www.nasa.gov/centers/goddard/home

Hands-On Universe
Award-winning astronomy site from the University of California, Berkeley.
> http://www.handsonuniverse.org

International Space Station
The European Space Agency's site for news and information about the International Space Station.
> http://www.esa.int/esaHS/iss.html

Jet Propulsion Laboratory (JPL)
Web site of the facility that builds most of NASA's interplanetary probes, managed by the California Institute of Technology.
> http://www.jpl.nasa.gov

Johnson Space Center (JSC)
The NASA center for human spaceflight.
> http://www.nasa.gov/centers/johnson/home

Kennedy Space Center (KSC)
NASA's primary spacecraft assembly and launch facility.
> http://www.nasa.gov/centers/kennedy/home

Lunar and Planetary Institute
An excellent source of maps of the Moon and other bodies in the solar system.
> http://www.lpi.usra.edu

Marshall Space Flight Center
A major NASA center for the development of space transportation and propulsion systems.
> http://www.nasa.gov/centers/marshall/home

NASA
The homepage of the National Aeronautics and Space Administration.
> http://www.nasa.gov

NASA Edspace
A highly interactive online experience for younger students.
> http://edspace.nasa.gov

NASA Human Spaceflight
NASA's human space travel front page.
> http://spaceflight.nasa.gov

INTERNET RESOURCES

NASA Planetary Photojournal
Awesome photographs of the planets.
http://photojournal.jpl.nasa.gov

National Air and Space Museum (Smithsonian Institution)
Web site of the leading aviation museum.
http://www.nasm.si.edu

National Center for Atmospheric Research
A center of research into Earth's atmosphere.
http://www.ncar.ucar.edu

National Space Science Data Center (NSSDC)
NASA's archive of space science mission data.
http://nssdc.gsfc.nasa.gov

Open Directory Project: Astronomy
A comprehensive listing of internet resources for astronomy.
http://dmoz.org/Science/Astronomy

Open Directory Project: Cosmology
A comprehensive listing of internet resources for the physical sciences underlying cosmological theories.
http://dmoz.org/Science/Physics/Cosmology

Open Directory Project: Space
A comprehensive listing of internet resources for the science of space and space travel.
http://dmoz.org/Science/Technology/Space

Planetary Science Research Discoveries
An educational site sharing the latest research on meteorites, planets, and other solar system bodies being made by NASA-sponsored scientists.
http://www.psrd.hawaii.edu

Rocket and Space Technology
An informative educational site bridging the gap between simplistic introductions and abstrusely academic rocket science.
http://www.braeunig.us/space

Russian Space Web
News about current Russian space programs and the history of aeronautics in the USSR.
http://www.russianspaceweb.com

Science Master's Space and Astronomy Home Page
Provides excellent science educational resources.
http://www.sciencemaster.com/space/space.php

Sky and Telescope
Useful astronomy resources from the popular magazine.
http://skyandtelescope.com

Solar System Simulator
Photographic views of the solar system simulated from the perspectives of its different members.
http://space.jpl.nasa.gov

Spaceflight Now
Online space news.
http://www.spaceflightnow.com

StarChild
A fun introduction to space and astronomy for younger students.
http://starchild.gsfc.nasa.gov

The Planetary Society
The Planetary Society's stated mission is to create ways for the public to participate in space exploration.
http://www.planetary.org

Today's Space Weather
Real-time weather in space from the Space Environment Center.
http://www.sel.noaa.gov/today.html

Views of the solar system
Multimedia representations and thorough representations of solar system objects.
http://www.solarviews.com

Virtual Space Museum
A photographic history of the Soviet/Russian space programs, in Russian and English.
http://vsm.host.ru/emain.htm

Welcome to the Planets
Some of the clearest images taken from NASA's planetary exploration programs.
http://pds.jpl.nasa.gov/planets

Index

Index of subject headings.